Righteous Violence

Righteous Violence

REVOLUTION, SLAVERY, AND THE AMERICAN RENAISSANCE

LARRY J. REYNOLDS

The University of Georgia Press
Athens & London

© 2011 by the University of Georgia Press

Athens, Georgia 30602

www.ugapress.org

All rights reserved

Designed by Walton Harris

Set in 10/14 New Baskerville

Printed and bound by Thomson-Shore

The paper in this book meets the guidelines for
permanence and durability of the Committee on
Production Guidelines for Book Longevity of the
Council on Library Resources.

Printed in the United States of America

15   14   13   12   11   P   5   4   3   2   1

Library of Congress Cataloging-in-Publication Data

Reynolds, Larry J. (Larry John), 1942–
Righteous violence : revolution, slavery, and the
American renaissance / Larry J. Reynolds.
       p.   cm.
Includes bibliographical references and index.
ISBN-13: 978-0-8203-2825-6 (hardcover : alk. paper)
ISBN-10: 0-8203-2825-1 (hardcover : alk. paper)
ISBN-13: 978-0-8203-4140-8 (pbk. : alk. paper)
ISBN-10: 0-8203-4140-1 (pbk. : alk. paper)
1. American literature—19th century—History and
criticism. 2. Social change in literature. 3. Political
violence in literature. 4. United States—History—
19th century. I. Title.
PS217.S58R49 2011
810.9'3552—dc22   2011012916

British Library Cataloging-in-Publication Data available

for Bob and Noni

CONTENTS

PREFACE

The foundational moment in American history was marked by a gunshot, or so we are told in Ralph Waldo Emerson's famous poem "Concord Fight," also known as "Concord Hymn"—a not uncommon overlay of violence and religion in national history. In the poem, Emerson asserts,

> Here once the embattled farmers stood,
> And fired the shot heard round the world.[1]

His glorification of civilian resistance to an occupying army offers us but one perspective on the event, of course. The British, obviously, had another. And Emerson's friend and rival Nathaniel Hawthorne another. In his unfinished romance "Septimius Felton," begun at the start of the Civil War, Hawthorne tells of the retreat of the British troops from Concord as the colonists shoot at them from behind trees and houses. One redcoat staggers and falls, and Hawthorne's protagonist-observer shudders because this apparently righteous violence "was so like murder that he really could not tell the difference."[2] The same could be said of almost all political violence resulting in death, and the epistemological challenge to "tell the difference" lies at the heart of the literary movement known as the American Renaissance.[3]

This book focuses on a series of key moments in American literature between 1830 and 1890, when the idea and fact of political violence provoked the emotions and imaginations of American authors and deeply informed their writings. *Righteous Violence* examines the various and variable ways that Margaret Fuller, Ralph Waldo Emerson, Frederick Douglass, Henry David Thoreau, Louisa May Alcott, Nathaniel

Hawthorne, and Herman Melville responded to acts of political violence such as rebellions, revolts, riots, insurrections, and revolutions, which were regarded as crimes by those in power but righteous deeds by their perpetrators and supporters. More often than not, these authors struggled with the moral complexities of the unlawful violence they encountered and produced stirring works that capture the intensity and difficulty of their efforts. The three main goals of *Righteous Violence* are to historicize and illuminate their struggles, to show the political and cultural work they performed, and to deepen and complicate our own understanding of political violence beyond the dichotomies of revolution and murder, liberty and oppression, good and evil.

This study began with a sense that existing criticism had not provided an adequate account of the profoundly contingent and morally complex perspectives found in the writings of these authors. The recent turn to issues of politics and ethics in American literary and cultural studies, especially with regard to the issue of radical social action, has, despite the revelation of past injustices and the admirable expansion of the literary canon, been accompanied by the tendency to position authors for or against a "politics of liberation," as currently defined. *Righteous Violence* goes against the grain of this scholarship by taking a culturally relative approach to the authors it treats and evaluating their shifting and troubled stances primarily in their own terms, within their own historical moments. *Righteous Violence* proceeds in roughly chronological fashion, within and between chapters. After an introductory historical overview, it focuses on its seven authors in sequence. The book does not aspire to provide a linear narrative or a comprehensive topical treatment, but rather a series of overlapping essays linked through their shared concern with the violence of slavery and revolution, "dark twins of a national ideology riddled with ambiguities and tensions," as Eric Sundquist has called them.[4]

The first chapter examines the nature and influence of Margaret Fuller's *Tribune* dispatches from Italy during the 1848–49 revolutions and argues that these writings may have indirectly inspired the Civil War. After Fuller; her husband, Marquess Giovanni Ossoli; and her son, Angelo, fled Rome for Florence, she remained a defiant supporter of the Italian *Risorgimento* and, in apocalyptic terms, prophesied the fiery destruction of tyranny by the forces of liberty. Her celebrated support of revolution and assassination, I argue, prefigured a major change in antislavery thinking and influenced the pro-war attitudes of some of its most important northern intellectual advocates, especially Thomas Wentworth Higginson, the key member of John Brown's "Secret Six."

My second chapter, "Emerson, Guns, and Bloodlust," seeks to illuminate the controversial issue of Emerson's support of political activism. With the publication of the Gougeon and Myerson edition of *Emerson's Antislavery Writings* in 1995, this important part of Emerson's career became consolidated and magnified. During the past decade, the topic has moved to the forefront of Emerson scholarship as a host of influential critics have emphasized the fervor and impact of Emerson's antislavery efforts. In this chapter, I trace Emerson's progression from a proponent of peace to an advocate of war, by focusing on moments in his life when guns occupied his attention. My goal is to show how his arguments supporting violence and warfare were gradually and tortuously constructed through the use of elision, rejection, and rationalization, until he could forcefully assert that "war exalts the age."[5]

My third chapter builds on the work of those scholars who have studied Frederick Douglass's relation to Garrisonian nonresistance, which gave way to his support of violent slave insurrection. This chapter traces the intellectual struggle that attended this movement on Douglass's part, given his peace principles on the one hand and his hatred of slavery on the other. Though wise enough to perceive the suicidal nature of John Brown's Harpers Ferry raid, Douglass nevertheless admired Brown inordinately and evinced regret at not having joined him. His support of black-on-white violence existed in tension with the hope that violence and warfare could lead to an integrated nation free of slavery and racial prejudice, and his lone work of fiction, *The Heroic Slave* (1853), dramatizes that tension.

Chapter 4, "Contemplation versus Violence in Thoreau's World," explores a related tension that Thoreau struggled with throughout his career, especially when the slavery controversy intruded upon his thought. The Bhagavad Gita, because it focuses on the dilemma of whether it is morally right to kill as the agent of divine principle, encouraged

Thoreau to entertain the idea that violence could be a means of purification and enlightenment, contributing to an ongoing and deathless
process. In *Walden*, as well as in his "Slavery in Massachusetts" and "A
Plea for John Brown," one can discern Thoreau's growing Eastern belief
that the forces of destruction are inseparable from the forces of creation
and that violence is not a matter of good or evil but, rather, one of several ways to advance toward spiritual Reality.

My fifth chapter argues that political violence served Louisa May Alcott
as an unstable means of defining both male and female development
and heroism, focusing on her novel *Moods*, written in the wake of John
Brown's execution. In this novel, Alcott bases her male heroes Geoffrey
Moor and Adam Warwick on Emerson and Thoreau, respectively, the
latter also displaying John Brown's physical ferocity. The two male characters compete for the hand of Alcott's impulsive heroine, Sylvia Yule,
based on Alcott herself. In the final chapters of the novel, Alcott sends
the two men to Italy, where Warwick fights alongside Garibaldi on behalf of Italian liberty before drowning in a shipwreck on his return to
America. This ending reveals the ways Alcott was influenced by her heroine Fuller and how revolutionary violence could appear romantic in her
eyes. Written before the Civil War, the first edition of *Moods* appeared in
1865 and ends with the heroine's death. The revised edition, published
in 1882, ends with Sylvia's recovery and a vast vision of a dark sky penetrated by glorious light and the benignant face of Warwick. Alcott thus
romantically conjoins warfare and luminous sanctification, as she does
with Warwick's name and her poem to John Brown, "With a Rose, That
Bloomed on the Day of John Brown's Martyrdom."

My sixth chapter examines what has been called Hawthorne's "last
phase," when he returned to Concord from Europe in 1860 and found
himself in the midst of admirers of John Brown, including the Alcotts,
who were eager to go to war with the slaveholding South. After tracing
the development of Hawthorne's pacifism, especially his use of the myth
of the dragon's teeth to critique the bellicosity of his countrymen, I examine how his last romances, inspired by the cult of Oliver Cromwell,
focus on the question of whether the killing of an oppressor is a righteous or lamentable act. Both John Brown and Bronson Alcott inform
this fiction in surprising ways, as Hawthorne tries to come to terms with

the possibility that a bloody hand and loving heart can combine within one character.

Melville was one of the few writers of the day who shared Hawthorne's nonpartisan perspective on the Civil War, and in the latter half of his career, he too became more and more troubled by violence and bloodshed. In my final chapter, I argue that *Billy Budd* becomes a site—charged by contemporary events—for Melville to revisit and review the issues of revolution and reform, violence and order, which had long concerned him, and to dramatize the value and cost of a conservative stance toward them. Responding to contemporary labor unrest, especially the strikes in New York City and the Haymarket bombing in Chicago, along with the hanging of the anarchists supposedly responsible, Melville reflects on his career-long ambivalence between a democratic faith in man in the ideal and his conservative distrust of the mass of mankind. The chapter traces Melville's desire for reform and fear of revolution throughout a series of his early works, where he captures the epistemological uncertainty underlying the issue of violent resistance to established authority. In later works, such as *Battle-Pieces* and *Clarel*, his growing appreciation for law and order emerges, and in *Billy Budd*, he makes a hard-won case on behalf of social stability, with Captain Vere demonstrating one response to popular violence—hanging—when times are revolutionary.

Billy Budd remained an unfinished work at Melville's death, so the case it makes has to be regarded as provisional, and in many ways the responses of all of these authors are embedded in their particular historical moments and can only be understood as such. The value they retain for us, however, is that their imaginative and, at times, extravagant treatments of the clash between human law and a "higher law" provide an abundance of fresh understanding of what is now called terrorism.

ACKNOWLEDGMENTS

It is a pleasure to thank my colleagues at Texas A&M University who provided support and encouragement while I was writing this book—namely, Marian Eide, Richard Golsan, Kate Kelly, David McWhirter, Anne Morey, Claudia Nelson, Mary Ann O'Farrell, and Mikko Tuhkanen. I am also grateful to those current and former graduate students who assisted with my research, especially Michael Beilfuss, Kohei Furuya, Sarah Jones, Yonggi Kim, Nick Lawrence, Joon Park, James Stamant, Gina Terry, Marina Trninic, and Anne-Marie Womack.

I am indebted to the helpful staffs at the Boston Public Library, the Houghton Library of Harvard University, the Huntington Library, and the Massachusetts Historical Society. The scholarship and generosity of a number of Americanists made this book possible, and I would like to thank in particular Brigitte Bailey, Evan Carton, Bell Chevigny, Wai Chee Dimock, Len Gougeon, Robert Habich, Robert Hudspeth, David Leverenz, Robert Levine, Richard Millington, Thomas Mitchell, Joel Myerson, Frederick Newberry, Leland Person, David Reynolds, David Robinson, John Rowe, Jeffrey Steele, and Brook Thomas. I also thank Albert von Frank, whose vigorous critiques of my Emerson chapter were especially helpful.

Earlier versions of chapters 1, 2, and 7 appeared, respectively, in *Margaret Fuller: Transatlantic Crossings in a Revolutionary Age*, edited by Charles Capper and Cristina Giorcelli (Madison: University of Wisconsin Press, 2008); *More Day to Dawn: Thoreau's "Walden" for the Twenty-first Century*, edited by Sandra Harbert Petrulionis and Laura Walls (Boston: University of Massachusetts Press, 2006); and *New Essays on "Billy Budd,"* edited by Donald Yannella (New York: Cambridge University Press, 2002). I am grateful to the editors of these volumes for their warm encouragement and expert advice.

Two outstanding Americanists in my own department, Jimmie Killingsworth and Dennis Berthold, kindly read the completed manuscript and offered astute suggestions for improving it, and I heartily thank them. I am also grateful to Nancy Grayson, executive editor at the University of Georgia Press, whose support of this project over the years has been inspirational. My children, Brian, Charlotte, Logan, Robin, and Sean, have my deep gratitude for their kindness and love, and finally, my wife, Susan Bolet Egenolf, I thank not only for her love and support but also for her wonderful example as a scholar and a person.

Righteous Violence

I, John Brown, am now quite *certain* that the crimes of this *guilty land: will* never be purged *away;* but with Blood.

— Charlestown, Virginia, December 2, 1859

Nobody was ever more justly hanged. He won his martyrdom fairly, and took it firmly.

— HAWTHORNE, "Chiefly about War-Matters," 1862

INTRODUCTION

Righteous Violence

Political violence permeated the nineteenth century, and the Civil War, of course, generated the preponderance of bloodshed and death during the period. A series of other violent events also captured the attention of American authors, at times in more subtle and complex ways, due to the moral ambiguities associated with them. Nat Turner's 1831 slave rebellion, the 1837 murder of antislavery editor Elijah Lovejoy, the 1841 slave revolt on the *Creole,* the 1854 murder of James Batchelder in Boston (during the attempted rescue of fugitive slave Anthony Burns), the 1856 Pottawatomie massacre in "Bleeding Kansas," John Brown's 1859 raid on Harpers Ferry, and the 1886 Haymarket Bombing in Chicago are examples of such specific provocative events. Despite their disparity, the question these events persistently raised was, Under what circumstances is it morally right to kill another human being? That is, when established authority and institutional power come into conflict with "natural" human rights such as freedom, whose violence can be considered "righteous" when bloodshed and death result? The ways in which the seven authors of this study address these questions vary considerably due to the authors' distinct personalities, perspectives, and politics; however, the authors shared the same cultural situation, and all attended to the moral challenge such violence posed. It engaged their imaginations, informed their writings, and in some cases, shaped their careers. This introduction provides a historical overview of the problematic violence of revolution and slavery, and the chapters that follow examine the specific ways these authors responded to it. As will become clear, the figure of John Brown looms large as an influence and challenge.

On August 1, 1844, five of the authors in this study found themselves in Concord, Massachusetts, at the celebration of the tenth anniversary of the emancipation of slaves in the British West Indies. In the years ahead, as the agitation over slavery grew in intensity, all of them would find themselves pondering the use of violence to free the slaves in the United States. August 1, 1844, marks a beginning. (Herman Melville, at the time, was celebrating his twenty-fifth birthday on board the man-of-war *United States*, making its way to Boston harbor. Louisa May Alcott was an eleven-year-old girl living in Still River, Massachusetts, with her family, who would soon move to Concord.) At the invitation of the Concord Female Anti-Slavery Society, Frederick Douglass came to the town on August 1 to speak at the celebration, alongside Samuel J. May, John Pierpont, Walter Channing, and Emerson. Douglass's topic was most likely his life as a slave. Within a year he would publish his best-selling *Narrative of the Life of Frederick Douglass, an American Slave, Written by Himself* (1845), which Margaret Fuller would review favorably in the *New-York Tribune.* Fuller was staying with the Emersons in the summer of 1844, visiting with the Hawthornes as well, collecting materials for her *Woman in the Nineteenth Century* (1845), which she would soon write. In her journal, she recorded the effect of Emerson's antislavery address upon her: "It was true happiness to hear him; tears came to my eyes. The old story of how the blacks received their emancipation: it seemed as if I had never heard before: he gave it such expression. How ashamed one felt ever to be sad, while possessing that degree of freedom which gave them such joy. I felt excited to new life and a nobler emulation by Waldo this day."[1] A nod to "champions of the enslaved African" would find its way into her new book.[2]

Members of the Concord Female Anti-Slavery Society had persuaded Emerson to give his address. This group included Mary Brooks; Emerson's wife, Lidian; and Henry Thoreau's mother and sisters, Cynthia, Sophia, and Helen Thoreau. Many Concord residents opposed the event, however, failing to recognize the relation between colonial liberty and slave liberty. As William Lloyd Garrison's *Liberator* reported, "The doors of every church in town were barred against the advocates of universal emancipation, and they were compelled to resort to the court-house, though not without being threatened in certain quarters, if they should presume to exercise their liberty!"[3] Despite its key role in the American Revolution, Concord in the 1830s and early 1840s "vigilantly upheld the status quo and avoided extremism of any kind, certainly abolitionism," as Sandra Petrulionis has shown.[4] Hawthorne, who disdained abolitionists but admired Emerson, offered the yard of his home, the Manse, as a site for the event, but because it rained that morning, the activities were moved to the courthouse. When no one else would ring the bell of the Unitarian meeting-house to summon people to the event, Thoreau took it upon himself to do so. Two years later he would cohost the August 1 celebration at his hut at Walden Pond. Garrison called the treatment of the speakers in August 1844 a "disgrace" and roared, "This is *the* Concord of revolutionary renown—Concord 'in the year of our Lord one thousand eight hundred and forty-four, and in the sixty-eighth year of American Independence'! Its ancient patriotism has utterly perished."[5] The insult was a mighty one, for despite its anti-abolitionism (which it shared with most of the country), Concord prided itself on its revolutionary past, its "ancient patriotism."

APRIL 19 IN CONCORD

Throughout the nineteenth century, the American Revolution provided the most prevalent model for justifying violent resistance to established authority. The revolt of slaves in the South, and the rebellion of the South itself, were both represented by supporters in terms of the American Revolution—that is, as a fight for liberty against the forces of tyranny. As Eric Sundquist has pointed out, "The vexed relationship between the revolutionary tradition and slavery animated almost every significant political and cultural issue of the antebellum years, often in fact providing the grounds on which politics and literature met."[6] Within this juncture, the task of discerning and establishing the moral high ground proved difficult, whether the use of violence was by those with power or those without it.

April 19, the date American minutemen fought with British troops in Lexington and Concord to start the Revolution in 1775, became known for carnage and heroism. The date equaled in significance the Fourth of July, at least in the small New England village of Concord. Everyone who visited Concord as a speaker mentioned its revolutionary past, including the Hungarian revolutionary Louis Kossuth and the radical abolitionist John Brown, who "twice addressed the sons of those yeomen who fought at Concord Bridge," as Franklin Sanborn, one of Brown's conspirators, put it.[7] Although the encounter at the North Bridge was merely a skirmish, it immediately acquired national significance because for the first time the colonists shed the blood of the king's troops.

The conflict began when British general Thomas Gage, with knowledge that the Americans were stockpiling weapons and provisions in Concord, dispatched 700–800 elite British regulars from Boston on the night of April 18, 1775, with orders to seize and destroy the hidden supplies. On the morning of the nineteenth, seventy armed minutemen in Lexington, who had been warned that the British were coming, assembled on the green as an advance unit of six British companies marched into town. The colonial captain John Parker had given his men orders not to fire unless fired upon, and the British major John Pitcairn gave the same order to his regulars. Pitcairn contemptuously ordered the Americans to disperse, but while they were doing so, several shots were fired (by whom remains unclear), and the British immediately fired a volley and wildly charged the militiamen, killing eight and wounding nine. Shortly thereafter, the British reorganized, held a brief celebration, and continued their march to Concord.

Having been alerted during the night, the people of Concord hid weapons and provisions in neighboring towns and in the nearby countryside. Minutemen and militiamen assembled in the town to protect it. When the redcoats entered, one British company was sent to the South Bridge, and six companies were dispatched toward the North Bridge. Seeing this, the American colonel James Barrett ordered the provincials to assemble at Major Buttrick's farm on high ground west of the

North Bridge. Three of the British companies went past the Bridge to the Barrett farmhouse to search it, leaving behind fewer than a hundred men at the bridge. The Americans eventually numbered about 400 and occupied the high ground.

The redcoats in the center of town looted, destroyed barrels of flour, threw musket balls into the mill pond, and made a bonfire of the town's liberty pole, which accidentally set fire to the courthouse. Seeing the smoke, the men at Buttrick's farm thought the British were burning down the town, and after a brief council, Colonel Barrett ordered the men to march toward the bridge in double file. The British retreated to the east side of the bridge, fired warning shots, and then a volley at the approaching Americans, killing two men. The Americans returned fire, killing three British soldiers and wounding twelve others. The rest of the redcoats panicked and ran toward town. The fight over, most of the militiamen dispersed.

At this point a slow-witted young man named Ammi White, who had been chopping wood at the Manse (the minister's home) some hundred yards away when the shooting took place, arrived on the scene, and when a dying redcoat moved, he struck him on the head with his axe, splitting open his head but not killing him immediately.[8] The redcoat lived an hour or two more. Hawthorne, in his preface to *Mosses from an Old Manse* (1846), relates this story and adds, "Oftentimes, as an intellectual and moral exercise, I have sought to follow that poor youth through his subsequent career, and observe how his soul was tortured by the blood-stain, contracted, as it had been, before the long custom of war had robbed human life of its sanctity, and while it still seemed murderous to slay a brother man."[9] Obviously for Hawthorne, none of the killing that day rose to the level of high-minded patriotism.

The British soldiers returning from Barrett's farm saw the mangled head of their colleague and spread the rumor that the Americans scalped their fallen enemies alive.[10] The shooting that the colonists engaged in during the rest of the nineteenth provoked a similar charge of savagery. As is well known, Massachusetts militia from across the province, whose numbers grew to roughly 4,000, harried the retreating British throughout the afternoon, shooting at them from behind trees, houses, and stone walls. Periodically, the British made a stand and fought back, but by the end of the day, they had suffered 73 killed, 174 wounded, and 26 missing. Among the Americans, 49 were killed, 39 wounded, and 4 were missing.

The tactics used by the Americans seemed dishonorable to the British; one soldier claimed that the rebels showed "the cowardly disposition . . . to murder us all."[11] John Hancock, for the Americans, boasted that the British had been "compelled to retreat by the country people suddenly assembled to repel this cruel aggression. Hostilities thus commenced by the British troops, have been since prosecuted by them without regard to faith or reputation. . . . The arms we have been compelled by our enemies to assume, we will, in defiance of every hazard, with unabating firmness and perseverance, employ for the preservation of our liberties, being with one mind resolved, to dye Freemen rather than to live Slaves."[12] As John McWilliams has pointed out, although the British secretary of state, the Earl of Suffolk, dismissed the events of April 19 as inconsequential, "the immediate effect of the confrontations at Lexington and Concord was to validate the patriots' collective identity as oppressed farmers and homespun martyr-heroes."[13] As victims of British oppression, their violent resistance was represented in narratives by American authors as not only righteous but also heroic.

When Emerson wrote his "Concord Hymn" for the dedication of the monument at the site of the old North Bridge on July 4, 1836, he was neither the first nor the last to celebrate the events of April 19, 1775. As McWilliams has observed, "There seemed to have been no end to the commemorating. At the very moment when fulsome oratory about Revolutionary forefathers died away in the breaking out of civil war, Longfellow sent Paul Revere on his midnight ride through so many schoolchildren's heads that the whole episode slowed to a poetic jog trot, broadly and badly recited."[14] Following the Civil War, Emerson participated in the commemoration of the "Soldiers' Monument" placed in the center of town. At this ceremony, held April 19, 1867, Emerson looked back upon the American Revolution more critically, identifying a "poison" that accompanied the founding of the nation. He began by observing that "[t]he day is in Concord doubly our calendar day, as being the anniversary of the invasion of the town by the British troops in 1775 and of the departure of the company of volunteers for Washington in 1861." "The old Monument," he declared, "a short half-mile from this house, stands to signalize the first Revolution, where the people resisted offensive usurpations. . . . But in the necessities of the hour, they overlooked the moral law, and winked at a practical exception to the Bill of Rights they had drawn up. . . . It turned out that this one violation was a subtle poison, which in eighty years corrupted the whole overgrown body politic, and brought the alternative of extirpation of the poison or ruin to the Republic."[15] For Emerson and other abolitionists, the Civil War finally instantiated the principles of liberty and equality announced in the Declaration of Independence.

These principles were persistently evoked in the antebellum period by abolitionists and women's rights advocates. At the first women's rights convention held in Seneca Falls, New York, in 1848, the "Declaration of Sentiments" asserted: "We hold these truths to be self-evident; that all men and women are created equal; that they are endowed by their Creator with certain inalienable rights; that among these are life, liberty, and the pursuit of happiness."[16] Not surprisingly, those engaged in the antislavery movement were at the forefront of the women's rights movement. In *Woman in the Nineteenth Century* (1845), Fuller observed that the antislavery movement, "partly from a natural following out of principles, partly because many women have been prominent in that cause, makes, just now, the warmest appeal in behalf of woman."[17] Frederick Douglass attended the Seneca Falls convention, signed the "Declaration of Sentiments," and was the sole male to vote for the women's suffrage resolution. He became a longtime friend of Elizabeth Cady Stanton, one of the convention's organizers. The only time tension arose in their relationship was after the Civil War when the issue of suffrage for black males and for women arose. Douglass supported the Fifteenth Amendment, for obvious reasons, yet Stanton felt he had abandoned the cause of votes for women in the process, which he did, to help the chances of black males.

Whenever outrage at the existing government arose in the antebellum period, the heroism of the Minutemen was evoked. Following John Brown's Harpers Ferry raid, vigilance committees were organized in the South, and local militias were formed and armed. The likelihood of the Republican Lincoln's election moved many in the South to prepare for secession and war, which they conceived as a new American revolution against tyranny, similar to that of 1776. In the fall of 1860, a group of citizens in Columbia, South Carolina, called themselves "Minutemen" and pledged, "We, the undersigned . . . in view of the impending crisis, necessarily incident upon the election of a Black Republican to the Presidency of those United States . . . , which must come in the event of the triumph of Northern fanaticism, hereby form ourselves into an association under the name and style of 'the minutemen': and do further solemnly pledge our lives, our fortunes and sacred honor, to sustain Southern constitutional equality in the Union, or, failing in that, to establish our independence out of it."[18] Whereas secession was treason in the North, it was patriotism in the South.

SAN DOMINGO

A second revolution in the New World almost as important as the American Revolution in terms of shaping the discourse about slavery and violent rebellion was the 1791 slave revolt in the French colony of Saint-Domingue (known in English as San Domingo and in 1804 as the Republic of Haiti). The Haitian Revolution became notorious for the horrific cruelty the combatants inflicted upon one another and on women and children. Jeremy Popkin has pointed out that "half the slaves in 1790 were survivors of the fearful Middle Passage, and the plantation owners of Saint-Domingue had a reputation for particularly brutal behavior,"[19] which made the rage and barbarism of the rebelling slaves unsurprising, if not righteous. As Joan Dayan has shown, the Black Code and official reports about the tortures, mutilations, and terror inflicted upon the slaves of Saint-Domingue by their French masters were direct sources of the Marquis de Sade's depraved, pornographic fictions.[20] Sadism bred Sadism.

The revolt began with a series of nocturnal meetings among slave leaders in the summer of 1791, and on the night of August 22 a massive insurrection began as the slaves killed, and in some cases tortured, every white person they could find. One proslavery account describes it as a time when "blood flowed in torrents; lust and violation were made things of custom; and the population lost almost the traits which distinguish humanity from the brute."[21] In 1833 the Quaker abolitionist John Greenleaf Whittier described the revolt thus:

> Dark, naked arms were tossed on high;
> And, round the white man's lordly hall,
> Trod, fierce and free, the brute he made;
> And those who crept along the wall,
> And answered to his lightest call
> With more than spaniel dread,
> The creatures of his lawless beck,
> Were trampling on his very neck!
> And on the night-air, wild and clear,
> Rose woman's shriek of more than fear;
> For bloodied arms were round her thrown,
> And dark cheeks pressed against her own![22]

Southern slaveholders saw the revolt as confirming their argument that blacks were beasts who could become wanton murderers and rapists ("with bloodied arms") if agitated by abolitionists. For abolitionists, the horrors of San Domingo served as an example of what a slaveholder could expect if he did not free his slaves: a dark foot on the neck of his writhing figure, much like the tableau on the stern of the *San Dominick* in Melville's "Benito Cereno." In the *Liberator*, Garrison warned that if "the glorious day of universal emancipation" did not arrive, "woe to the safety of this people! . . . A cry of horror, a cry of revenge, will go up to heaven in the darkness of midnight, and re-echo from every cloud. Blood will flow like water—the blood of guilty men, and of innocent women and children. Then will be heard lamentations and weeping, such as will blot out the remembrance of the horrors of St. Domingo."[23] Though a Christian pacifist, Garrison specialized in bloodthirsty rhetoric, which earned him the reputation as a fanatic.

During the Haitian Revolution, lasting from 1791 to 1804, countless plantations were destroyed and chaos prevailed as slaves, mulattos, the French, the Spanish, and the British fought for dominance and used all means to attain it. Out of the chaos, a well-educated ex-slave named

Toussaint Louverture rose to leadership. According to most accounts, he did not participate in the massacre of whites in the initial revolt. In fact, he apparently helped his French master, Bayon de Libertat, and his family escape.[24] Referring to this kindness, Whittier, in his poem "Toussaint L'Ouverture," offers

> A tribute for thy lofty mind,
> Amidst whose gloomy vengeance shone
> Some milder virtues all thine own,
> Some gleams of feeling pure and warm,
> Like sunshine on a sky of storm,
> Proofs that the Negro's heart retains
> Some nobleness amid its chains,—
> That kindness to the wronged is never
> Without its excellent reward,
> Holy to human-kind and ever
> Acceptable to God.[25]

By the beginning of 1793, Toussaint had emerged as a brilliant military commander and astute politician. He organized the slaves and fought with the Spanish, then switched his allegiance to the French and fought against the Spanish and the British, driving the latter from the island. Claiming loyalty to France but asserting his independent authority, Toussaint conquered Spanish Santo Domingo in the east, put down a mulatto uprising in the west and the south with the aid of American forces, and took control of all of Hispaniola in 1801, restoring peace and order. The constitution he wrote, without consulting France, guaranteed liberty and equality to all people, regardless of race, and named himself governor for life. Napoleon, outraged and determined to reestablish slavery in the French West Indies, sent an army of 20,000 men to Haiti, forcing Toussaint to surrender. After he signed a peace treaty, Toussaint was betrayed, bound, transported to France, and imprisoned in the dungeon of Fort de Joux, where he died in 1803.

With the help of yellow fever, Toussaint's successor, Jean-Jacques Dessalines, drove the French from the island, killed all remaining whites, and completed the revolution. As C. L. R. James famously declared, this was "the only successful slave revolt in history, and the odds it had to overcome is evidence of the magnitude of the interests that were involved. The transformation of slaves, trembling in hundreds before a single white man, into a people able to organize themselves and defeat the most powerful European nations of their day, is one of the great epics of revolutionary struggle and achievement."[26] Hawthorne's *Peter Parley's Universal History on the Basis of Geography* (1837), written for children, describes how "the negroes . . . slaughtered the white people by thousands, pillaging their houses, and then setting them on fire," but it too offers a surprisingly positive description of the outcome: "After various revolutions, the whole island was formed into a republic, the officers of which were negroes or mulattoes, and so it continues to this day. The people are, on the whole, well governed, the state of society is improving, and attention is being paid to education. Nearly all the inhabitants are people of colour, but many of them are intelligent, and carry on the various concerns of agriculture and commerce with skill and success."[27] The popular Peter Parley series helped schoolchildren in New England understand the wrongs of slavery and the benefits of liberty.

As enlightened rebel, Toussaint became an iconic figure for romantic writers on both sides of the Atlantic. He was represented as almost immortal in Wordsworth's famous sonnet "To Toussaint L'Ouverture," published in 1803, and in the United States he became a role model for ex-slaves such as Frederick Douglass. Emerson, too, was impressed, and in his 1844 Antislavery Address declared that "the arrival in the world of such men as Toussaint, and the Haytian heroes, or of the leaders of their race in Barbadoes and Jamaica, outweighs in good omen all the English and American humanity."[28] In his essay "Character" (1844), Emerson likewise extended respect to the rebel slave leader, asking, "Suppose a slaver on the coast of Guinea should take on board a gang of negroes, which should contain persons of the stamp of Toussaint L'Ouverture: or, let us fancy, under these swarthy masks he has a gang of Washingtons in chains. When they arrive at Cuba, will the relative order of the ship's company be the same?"[29] Toussaint and Madison Washington, leader of a slave revolt on the ship *Creole* in 1841, attained heroic status by their successful use of force to achieve liberty. George Washington, Emerson may have thought, did the same.

INSURRECTION, MOBS, AND MARTYRDOM

Although the United States abolished trade with Haiti in 1805 (because France still claimed it as its colony), black slaves throughout the Americas were inspired by its example. Gabriel Prosser's slave conspiracy of 1800 near Richmond, Virginia, was inspired by the slaves of Saint-Domingue, as was Denmark Vesey's abortive revolt of 1822 in Charleston, South Carolina, at least according to his followers.[30] The inspiration for Nat Turner's notorious Southampton, Virginia, insurrection in 1831, however, came not primarily from Haiti but the Bible, particularly the visions and voices it evoked. According to his supposed *Confessions* (1831), transcribed by local lawyer Thomas Gray, Turner declared: "I had a vision—and I saw white spirits and black spirits engaged in battle, and the sun was darkened—the thunder rolled in the Heavens, and blood flowed in streams—and I heard a voice saying, 'Such is your luck, such you are called to see, and let it come rough or smooth, you must surely bare it.'"[31]

In the early morning hours of August 22, 1831 (coincidentally, the anniversary of the Haitian Revolution), Turner and his band of seven, armed with crude weapons, began breaking into local houses, killing every white man, woman, and child they could find. They began with Turner's owner, Joseph Travis. Turner reportedly said, "armed with a hatchet, and accompanied by Will, I entered my master's chamber, it being dark, I could not give a death blow, the hatchet glanced from his head, he sprang from the bed and called his wife, it was his last word, Will laid him dead, with a blow of his axe, and Mrs. Travis shared the same fate, as she lay in bed."[32] During the next two days, as the rebels moved along, they recruited followers, some seventy in all, mostly enslaved blacks, and they killed at least fifty-seven whites. When word spread throughout Southampton County, a party of militia formed, and they successfully confronted, chased down, and arrested most of the rebels. Seventeen were executed and the rest were transported. Turner hid out for two months but was discovered, arrested, tried, and hanged on November 11, 1831. The revolt generated suspicion and panic throughout the South, and countless blacks were tortured and killed in retaliation. In an 1861 essay in the *Atlantic Monthly*, Thomas Wentworth

Higginson, using southern newspapers as his sources, reports that many innocent negroes were killed every day: "Men were tortured to death, burned, maimed, and subjected to nameless atrocities. The overseers were called on to point out any slaves whom they distrusted, and if any tried to escape they were shot down."[33]

To blacks, Nat Turner became a heroic figure, and Douglass in particular praised him time and again, arguing that he brought emancipation closer through his violence. Douglass in a speech in 1848 asserted that Turner endeavored "to gain his own liberty, and that of his enslaved brethren, by the self-same means which the Revolutionary fathers employed." With more passion than accuracy, Douglass conveyed Virginia's hatred of Turner by adding: "When taken by his enemies, he was stripped naked, and compelled to walk barefooted, some thirty yards, over burning coals, and when he reached the end, he fell, pierced by a hundred American bullets!"[34] Garrison, whose *Liberator* was blamed for inciting Turner's revolt, responded in a self-divided way. On the one hand, because he had argued for nonresistance in the face of violence, Garrison insisted that slave insurrections such as Turner's were morally wrong and ineffectual. On the other hand, he extended understanding and sympathy to slaves who did revolt. In a piece written two months before Turner's execution, he condemned the "white butchers" who "are slaying their victims in a most ferocious manner, and exhibiting a cannibal thirst for human blood. They have not the excuse of the infuriated slaves—ignorance and a deprivation of liberty."[35] Garrison received assassination threats from the South and New England both.[36]

Although members of the Massachusetts Anti-Slavery Society under Garrison's leadership in the 1830s practiced nonresistance and discouraged slave revolts, they provoked mobs that attacked their speakers as well as mobs that attacked free blacks. Leonard I. Richards in his *"Gentlemen of Property and Standing": Anti-Abolition Mobs in Jacksonian America* reports sixty-one "anti-abolition and anti-Negro mobs" in New England between 1833 and 1837.[37] In 1835 a mob dragged Garrison through the streets of Boston with a rope around his neck, and in 1838, an anti-abolition mob burned down Pennsylvania Hall. Race hatred took precedence over the hatred of abolitionists, and stereotypes of negroes as savage and demonic fueled riots directed at both. Perhaps the most horrific mob attack occurred in Saint Louis in April 1836, resulting in the lynching of Francis L. McIntosh, a free mulatto boatman.

McIntosh was arrested by Deputy Sheriff George Hammond and Deputy Constable William Mull for interfering with their attempt to arrest two sailors on McIntosh's boat. As McIntosh was being taken to jail, he drew a knife and wounded both the officers, Hammond mortally. McIntosh fled, but a crowd pursued and caught him and took him to jail. As word spread of his deed, an angry mob formed outside the jail, and after the sheriff and his family left, they broke into the jail that night and took their victim to a large locust tree on the edge of town, chained him to it, and set fire to wood piled at his feet, slowly burning him to death. Later, a rabble of boys amused themselves by throwing stones at his burned corpse trying to break its skull.

Most of the Missouri papers chose not to print the gory details of this violence, but the editor of the *St. Louis Observer*, a thirty-four-year-old Presbyterian minister and moderate abolitionist named Elijah Parish Lovejoy, did. At one point he related that McIntosh, as he was burning, "commenced singing a hymn and trying to pray. Afterwards he hung his head and suffered in silence, until roused by some one saying, that he must be already out of his misery. Upon this, though wrapped in flames, and though the fire had obliterated the features of humanity, he raised his head, and spoke out distinctly, saying, 'No, no; I feel as much as any of you, I hear you all; shoot me, shoot me.' He was burning about twenty minutes, before life became extinct."[38] In addition to publishing this shameful account, Lovejoy also criticized Judge Luke E. Lawless for charging a grand jury not to indict those responsible for murdering McIntosh. Consequently, a mob of citizens destroyed Lovejoy's press and threatened to tar and feather him, if not worse. To protect his family and himself, he moved twenty-five miles northeast of St. Louis to Alton, Illinois (a free state), where he attempted to edit the *Alton Observer*.

In Alton, Lovejoy, a native of Massachusetts, was followed by anti-abolitionist mobs who threatened his life and destroyed three of his presses within four months. Determined to protect a fourth press, Lovejoy enlisted the aid of the mayor and a volunteer militia made up of family, friends, and sympathetic citizens. Shortly before the arrival of the press, he wrote a letter to the *Liberator* relating that "I am writing by the bedside of Mrs. L[ovejoy] whose excitement and fears have measurably returned with the darkness. A loaded musket is standing at my bedside, while my two brothers, in an adjoining room, have *three others*, together with *pistols, cartridges*, etc. I have had inexpressible reluctance to resort to this method of defense. But dear-bought experience has taught me, that there is at present no safety for me, and no defense in this place either in the laws or the protecting aegis of public sentiment."[39] By plan, at 3:00 a.m. on the morning of November 7, 1837, the press arrived on a Mississippi steamboat and was quickly transported to a stone warehouse on the banks of the river, where it was guarded by thirty to forty of Lovejoy's armed supporters. During the day, as news spread about the arrival of the press, a mob formed, and around nine o'clock in the evening some twenty to thirty men, armed with stones, pistols, and guns, gathered outside the building, demanding the press. They threw stones and fired several shots into the warehouse, threatening to blow it up or burn it down unless the press was turned over to them. The nineteen men inside, including Lovejoy and Winthrop Gilman, an owner of the warehouse, refused to comply, and Lovejoy or one of his men shot and killed a young carpenter named Lyman Bishop, who was throwing stones at the windows.

After Bishop was carried to a doctor, the mob dispersed, but an hour later, according to an Ohio newspaper, they "returned with increased numbers, and armed with guns and muskets, &c. &c. and recommenced the attack with renewed violence."[40] Near midnight the mob raised a ladder on one of the windowless sides of the building and tried to start a fire on the wooden roof. Lovejoy and three or four volunteers came around a corner of the building, fired at those manning the ladder, shot at and wounded the boy on the ladder, who fell to the ground, and pushed the ladder over before retreating inside. When another attempt was made to set fire to the roof, two of the mob hid behind a woodpile facing the door, and when Lovejoy stepped out, pistol in hand, one of them shot him with a double-barreled shotgun. Five buckshot entered his chest, abdomen, and arms; he made his way up a flight of stairs to the second floor of the building and died within minutes. Those guarding the press soon decided to make their escape after arranging a tentative truce with the mob, who nevertheless shot at them as they fled. Others in the mob rushed into the empty building, threw the press out the window to the riverbank, broke it into pieces, and threw it in the river.[41]

News of this event shocked many in the country and provoked widespread commentary. As John Demos has said, it was "the first clear-cut breach of non-violent principles" by a formerly nonresistant abolitionist.[42] Those supporters of Lovejoy inside the warehouse were arrested and tried because they "unlawfully, riotously, routously, and in a violent and tumultuous manner defended and resisted an attempt . . . to force open and enter the store-house."[43] (They were acquitted, as were the assailants.) John Quincy Adams observed that Lovejoy's death sent "a shock as of an earthquake throughout the continent, which will be felt in the most distant regions of the earth."[44] Emerson, as Len Gougeon has pointed out, "was so moved by the event in Alton that in his lecture 'Heroism,' delivered in January 1838, and again in his 1841 essay of the same title, he heralded Lovejoy as an authentic hero."[45]

Many southerners and anti-abolitionist editors blamed Lovejoy for his own death, claiming he should not have provoked the citizens of Alton. At a meeting in Faneuil Hall in Boston, even Attorney General James Austin of Massachusetts asserted that Lovejoy had "died as the fool dieth" and compared the mob to the patriots who threw the tea overboard in the Boston Tea Party. Lovejoy's sympathizers, however, who were in the majority at this meeting, defended his right to free speech and castigated mob rule. Wendell Phillips, an aristocratic young Bostonian about to become an ardent abolitionist, declared that "you must read our Revolutionary history upside down" to arrive at the comparison of the Alton mob with the Boston tea partiers. In response to the charge that Lovejoy's behavior was imprudent, Phillips responded, "*Imprudent* to defend the liberty of the press! Why? Because the defence was unsuccessful? Does success gild crime into patriotism, and the want of it change heroic self-devotion to imprudence?"[46]

At a prayer meeting in Hudson, Ohio, a professor of theology, Laurens P. Hickok, made an eloquent speech about Lovejoy's murder, declaring: "The crisis has come. The question now before the American citizens is no longer alone, 'Can the slaves be made free?' but, 'Are we free, or are we slaves under Southern mob law?'" As the meeting came to a close, one man who had sat silent in the back of the room stood up, lifted his right hand, and declared, "Here, before God, in the presence of these witnesses, from this time, I consecrate my life to the destruction of slavery!"[47] His name was John Brown. As Stephen Oates has said, "The vow was no idle gesture."[48]

In the 1840s Garrisonian abolitionists found it more and more difficult to maintain their commitment to nonresistance, especially in the face of arguments referencing the events and ideas of the American Revolution. Garrison called the revolution "selfish, revengeful, murderous" and objected to the claim that it was a Christian undertaking.[49] In 1841, however, the successful slave revolt on the American brig *Creole* led by Madison Washington added to the appeal of the revolutionary tradition. The facts of this revolt became famous within the abolitionist movement, and Frederick Douglass praised and identified with the rebel leader, mentioning him frequently in his fiery speeches. In 1853 Douglass published *The Heroic Slave*, a novella about Washington (discussed in chapter 2), and imbued Washington's violence with righteousness.

The actual revolt occurred on the evening of November 7, 1841, as the *Creole* was sailing from Virginia to New Orleans with a cargo of 135 slaves, including Washington, the slaves' cook. He was discovered by the chief mate, Zephaniah Gifford, in the main hold with the female slaves, and when Gifford and the white overseer of the slaves, William Merritt, tried to seize him, he sprang on deck and called for others to join him. Three other leaders of the revolt, along with fifteen armed slaves, responded and overpowered the eight-man crew, severely wounding the captain, Robert Ensor, and killing John Hewell, owner of thirty-nine slaves, who, while trying to fire a pistol, was knocked down and stabbed repeatedly. Two slaves were seriously wounded in the fighting; one of them later died. Washington and a fellow slave leader, Elijah Morris, prevented the killing of more whites after the revolt, and two injured white sailors had their wounds dressed by the blacks. With the forced assistance of Merritt, the mutineers sailed to the British port of Nassau, in the Bahamas, arriving on the morning of November 9, and British officials, over the United States' objections, eventually allowed all the slaves, including Washington, to go free.[50]

THE AMERICAN AND EUROPEAN 1848S

France followed Britain in freeing all of its slaves—again—in its West Indian colonies in 1848, after the successful French Revolution in the spring of that year, which ousted King Louis Philippe and established a provisional republic headed by the celebrated poet, historian, and statesman Alphonse de Lamartine (the first French Revolution had abolished slavery, but Napoleon had reinstituted it). Michael Rogin was one of the first scholars to discuss the transatlantic features of the year 1848, and he coined the term "the American 1848" as he pointed out that "the news that Mexico and the United States had agreed to peace reached President Polk on February 19, 1848. Three days later, revolution broke out in Paris. While the Senate was considering the Mexican peace treaty, a Parisian mob forced Louis Philippe to abdicate."[51] In Europe, liberty seemed to be advancing, but suffering losses in the United States. All the abolitionists opposed war with Mexico, because they saw it as an attempt to extend slave territory. James Russell Lowell's *Biglow Papers*, featuring "letters" from Lowell's young Birdofredom Sawin, "Private in the Massachusetts Regiment," directs cutting satire at the Polk administration's war propaganda:

> Ez fer war, I call it murder,—
>> There you hev it plain an' flat;
>> I don't want to go no furder
>> Than my Testyment fer that.[52]

Margaret Fuller, in Italy, writing dispatches for Horace Greeley's *New-York Tribune*, also opposed the Mexican War. When the revolutions broke out all over Europe in the spring of 1848, she imagined the spirit of liberty being more alive there than in the United States: "My country is at present spoiled by prosperity, stupid with the lust of gain, soiled by crime in its willing perpetuation of Slavery, shamed by an unjust war." Thus she argues that America, which "is not dead, but in my time she sleepeth," must heed Europe's example. "I hear earnest words of pure faith and love. I see deeds of brotherhood. This is what makes *my* America."[53] Fuller's dispatches from Italy in 1848–49 exerted a strong influence on Americans, especially abolitionists, encouraging them to regard violence as a legitimate means of dealing with oppressive government. She applauded the assassination of Count Pellegrino Rossi on November 15, 1848, when he was fatally stabbed in the neck with a dagger by Luigi Brunetti, son of Angelo Brunetti, a fervent democrat. Fuller and the radicals in Rome represented the killing as necessary tyrannicide.

Such violent events and the rhetoric associated with the European revolutions of 1848–49 persuaded a number of abolitionists to accept the use of force to oppose tyranny and oppression. Thus Theodore Parker asserted, "All the great charters of humanity have been *writ in blood*, and must continue to be so for some centuries."[54] Not everyone agreed, because France's revolutionary tradition, with its Reign of Terror and the rise of Napoleon, struck many Americans as fraught with unintended consequences. Fuller was criticized for her radicalism, and in November 1848 the *New York Herald* attacked Parker and compared him to those "thoroughgoing radicals who have eliminated the Bible to suit their theories, and, in imitation of some of the French and English infidels, changed Jesus Christ from the meek and lowly Messiah . . . into a great democratic reformer . . . [thus pleasing] the wildest of the Parisian populace."[55] Melville, who harbored deep-seated animosity toward the atheism of French radicals, likewise saw dangers in the French model of revolution.

While William Lloyd Garrison and most of his followers continued to argue for nonresistance in the 1850s, prominent activists such as Angelina Grimké Weld, Samuel J. May, Wendell Phillips, Thomas Wentworth Higginson, and Parker Pilsbury all abandoned their peace principles and argued for armed resistance.[56] Congressional passage of the Compromise of 1850 (containing the Fugitive Slave Act), coming on the heels of the siege of Rome by France, evoked a new spirit of defiance among abolitionists, which can be seen in the letter Angelina Grimké Weld wrote a friend in Brookline, Massachusetts: "[A]lthough the shedding of human blood is utterly abhorrent to my mind, as barbarous and unchristian, yet the tame surrender of a helpless victim up to the fate of the slave is far more abhorrent: as slavery is equally, if not more, abhorrent to Christianity, than murder. In this case, it seems as though we are compelled to choose between two evils, and all that we can do is to take the *least*, and baptize liberty in blood, if it must be so. . . . I sincerely hope that the arrest of every fugitive may be contested even unto blood."[57] Even the sedate Emerson in his journal called the Fugitive Slave Act "the most detestable law that was ever enacted by a civilized state" and swore, "I will not obey it, by God."[58]

Emerson gave financial support to the Vigilance Committee in Boston formed to protect fugitives from slave hunters, but he did not personally participate in their activities. Theodore Parker, Unitarian minister and head of the committee, did. In his sermon "The Function and Place of Conscience in Relation to the Laws of Men," he told his congregation: "It is the natural duty of citizens to rescue every fugitive slave from the hands of the marshal who essays to return him to bondage; to do it peaceably if they can; forcibly if they must, but by all means to do it . . . if I were a fugitive, and could escape in no other way, I would kill him [the slave-catcher] with as little compunction as I would drive a mosquito from my face. It is high time this was said."[59] When two slave catchers from Macon, Georgia, arrived in Boston in mid-October 1850 seeking the fugitive slaves William and Ellen Craft, Parker stood ready to defend these parishioners, with violence if necessary: "Yes, I have had to arm myself. I have written my sermons with a pistol in my desk, — loaded, a cap on the nipple, and ready for action. Yea, with a drawn sword within reach of my right hand. . . . My grand-father drew the first sword in the Revolution; my fathers fired the first shot; the blood which flowed there was kindred to this which courses in my veins to-day."[60] Another member of the Vigilance Committee, Lewis Hayden, a fugitive slave from Kentucky living in Boston, "threatened to set off two kegs of dynamite in the basement of his Southac Street home rather than give up Craft or any other fugitive."[61] The Crafts traveled to England for safety and ending up living there for seventeen years, returning after the Civil War.

Lewis Hayden would become the most violent member of Boston's Vigilance Committee, committing what most would consider murder, the shooting of a deputy marshal. He had been born a slave in Lexington, Kentucky, and witnessed the sale of his wife and a son to Senator Henry Clay, who sold them into the deep South, devastating Hayden, who never saw them again. In 1844 he escaped with his second wife and their son to Canada, and they later made their way to Boston, where Hayden ran a clothing store. (His narrative appears in chapter

5 of Stowe's *A Key to Uncle Tom's Cabin.*) He helped in the rescue of the fugitive Shadrach Minkins in 1851, and in 1854 joined Higginson in an attack on the Boston courthouse to try to free the fugitive Anthony Burns (discussed more fully below). Armed with two pistols, he shot and killed one of the deputized guards, the twenty-four-year-old Irish truckman James Batchelder.

Higginson was the leader of the attempted rescue of Burns.[62] Despite being a Unitarian minister, he gloried in violent confrontations. Inspired by Margaret Fuller and Theodore Parker, he sought adventure and action; he subsequently gained fame during the Civil War as commanding officer of the 1st South Carolina Volunteers, the first African American regiment in the Union army. Before the war, he was the most committed member of John Brown's "Secret Six," the abolitionists who provided Brown with support and weapons for his guerrilla warfare. Higginson subscribed to a cult of masculinity, and his actions sometimes lacked political motivation. In a notebook he kept during his ride through "Bleeding Kansas" in 1856, he wrote: "I enjoy danger. Enjoy sitting in a hotel & hearing men talking about me etc. . . . while I know that I have incurred the penalty of death for treason under U.S. laws & for arming fugitives to Kansas."[63] Under the influence of a revolutionary ethos, Higginson argued for the use of force to try to free Anthony Burns.

THE ANTHONY BURNS CASE

The Burns case began for Higginson on the afternoon of Thursday, May 25, 1854, when he received a letter from the abolitionist Samuel J. May and a visit from the transcendentalist philosopher Bronson Alcott, both informing him that the fugitive Burns was being held at the Boston courthouse and a trial had been set for Saturday. After making it to Boston from Worcester, Higginson and six other leaders of the Vigilance Committee agreed to stage a meeting at Faneuil Hall the next day and lead an attack on the courthouse. To surprise the authorities, Higginson came up with the idea of timing the attack to coincide with the height of the Faneuil Hall meeting. Those at the meeting, informed that an attack was underway, were to surge to the courthouse next door and assist. The speakers at the meeting, his friends Parker, Phillips, and Samuel Gridley

Howe, did not quite comprehend the hastily conceived plan; plus, the young man who was to burst in and announce that the attack was underway could not get into the hall because it was packed. According to Higginson, he, the black abolitionist Martin Stowell, and several others used a beam to knock in the door, where they confronted six or eight policemen who resisted with clubs. Higginson, using the passive voice, relates that "a shot had been fired" and "one of the marshall's deputies, a man named Batchelder, had fallen dead."

For years there was uncertainty about who had killed Batchelder and whether the weapon was a pistol or a knife. Parker, of course, claimed that Commissioner Loring, who had ordered Burns's return, was responsible, but he knew more than he let on. Higginson, in a private, unpublished notebook entry made on April 6, 1874, relates that Lewis Hayden went to a mutual friend, William F. Channing, the day after the shooting and told him that he saw Higginson being beaten inside the courthouse door and thought his (Higginson's) life was in danger, so he fired and Batchelder fell. On Sunday, Channing and Hayden spoke with Parker, after his service, and told him what had happened. Parker advised Hayden to leave town, which he did. Channing drove him to William I. Bowditch's house in Brookline that evening. As for the wound, Hayden "had not a revolver but two common pistols; one of which — the one he fired — was loaded with a slug" and the "long & jagged" wound, Channing says, "was clearly produced by the slug, entering crosswise." Higginson concludes, "I now for the first time understand B's death, which has been a puzzle to me all these years. L. H. told me afterward, rather mysteriously, as if I should understand it, that he had thought it safer, to be out of town. I am ashamed today that I was inclined to think it a bit of brag on his part. Now I feel perfectly sure of the truth of this statement; it explains all the facts & perhaps I owe him my life, or at least preservation from a worse pounding & slashing than I had."[64]

Rather than express dismay at the death of Batchelder, Higginson at the time exulted in it. In a letter to the *Liberator*, he defended his actions by saying that if an "attempt had not been made, *none would have been made;* that, if no attempt had been made, we should have had the ineffable disgrace of seeing Burns marched down State street under a corporal's guard only, amidst a crowd of irresolute semi-abolitionists, hooting, groaning, and never striking a blow."[65] One of the *Liberator*'s readers responded to Higginson's self-serving letter by pointing out that what was needed was "not to nullify the law by assault and brute force, but by the strong will of the people, acting deliberately and intelligently, rising up in their strength, and forbidding its execution in such tones that the Federal Government shall not dare to undertake it here. When the law is to be defeated by brute force . . . the question turns on the point of strength, and victory will generally result to the side bringing the strongest force into the field at the time; and for a long time the government can command more brute strength than its opponents, whether 'semi' or whole abolitionists."[66]

One reason Higginson failed in his charge on the courthouse was the lack of followers. The Faneuil Hall crowd did not participate as planned. After the first attempt and the shooting, the mob fell back. One admirer, however, did step forward after the initial repulsion, Bronson Alcott. As Higginson later narrated, "In the silent pause that ensued there came quietly forth from the crowd the well-known form of Mr. Amos Bronson Alcott, the transcendental philosopher. Ascending the lighted steps alone, he said tranquilly, turning to me and pointing forward, 'Why are we not within?' 'Because,' was the rather impatient answer, 'these people will not stand by us.' He said not a word, but calmly walked up the steps,—he and his familiar cane. He paused again at the top, the centre of all eyes, within and without; a revolver sounded from within, but hit nobody; and finding himself wholly unsupported, he turned and retreated, but without hastening a step."[67]

Higginson compares Alcott at this moment to Hawthorne's Gray Champion, though Hawthorne would surely have objected to the comparison if he had known about it. He found Alcott misguided and dangerous, although likable. (In the aftermath of the attack on the courthouse, Alcott carried a pistol, as did other members of the Vigilance Committee, as they defended Wendell Phillips's home, a target of antiabolitionists.) Hawthorne and his wife, Sophia, were apparently appalled at the violence committed by their New England friends and acquaintances, whom they read about in England. On July 4, 1854, Sophia Hawthorne wrote her father, saying: "We have seen in the papers accounts on all sides of the great slave case in Boston. The abolitionists certainly seem raving distracted, but not in the least brave. . . . Oh how much harm to the wretched slave these crazy men do! Mr Parker was far more the murderer of that officer than the man who shot him. How bloodthirsty he is. How like madmen they behave—& all to no purpose."[68] The Hawthornes' friend Thoreau, on the other hand, praised the attempted rescue as "bloody & disinterestedly heroic,"[69] and it inspired one of his most polemical essays, "Slavery in Massachusetts."

At the annual meeting of the abolitionists on July 4, 1854, in Framingham Grove, Massachusetts, three thousand people attended, and all the speakers, including Thoreau, denounced the Kansas-Nebraska Bill and the rendition of Burns. Moncure Conway, the Virginia abolitionist minister, in his *Autobiography*, provides a fascinating eyewitness account. He relates, "A very aged negro woman named 'Sojourner Truth,' lank, shriveled, but picturesque, slowly mounted to the platform, amid general applause, and sat silently listening to the speeches. After some stormy speaker a young Southerner rose in the audience and began to talk fiercely. . . . [I]n the course of his defence of slavery and affirming his sincerity, [the young man] twice exclaimed, 'As god is my witness!' 'Young man,' cried Sojourner Truth, 'I don't believe God Almighty ever hearn tell of you!' Her shrill voice sounded through the grove like a bugle; shouts of laughter responded, and the poor Southerner could not recover from that only interruption."[70] Conway says of Thoreau that "it was a rare thing for him to attend any meeting outside of Concord, and though he sometimes lectured in the Lyceum there, he had probably never spoken on a platform. . . . Alluding to the Boston commissioner who had surrendered Anthony Burns, Edward G. Loring, Thoreau said, 'The fugitive's case was already decided by God—not Edward G. God, but simple God.' This was said with such serene unconsciousness of anything shocking in it that we were but mildly startled."[71]

Although Thoreau's speech was reported as "Words that Burn" in the *National Anti-Slavery Standard*, it was Garrison who literally burned words at the event: "the Fugitive Slave Law, the judgment of Loring surrendering Anthony Burns, and a charge of United States Judge Curtis on the 'treasonable' attempt to rescue Burns. Lighting matches, he burned successively these documents, after each crying, 'And let all the people say Amen!' The Amens were loudly given, but at last Garrison uplifted a copy of the Constitution of the United States, and read its compromises with slavery and the slave trade; he then declared it the source of all the other atrocities, the original 'covenant with death and agreement with hell,' and held it up burning until the last ash must have singed his fingers. 'So perish all compromises with tyranny!' he cried."[72]

In an inflammatory sermon after the event, titled "Massachusetts in Mourning," Higginson stressed the importance of his violent actions trying to free Burns: "If men array brute force against Freedom—pistols, clubs, drilled soldiers, and stone walls—then the body also has a part to do in resistance. . . . The strokes on the door of the Court House that night . . . went echoing from town to town, from Boston to New Orleans, like the first drum beat of the Revolution."[73] In his *Cheerful Yesterdays*, he recalled with pride, "In all the long procession of events which led the nation through the Kansas struggle, past the John Brown foray, and up to the Emancipation Proclamation, the killing of Batchelder was the first act of violence. It was, like the firing on Fort Sumter, a proof that war had really begun."[74] Higginson and Brown made a good match.

POTTAWATOMIE

As is well known, the Kansas-Nebraska Bill led to "Bleeding Kansas," as settlers from the free states fought with Missouri "Ruffians" who came into the territory to affect the outcome of elections. Propaganda from Kansas inflamed readers in the East, provoking them to speak in terms of overthrowing the United States government. On June 9, 1855, Higginson asked members of the New England Anti-Slavery Convention, "Where on earth are there such materials for revolution as here?" A month later, Samuel J. May declared, "Nothing but revolution will save us. . . . Revolution, I fear is the only road to the death of slavery."[75] Higginson's reports to the *New-York Tribune* from Kansas contributed to the sensationalism and propaganda that surrounded the violence there. David Potter points out that "by far the most active newspaper in reporting affairs in Kansas was the New York *Tribune* edited by Horace Greeley, who proved a true field marshal in the propaganda war."[76] Both antislavery settlers and proslavery settlers in Kansas were being killed, and on May 30, 1856, a dispatch that appeared in the *Tribune* accurately observed, "No man's life is safe; no kind of property secure. A Guerrilla war exists in Kansas, and unless the people in the States come to our rescue and relief speedily, we shall all likewise perish."[77]

John Brown and his sons were among those who responded to the call to make Kansas a free state. On May 21, 1856, the town of Lawrence, Kansas, headquarters of the free-state party, was sacked by Sheriff Jones and a large "posse" of Missouri "Ruffians." They destroyed two free-state newspapers, looted shops and homes, and burned the hotel and free-state Governor Robinson's house. By design, the free-staters offered no resistance. On May 22, the day after the sack of Lawrence, South Carolina congressman Preston Brooks assaulted Charles Sumner without warning in the Senate chamber, beating him with a heavy cane until he was lying bloody and unconscious on the floor. Sumner had offended southerners with his inflammatory "Crime Against Kansas" speech. His injuries, both physical and psychological, were severe, and he did not return to the Senate for three and a half years.

Outraged by both events, John Brown decided to take action. He had frequently stated that "without shedding of blood there is no remission of sin" (Hebrews 9:22), and with this in mind, he led a party of seven men along the Pottawatomie Creek in Kansas in the middle of the night of May 24–25, and they used small, heavy broadswords to kill five southern settlers. The first was James P. Doyle, living with his wife, daughter, and three sons. He was dragged from his cabin, along with his two older sons, and hacked to death by Brown's men. For good measure, Brown shot him through the head. Doyle's twenty-year-old son, Drury, who tried to run, was found the next morning with his head gashed open and his arms cut off. The two other victims of this raid, Allen Wilkinson, who lived with his wife and two children, and William Sherman, a bachelor, were likewise hacked and dismembered. None was armed; none owned slaves.

The *New York Herald* reported, "These devils in human form dragged their captives just outside" their cabins and left them "cold and dead upon the ground, gashed, torn, hacked and disfigured to a degree at which even Indian barbarity would shudder. The windpipe of the old man, for instance, was entirely cut out, his throat cut from ear to ear. The body of one young man has the face and head sacrificed, and the hands are cut and chopped up with a bowie knife."[78] Whether these killings were justified or not remains a matter of debate. The facts are that Wilkinson and Sherman were proslavery partisans who had harassed free-state settlers and threatened to kill them. The first victim, James Doyle, was an illiterate carpenter who had emigrated from Tennessee with his family seeking work in free-soil territory. Doyle's wife, Mahala, later explained that "her husband had often said that Slavery was ruinous to white labor and that they had a large family of boys and would go there and settle and try to get comfortable homes for their children." Her husband despised blacks and abolitionists and was a willing participant as a juror in a proslavery territorial court convened to issue warrants for settlers who had violated laws against antislavery speech. Wilkinson acted as the district attorney.[79] When Mahala Doyle was asked why she thought Brown killed her husband and sons, she replied, "Just we were southern people I reckon."[80] She knew, however, that her husband had allied himself with Wilkinson and Sherman. Salmon Brown recalled her saying to her husband as he was dragged out the door, "I told you what you were going to get."[81]

The Pottawatomie killings look very much like murder, yet a case has been made for them as acts of self-defense and as acts of war. That is, the victims were allied with the group of proslavery Ruffians who had engaged in murder, intimidation, and the sacking of Lawrence. As such, they posed a growing threat to the lives and well-being of free-state settlers. Many observers regarded Kansas as in a state of war in 1856; in fact, Brown viewed slavery itself as a one-sided war waged by brutal slaveholders against African Americans. As David Reynolds has explained, Brown saw himself serving the Old Testament God of Battles: "In this sense he followed the example of his greatest hero among white Christians, Oliver Cromwell." Reynolds adds, "The most positive way to view Cromwell's and Brown's crimes is to regard them as what Doris Lessing calls 'good terrorism'—that is, terrorism justified by obvious social injustice. Terrorism is violence that avoids combat, is used against the defenseless (often civilians), and is intended to shock and horrify, with the aim of bringing about social change."[82] Late in life, Higginson spoke to the success of Brown's methods and claimed that during his ride through Kansas in 1856, he "heard of no one who did not approve of the act, and its beneficial effects were universally asserted," for "it had given an immediate check to the armed aggressions of the Missourians."[83] When questioned about the Pottawatomie killings by his New England supporters, Brown denied involvement.

At the meeting of the Massachusetts Anti-Slavery Society in February 1859, the activities of Brown in Kansas received considerable praise. A Mr. R. J. Hinton of Kansas read a letter from Brown telling of his rescue of eleven slaves from Missouri. A number of speakers, including Higginson, Phillips, and Parker Pillsbury, agreed with one another that "whoever believes in the use of the sword, and is not preparing himself for its use, is not up to the exigencies of this hour."[84] On the other hand, Garrison and several others at the meeting remained nonresistants, and they questioned the righteousness of such violence. Garrison declared that the New England emigrants to Kansas "went to make money. I do not think them worthy of imitation, and I do not see that Kansas has given us any lessons of wisdom in regard to the management of the warfare against slavery. . . . My voice is still for peace."[85] Similarly, a Mr. Holden of Lynn, Massachusetts, spoke up to say:

> When I hear our friends counseling armed resistance as the only means of establishing universal liberty, I am not only opposed to them on mere policy, but also from principle; for is not the right to life as inalienable as that to liberty? When, at one of our previous meetings, I heard our good friend Pillsbury say, that he "longed to see the time come, when Boston streets should run with blood from Beacon Hill to the foot of Broad street," I could not but shudder at the spirit of vindictiveness, and doubt the sincerity of our friend, although he thought himself sincere at that time. Then again, yesterday afternoon, I was grieved to hear our friend Phillips say, "he was glad that every five minutes gave birth to a black baby, for in its infant wail he recognized the voice which should yet shout the war cry of insurrection; its baby hand would one day hold the dagger which should reach the master's heart." More in unison with my sentiments are the principles of our great leader. This movement of ours is not so much political as moral, and by all means, when we are engaged in a great moral enterprise, let us pay equal regard to the means to be employed as well as the end in view.[86]

The influence of such sentiments was almost at an end, for as Demos has shown, "the decline of non-violent abolitionism in the 1850s was nothing short of a total collapse."[87]

HARPERS FERRY

In the fall of 1859, Parker, Sanborn, and Higginson—transcendentalists all—went beyond rhetoric by conspiring with John Brown as part of his "Secret Six" and provided him with money and arms for the Harpers Ferry raid, which began on the evening of October 16, 1859. After it failed, Alcott, Thoreau, and Emerson sanctified Brown, praised his service to "a higher law," and beat the drums of war.[88] When Brown started for Harpers Ferry, he had 21 men, 950 pikes, 200 revolvers, and 198 Sharps repeating rifles. The pikes, six-foot poles with Bowie knives at their ends, had been specially ordered by Brown from a Connecticut forge-master for a dollar apiece. Effective for silent and repeated use at a distance of six feet or less, they were intended to arm the slaves Brown expected to join him in an insurrection. The Sharps rifles, purchased by donations from the "Secret Six" and others in the North, were intended to kill anyone who tried to stop the raiders. Thoreau, who had almost certainly read reports about the Pottawatomie massacre,[89] said of the Harpers Ferry raid: "I know that the mass of my countrymen think that the only righteous use that can be made of Sharps' rifles and revolvers is to fight duels with them, when we are insulted by other nations, or to hunt Indians, or shoot fugitive slaves with them, or the like. I think that for once the Sharps' rifles and the revolvers were employed in a righteous cause. The tools were in the hands of one who could use them."[90]

Ironically, the first person Brown and his men killed at Harpers Ferry was Hayward Shepard, a free black who worked as the porter at the Harpers Ferry train station. He was shot in the back and died a lingering death after being taken inside the station. Brown and his men took sixty hostages and held them in the federal armory, where they were pinned down by local townspeople, with whom they exchanged fire throughout the next day. When a company of militia closed in, Brown's men retreated with nine prisoners to the armory's small engine house. In the evening, a unit of eighty-six United States marines under the leadership of Colonel Robert E. Lee arrived and the next morning stormed the engine house. By the time Brown was captured, ten of his men were dead (including two of his sons), plus three townsmen, two slaves, one slaveholder, and one marine. Brown was tried for treason by the state of Virginia and hanged on December 2, 1859, but not before writing a number of eloquent letters defending his actions.[91]

Because Brown had the opportunity to burnish his image before his execution by unsolicited speeches and public letters, he influenced responses to his actions, which were perceived as murderous and insane by many yet principled and heroic by some, especially by abolitionists in the North. The staunch pacifist Garrison at first called the raid "misguided, wild, and apparently insane, though disinterested and well-intended," adding, "Our views of war and bloodshed, even in the best of causes, are too well known to need repeating here; but let no one who glories in the Revolutionary struggle of 1776 deny the right of the slaves to imitate the example of our fathers."[92] On December 2, 1859, the day of Brown's execution, Garrison reconsidered and declared, "As a peace man,—an 'ultra' peace man—I am prepared to say, 'Success to every slave insurrection in the South, and in every slave country.' . . . Give me, as a non-resistant, Bunker Hill, and Lexington, and Concord, rather than the cowardice and servility of a Southern slave plantation."[93]

Harpers Ferry encouraged the radical abolitionists, who had long hoped that Brown's activities would lead to civil war. As Edward J. Renehan Jr. benignly puts it, "As amateur boxer, Higginson itched to see slave and free states go at it with the gloves off. And he was intrigued by Brown's propensity for making fists fly."[94] The only regret Higginson later expressed was that Brown lost his life as a result of the Harpers Ferry raid. "In retrospect," Higginson recalled, "I think the bombing of a few fine southern buildings, or a few famous southern men, with notes crediting the blasts to some choice northern abolitionist groups, would have done the job."[95] Thoreau, who had responded to the Fugitive Slave Law by privately vowing to "touch a match to blow up earth & hell together,"[96] saw his young neighbor Sanborn, another of Brown's "Secret Six," as a kindred insurrectionist. He apparently told

Higginson that Sanborn's "quiet, steadfast earnestness and ethical fortitude are of the type that calmly, so calmly, ignites and then throws bomb
after bomb."[97]

The transcendentalists Emerson and Thoreau heaped praise on
Brown and were recognized for their efforts. James Redpath's best-
selling biography, *The Public Life of Captain John Brown*, which appeared
in April 1860, was dedicated to Wendell Phillips, Emerson, and Thoreau,
"Defenders of the Faithful, who, when the mob shouted, 'Madman!'
said, 'Saint!'" Other residents of Concord supported the notion of
Brown as a Christ-like martyr. Bronson and Louisa May Alcott contributed to Redpath's collection of tributes to Brown titled *Echoes of Harpers
Ferry*, and in the summer of 1860 the family hosted a tea for his widow,
Mary, and the following spring and summer they boarded his daughters, Anne and Sarah. The political activities of Hawthorne's Concord
neighbors played a major role in disconcerting him and in provoking
southern anger and paranoia. As Betty Mitchell has observed, "The well-
publicized words of New England transcendentalists like Emerson and
Thoreau who glorified Brown led traumatized southerners to mistak-
enly identify these individual sentiments with the main body of northern
opinion."[98]

Following the Harpers Ferry raid and the election of the Republican
candidate Abraham Lincoln to the presidency, the independence movement in South Carolina reached fever pitch, and Charleston became
alive with "anxious vigilance patrols, drilling militia, and ceaseless rumors and evidences of black unrest."[99] On the night of November 13,
1860, the fire-eating congressman Lawrence Keitt voiced the sentiments
of many southerners when he declared to an enthusiastic crowd that
"South Carolina should shatter the accursed Union. If she could not
otherwise accomplish it, she should throw her arms around the pillars
of the Constitution, and, by pulling it down from turret to foundation-
stone, involve the States in the common ruin!"[100]

Both northerners and southerners alike at the end of 1860 envi-
sioned an imminent heroic struggle on their part against the forces of
darkness. In retrospect, Brown seemed a prophetic figure, as he sought
to be. In a poem titled, "Year of Meteors, 1859–60," first published in
1867, Whitman wrote:

YEAR of meteors! brooding year!

I would bind in words retrospective, some of your deeds and signs;

I would sing your contest for the 19th Presidentiad;

I would sing how an old man, tall, with white hair, mounted the scaffold
   in Virginia;

(I was at hand—silent I stood, with teeth shut close—I watch'd;

I stood very near you, old man, when cool and indifferent, but trembling
with age and your unheal'd wounds, you mounted the scaffold;)[101]

Whitman's imaginative participation at Brown's hanging not only elevates the event (as Brown "mounts" the scaffold), but its focus on Brown's debility and wounds makes the old man seem the victim, not the perpetrator, of violence.

Brown saved the letters of support he received in prison awaiting his execution. He threw one letter away, however, which his jailer retrieved. It was from Mahala Doyle and read in part, "You can now [having lost two sons] appreciate my distress in Kansas when you then and there entered my house at midnight and arrested my husband and two boys, and took them out in the yard, and in cold blood shot them dead in my hearing. You can't say you did it to free our slaves; we had none, and never expected to own one; but it has only made me a poor desolate widow, with helpless children. While I feel for your folly, I do hope and trust you will meet with your just reward. Oh, how it pained my heart to hear the dying groans of my husband and children. If this scrawl gives you any consolation you are welcome to it."[102] Obviously, Mrs. Doyle's opinion of Brown jarred with the public image he was successfully creating.

Melville, in his powerful poem about Brown titled "The Portent" (1859), captures, like Whitman, the pathos of Brown's hanging and the violence it portends:

HANGING from the beam,
   Slowing swaying (such the law),
Gaunt the shadow on your green,
   Shenandoah!
The cut is on the crown
   (Lo, John Brown),
And the stabs shall heal no more.

> Hidden in the cap
>> Is the anguish none can draw;
> So your future veils its face,
>> Shenandoah!
> But the streaming beard is shown
>> (Weird John Brown),
> The meteor of the war.[103]

By focusing on Brown's lifeless body and hidden face, Melville suggests the enigmatic character of the man. The future anguish of Brown or Shenandoah (the pronoun "your" is ambiguous), "none can draw." For Robert Milder, "The cap covering Brown's face suggests a veiled future that even in Northern victory remains problematic."[104]

Melville and the other writers discussed in this study struggled to comprehend in retrospect the massive death and trauma of the Civil War, and Melville in the supplement to *Battle Pieces* expressed the belief that emancipation of the slaves was worth it: "Only through agonized violence could so mighty a result be effected," he declared.[105] Nevertheless, citizens on both sides were distraught at the cost of the war (the loss of some 620,000 lives), because they anticipated it would resemble the Revolutionary War, which resulted in the deaths of 8,000 Americans in battle. This study does not presume to attend to the many aspects of a war that has been the subject of voluminous historical and literary scholarship. For the most part, the violence of the Civil War was viewed as justified by those fighting on both sides. The motives and actions of politicians and soldiers were questionable, of course, and have been debated for years, yet the most problematic engagement on the part of writers and other intellectuals occurred when their commitments to peace on the one hand and freedom on the other came into conflict.

THE HAYMARKET BOMBING

The Civil War obviously marked the end to the problematic violence associated with abolitionism, slave insurrections, and fugitive slaves, yet the failure of Reconstruction visited new forms of terror upon former slaves, most notably the horrific lynchings of black men in the South, which

Frederick Douglass, at the urging of Ida Wells, spoke out against.[106] In the North, the most explosive political violence occurred in clashes between workers (many foreign born) and the police, which Melville, living in New York City, found himself in the midst of. As James Green has shown, "Workingmen, the very mechanics who benefited most from the free labor system Lincoln had extolled, began to doubt the nature of their liberty."[107]

The French Revolution of 1871 ignited three decades of bitter class struggle in the United States as workers, influenced by the worldwide socialist movement, struck for better wages, shorter hours, and improved working conditions. The vast influx of eight million immigrants into the United States during the years 1870–90 led to a cycle of wage-cutting, union organization, strikes, and reaction. "The times are revolutionary," declared John Swinton, the former editor of the *New York Sun*,[108] and the times were the mid-1880s, during which the United States experienced one of the most sustained periods of violent labor unrest in its history. During the peak years of upheaval (1877, 1886, and 1892–93), tens of thousands of strikes, involving hundreds of thousands of workers, occurred in a number of industries across the country.[109] Owners, employers, and their representatives in city, state, and federal governments called the strikes "insurrections," linked them to the "Paris Commune," and denounced the strikers as "anarchists," "communists," "Reds," "foreign agitators," and "bomb-throwers." Meanwhile, urban newspapers and magazines depicted union workers as dark, unshaven men arriving from abroad, armed with swords, bombs, rifles, and cannon. As Melville developed his narrative about what befell Billy Budd during the year of "the Great Mutiny," he did so in a society anxious about violence, eager for order, and willing to use armed force to impose it.

On May 4, 1886, a deadly and explosive confrontation between workers and police occurred in Chicago at Haymarket Square, which received widespread newspaper coverage and led to the most sensational trial of the decade. "No disturbance of the peace that has occurred in the United States since the war of rebellion," claimed the *New York Times*, "has excited public sentiment throughout the Union as it is excited by the Anarchists' murder of policemen in Chicago on Tuesday night."[110] On May 3 strikers had fought with scabs at the

FIGURE 1. T. De Thulstrup, *The Anarchist Riot in Chicago—A Dynamite Bomb Exploding among the Police.* From *Harper's Weekly* 30 (May 15, 1886): 312–13.

McCormick Harvester Company, and the Chicago police fired on the strikers, killing four men and wounding many more. In protest, some three thousand people gathered in Haymarket Square the next evening and listened to speeches condemning the police and their actions. As the crowd was breaking up, the police moved in with raised clubs. A dynamite bomb exploded in their midst, and they opened fire on the crowd. Six policemen were killed by the bomb, and some fifty were injured; several workers were killed by the police and at least two hundred were wounded.[111] Public outrage and blame about this bloodshed were directed toward the anarchists who had spoken out on behalf of the strike. A widely circulated illustration in *Harper's Weekly* (see figure 1) dramatized the perceived ties between the anarchists and the violence, as speaker and bomb mirror one another in the picture's horizontal composition.

After the bombing, the Chicago police raided meeting halls, printing offices, and private homes, arrested hundreds of workers, and charged eight leading anarchists with murder. Although no evidence linked them directly to the bombing, the eight men were accused of having incited the unknown bomb-thrower. A few prominent citizens, such as William Dean Howells, spoke out on their behalf, but public opinion ran strongly against them. The majority view was expressed by the owner of a Chicago clothing firm who declared, "No, I don't consider these people to have been found guilty of any offense, *but they must be hanged . . . the labor movement must be crushed!*"[112]

In the wake of the Haymarket bombing, New York and other cities witnessed judicial reaction. As Philip Foner has explained, "The police and the courts were assigned an important role in the employers' counter-offensive; police activity was matched by judicial tyranny. Arrests and imprisonment of strikers and boycotters on the spurious charge of 'conspiracy' occurred all over the country."[113] An editorial in *Harper's Weekly* entitled "The Anarchists at Chicago" rationalized the contemporary legal severity by declaring, "Anarchists who justify and counsel murder as necessary to the overthrow of society, when murder begins in consequence of that incitement, cannot be held guiltless. . . . It is the welfare of society and the security of liberty under law which alone should determine the kind and degree of the penalty!"[114] With even less moderation, an editorial in the November 25 *New York Times* called the anarchists "a gang of villains" and "mad dogs," and then declared: "In such a case even Judges may be expected to be guided by a sense of stern justice, and to regard it as desirable that the wretched brood should be exterminated."[115]

Judge Joseph E. Gary, who presided over the Haymarket trial, displayed extraordinary bias. He refused to disqualify prospective jurors who admitted their prejudice against the defendants; he allowed the relative of one of the slain policemen to serve on the jury; and he ruled in favor of the prosecution on every contested point.[116] Not surprisingly, the anarchists were found guilty, and seven were sentenced to death. Governor Oglesby commuted the sentences of two to life imprisonment; one committed suicide in his cell, and on November 11, 1887, four of them were hanged. "Law and order must be maintained when revolution threatens," declared the author of an article entitled "The Lesson of Chicago."[117] When Illinois governor John Peter Altgeld issued his famous pardon on June 26, 1893, declaring the defendants completely innocent victims of a biased judge and packed juries, he became one of the most reviled men in America.[118]

The issues of conspiracy, rebellion, armed force, and injustice figure prominently in *Billy Budd* and are responses to the contemporary scene. Melville, like all the other writers of this study, found political violence, especially when committed by civilians, worthy of careful examination, not only because of what it revealed about human nature and political behavior but also because of the way it forced all deeply thinking persons to ponder how their principles clashed with historical actuality or, more subtly, with one another. As Angelina Grimké Weld said, sometimes "it seems as though we are compelled to choose between two evils, and all that we can do is to take the *least.*" What remains is the challenging struggle to determine which one that is.

She rose before me at times into heroical
& godlike regions.
— Emerson journal entry about Fuller, 1843

The men thought she carried too many guns. . . .
— EMERSON, Memoirs of Margaret Fuller Ossoli, 1852

CHAPTER ONE

Margaret Fuller's Revolutionary Example

In her dispatches from Italy during 1848 and 1849, Margaret Fuller spoke as an American on behalf of what she called "my Italy" and celebrated the romantic heroism of the defenders of the Roman Republic. "The voice of this age," she wrote after the republic fell, "shall yet proclaim the names of some of these Patriots whose inspiring soul was JOSEPH MAZZINI — men as nobly true to their convictions as any that have ever yet redeemed poor, stained Humanity" (*SG* 315). After she, her husband, and their son fled Rome for Florence, she remained a defiant supporter of the *Risorgimento*. Uncertain of the future yet retaining a sense of divine mission, she assumed the role of a prophetess in her dispatches and created a vision of righteous violence and destruction that echoes Isaiah on the coming era of Emmanuel. In her last dispatch, on January 6, 1850, she fiercely declares:

> The seeds for a vast harvest of hatreds and contempts are sown over every inch of Roman ground, nor can that malignant growth be extirpated,

till the wishes of Heaven shall waft a fire that will burn down all, root and branch, and prepare the earth for an entirely new culture. The next revolution, here and elsewhere, will be radical. . . . Sons cannot be long employed in the conscious enslavement of their sires, fathers of their children. That advent called EMMANUEL begins to be understood, and shall no more so foully be blasphemed. . . . Do you laugh, Roman Cardinal, as you shut the prison-door on woman weeping for her son martyred in the cause of his country? Do you laugh, Austrian officer, as you drill the Hungarian and Lombard youth to tremble at your baton? Soon you, all of you, shall "*believe* and tremble." (*SG* 321–22)

Of all American authors, Fuller alone "had the opportunity, the inclination, and ultimately the resolve to align herself wholeheartedly with European democratic liberalism."[1] This alignment, moreover, sharpened rather than clouded her vision, and her dispatches remain one of the most stirring accounts of the people and events involved in the Italian revolutions of 1848–49. As Barbara Packer has pointed out, they are also "one of the most absorbing, brilliant, and far-ranging of all texts written by the transcendentalists."[2] My goal in this chapter is to trace their more remarkable effects on American thought and writing in the period from their appearance to the Civil War. Fuller's example, I suggest, may have indirectly led to that war. Her support of political violence in Europe prefigured a major change in antislavery thinking in the United States and influenced the prowar attitudes of some of its most important northern intellectual advocates.

FULLER'S CONTEMPORARY REPUTATION

Fuller spent the early part of her career among a select group of friends devoted to the ideal of self-culture. As editor of the *Dial* from 1840 to 1842, as leader of her Boston "Conversations" for women in the winters of 1839 to 1843, and even as author of *Woman in the Nineteenth Century*, published in 1845, Fuller sought to encourage her audiences to attend to their individual intellectual and spiritual growth. The story of the prodigal son told in Luke 15:11–32 fascinated her, and she interpreted it in such a way that the prodigal becomes a spiritual leader through his suffering and enlightenment. As she puts it at the beginning of *Woman in the Nineteenth Century*, "We see that in him the largest claim finds a due foundation. . . . He feels himself called to understand and aid nature, that she may, through his intelligence, be raised and interpreted; to be a student of, and servant to, the universe-spirit; and king of his planet, that as an angelic minister, he may bring it into conscious harmony with the law of that spirit."[3] Even after she moved to New York City and began working for Horace Greeley's *New-York Tribune*, Fuller clung to her belief that each individual needed to concentrate first and foremost on the self. Only by first becoming a better person could one begin to address public problems calling for solution. In the summer of 1845, in an essay for the *Tribune*, she lamented the existence of slavery but asserted that "in private lives, more than in public measures must the salvation of the country lie." At present, she claims, the country lacks "men ripened and confirmed for better things. They leaned too carelessly on one another; they had not deepened and purified the private lives from which the public must spring."[4]

In Italy, in the midst of the Italian revolutionary movement, about which she hoped to write a major history, Fuller transformed into a political activist. Consequently, when she died in the shipwreck of the *Elizabeth* on July 19, 1850, she indeed rose "into heroical and godlike regions" as Emerson anticipated in 1843. In her European dispatches Fuller had celebrated the heroism of Mazzini, Garibaldi, and the Roman republicans who fought unsuccessfully against the French army that restored Pope Pius IX to power, yet her own sustained commitment to the revolution struck many in America as heroic, especially after her tragic death. In his 1852 introduction to a reprinting of Fuller's *Papers on Literature and Art*, Horace Greeley refers to "Italy's last struggle for liberty and light" and credits Fuller with having been "a portion of its incitement, its animation, its informing soul. She bore more than a woman's part in its conflicts and its perils; and the bombs of that ruthless army which a false and traitorous government impelled against the ramparts of Republican Rome, could have stilled no voice more eloquent in its exposures, no heart more lofty in its defiance, of the villany [*sic*] which so wantonly drowned in blood the hopes, while crushing the dearest rights, of a people, than those of Margaret Fuller."[5] Fuller's brother Arthur, who would distinguish himself as a fighting chaplain in the Civil War, similarly credited Fuller's *At Home and Abroad* (1856) (the first reprinting of her *Tribune* dispatches) with the potential to "inspire its readers with an increased love of republican institutions, and an earnest purpose to seek the removal of every national wrong which hinders our beloved country from being a perfect example and hearty helper of other nations in their struggles for liberty."[6] The main "wrong" he alludes to, of course, is slavery, or "this horrible cancer of Slavery," as his sister called it in her December 1847 dispatch from Europe (*SG* 165).

Although Greeley and Arthur can be suspected of bias because of their attachment to Fuller, her defiant voice and heart indeed inspired many Americans in the decade following her death, especially those in New England who turned to political violence as a means to rid the country of slavery. In the early 1840s, Fuller had kept her distance from the abolitionists, considering them too fanatical in their activities. In 1845, encouraged perhaps by Emerson's 1844 antislavery address, she published seven pieces in the *Tribune* against slavery, and in Europe, surely encouraged by her traveling companions, the abolitionist Quakers Rebecca and Marcus Spring, she had a change of heart. "How it pleases me here to think of the Abolitionists!" she wrote from Italy in late 1847. "I could never endure to be with them at home, they were so tedious, often so narrow, always so rabid and exaggerated in their tone. But, after all, they had a high motive, something eternal in their desire and life; and, if it was not the only thing worth thinking of it was really something worth living and dying for to free a great nation from such a terrible blot, such a threatening plague. God strengthen them and make them wise to achieve their purpose!" (*SG* 77).

When Fuller's *Tribune* dispatches from Italy first appeared in America, they evoked massive public sympathy for the defenders of Rome and antipathy for Pope Pius IX and the French army that came to his aid. They also fed into the growing resistance to slavery by Fuller's abolitionist readers. Throughout June and July of 1849, Fuller's reports inspired sympathy meetings in New York City, New Orleans, and elsewhere. (Southern defenders of slavery and conservative New England Whigs condemned the European revolutions privately.)[7] Crowds of supporters adopted numerous resolutions calling for the United States to support the republican struggle "by every means possible." And a number of American writers, including the abolitionists James Russell Lowell and John Greenleaf Whittier, joined Fuller in her commitment to the Roman republicans. In his poem "Freedom," Lowell alludes to the issue of American slavery as he depicts Italy as a beautiful pearl lying before the swine of Austria and declares,

> Welcome to me whatever breaks a chain,
> That surely is of God and all divine.[8]

Whittier's "To Pius IX," written after the fall of the Roman Republic, depicts the pope as a cowardly tyrant and extends the following sarcastic challenge:

> Stand where Rome's blood was freest shed,
> Mock Heaven with impious thanks and call
> Its curses on the patriot dead,
> Its blessing on the Gaul![9]

Walt Whitman, too, inspired by Fuller's dispatches, wrote in "Resurgemus," which became the first poem of *Leaves of Grass:*

> Not a grave of the murdered for freedom but grows seed for
> freedom. . . . in its turn to bear seed,
> Which the winds carry afar and re-sow, and the rains
> And the snows nourish.[10]

The "grass" of *Leaves of Grass* has one of its origins in Italian soil, though transformed into a symbol of American democracy by an aspiring national bard.

As Timothy Roberts has shown, Americans manifested complicated responses to the European revolutions, which nevertheless allowed them "to assert a unified public revolutionary identity amid an uncertain Atlantic and domestic political atmosphere."[11] Among Catholics, the Italian revolutions became particularly unsettling, for obvious reasons, and they resented Fuller's criticism of the pope. Bishop Hughes of New York in a widely reprinted letter to the *New York Courier and Inquirer* denounced the "revolutionists in Rome" and asserted that they had established "a reign of terror over the Roman people." Hughes pointed out that no ambassador had recognized the Roman Republic, "except it be the female plenipotentiary who furnishes the *Tribune* with diplomatic correspondence."[12] (The U.S. government had instructed the new chargé d'affaires in Rome, Lewis Cass Jr., to delay recognition of the Roman Republic until it showed it could sustain itself, a reticence Fuller found especially galling.) Fuller responded to Hughes's denigration of the Roman republicans by declaring the city safe, asserting, "I, a woman, walk everywhere alone, and all the little children do the same, with their nurses" (*SG* 294). What she omitted, though, was that indeed priests had been murdered. According to the historian George Macaulay Trevelyan, one of the Roman republicans, Callimaco Zambianchi, in early May 1849, massacred "six persons in holy orders, whom he declared to have been preaching sedition and conspiring against the Republic."[13]

The limited opposition in America to the Roman Republic was fueled by columns reprinted from the ultraconservative London *Times*. During the siege of Rome, the reporter for the *Times*, who traveled with the French army, claimed the city was defended by "the degenerate remnant of the Roman people" and by "a nest of adventurers, from every part not only of Italy but of Europe."[14] The *Times* became another target of Fuller's hostility. "There exists not in Europe a paper more violently opposed to the cause of freedom than the *Times*," she informed her readers, "and neither its leaders nor its foreign correspondence [*sic*] are to be depended upon" (*SG* 294). The American poet Henry Wadsworth Longfellow agreed that the *Times* "falsified and adulterated the generous wine of Truth," and he marveled "that it should be sent over here, as the genuine article, and that the good people here should smack their lips over it, and twirl it round in their little hearts, as in small glasses, and say 'How delightful!'"[15] The *New York Herald*, a rival of the *Tribune*, drew most heavily from the *Times* for its coverage. Ironically, it was Fuller's good friend Emerson who most enthusiastically promoted the *Times*, calling it in 1848 "the best newspaper of the world."[16]

Throughout 1849, after he had returned from his trip abroad, Emerson prepared lectures based on his stay in England that would form chapters of his book *English Traits*. He devotes an entire chapter to the *Times*, calling it "a living index of the colossal British power. Its existence honors the people who dare to print all they know, dare to know all the facts."[17] It was not just the ultraconservative coverage of this English paper, though, that made Emerson skeptical of the European revolutions of 1848–49. His faith in individualism also shaped his attitude, which most often took the form of sarcasm and condescension. At the very moment Fuller was ardently asking for American support of the revolutionary effort in Rome, Emerson was entering comments such as the following in his journal: "There will be no revolution 'till we see new men"; "Hungary, it seems, must take the yoke again, & Austria, & Italy, & Prussia, & France. Only the English race can be trusted with Freedom" (*JMN* 11: 94, 98, 148).

FULLER AND EMERSON

The wide gulf separating Emerson's fatalism and Fuller's activism in the late 1840s had developed over the course of the decade, and it grew out of a small difference in the transcendental idealism they once shared. Both authors during the early 1840s subscribed to the central concept of the Romantic movement—organicism—and they believed that the singular soul, like the human race itself, was involved in an ongoing process of perfection whereby the seed of the divine at the center of the self and humanity was being impelled toward a perfect form; however, for Emerson the self was primary, social institutions secondary, for he believed that as one perfected the self, the world would change for the better. As he explained, "Spirit alters, moulds, makes" the world we live in.[18] Fuller, however, came to believe that social conditions could thwart the spiritual growth of the individual, and one needed to strive to perfect society to allow for the more important perfection of the self. She develops this thesis in *Woman in the Nineteenth Century*, using Goethe to make her point. As she puts it, "Goethe thinks, As the man, so the institutions! . . . A man can grow in any place, if he will. Ay!, but Goethe, bad institutions are prison walls and impure air that make him stupid, so that he does not will."[19] So, while Emerson in the midst of the European revolutions declares "we are authorized to say much on the destinies of one, nothing on those of many" (*JMN* 10: 310), Fuller insists upon "the necessity of some practical application of the precepts of Christ" (*SG* 119).

After Fuller's death, Emerson, as one of the three editors of her

Memoirs (1852), struggled to come to terms with her life, as it was re-vealed to him through the journals, letters, and other materials that came into his hands from various sources, and her memory informed his own growing political engagement. To read through the collection *Emerson's Antislavery Writings* (1995) is to be impressed by the extent and fervor of his participation, even knowing that Emerson's journal entries periodically disdain his efforts. At the time, Fuller figured prominently in his thought, as his essay "Fate" reveals. Published in *The Conduct of Life* (1860), "Fate" discloses the shift in Emerson's attitude regarding the limitations one must confront to attain freedom, as he declares, "We must see that the world is rough and surly, and will not mind drowning a man or a woman, but swallows your ship like a grain of dust." His ref-erence to shipwreck and drowning suggests he may have been thinking of Fuller, and he not only arrives at Fuller's position on political oppres-sion by declaring "every spirit makes its house; but afterwards the house confines the spirit,"[20] he also, as Cristina Zwarg has shown, uses Fuller as the undisclosed heroine of his essay, as he lauds the power of the excep-tional person to overcome fate. Zwarg notes "Emerson's confession in the *Memoirs* that [Fuller's] 'personal influence' was the strongest he had ever experienced."[21] In his journal, Emerson cites Fuller by name, writ-ing: "A personal influence towers up in memory the only worthy force when we would gladly forget numbers or money or climate, gravitation & the rest of Fate. Margaret, wherever she came, fused people into soci-ety, & a glowing company was the result. When I think how few persons can do that feat for the intellectual class, I feel our squalid poverty" (*JMN* 11: 449).

In "Fate," Fuller's name is removed, and her gender altered, as she becomes Emerson's "hero": "Society is servile from want of will, and therefore the world wants saviours and religions. One way is right to go; the hero sees it, and moves on that aim, and has the world under him for root and support. He is to others as the world. His approbation is honor; his dissent, infamy. . . . A personal influence towers up in memory only worthy, and we gladly forget numbers, money, climate, gravitation, and the rest of Fate."[22] Emerson's need to turn heroism into a masculine quality, though informed by Fuller's example, responds to the dominant assumptions of the day, of course, and almost all of his contemporaries, including women, shared this assumption. For example, Louisa May Alcott, in her novel *Moods*, paid tribute to Fuller, her role model, by having two of her male protagonists go to Italy to fight alongside Garibaldi on behalf of the Roman Republic. Her female heroine stays at home.

Despite his inability to go beyond his gendering of political power,[23] Emerson revealed in a lecture in 1855 that his thinking about collective effort had changed: "Whilst I insist on the doctrine of the independence and the inspiration of the individual, I do not cripple but exalt the social action." He added, "It is so delicious to act with great masses to great aims" (*AW* 103, 105). Ten years previously, such a sentiment would not have escaped his lips, given his commitment to self-reliant individualism. During the late 1850s, Emerson also altered his views on violent means, becoming more and more outraged at southern intransigence and aggression. By the time the Civil War began, he had become "merciless as a steel bayonet,"[24] according to Hawthorne, and this was not an overstatement. "Ah! Sometimes gunpowder smells good," Emerson declared while visiting the Charlestown Navy Yard.[25]

FULLER'S RADICALISM AND ITS EFFECTS

Years before her friend Emerson turned radical, Fuller in her dispatches revealed a fierceness about achieving the utopian ends she sought, and she defended violence as a means to resist oppression and bring about justice. She had met Mazzini in England before journeying to Italy, and her willingness to accept violence partly flowed from her support of his radical position with the *Risorgimento*. Mazzini had plotted a number of insurrections against Italian rulers throughout the 1820s and 1830s, and he was living in exile under sentence of death. His revolutionary nationalism, calling for a unitary Italian republic, stood in sharp contrast to the conservative federalism of the Neo-Guelph movement, which sought a federation of Italian states under papal leadership, and to the moderate constitutionalism of northern Italian progressives who sought a free and united Italy under a constitutional monarch.[26]

In the spring of 1848, Fuller regarded the revolution in Paris as prophetic. "The news from France," she wrote in her dispatch for March 29, 1848, "sounds ominous, though still vague; it would appear that the political is being merged in the social struggle: it is well; whatever blood is to be shed, whatever altars cast down. Those tremendous problems MUST be solved, whatever be the cost!" (*SG* 211). In her commentary on Italian politics, she likewise accepted violence and bloodshed as the necessary cost of liberty. She disparaged the so-called Moderate Party and the Neo-Guelphs, and supported Mazzini's radicalism.

The most dramatic and central example of this was her approval of the assassination of Count Pellegrino Rossi. After Rossi's stabbing on November 16, 1848, as he entered the Chamber of Deputies, Fuller reported that afterward soldiers and citizens joined in singing "Blessed the hand that rids the earth of a tyrant," and, she added, "Certainly, the manner was grandiose" (*SG* 240). This was her private sentiment as well, and she told her mother, "For me, I never thought to have heard of a violent death with satisfaction, but this act affected me as one of terrible justice."[27] To some Americans, such as her friends the Springs, Fuller had gone too far in applauding a political assassination, but she defended her position in a letter to them: "What you say is deeply true about the peace way being the best. If any one see clearly how to work in that way, let him in God's name. . . . Meanwhile I am not sure that I can keep my hands free from blood. I doubt I have not the strength. . . . You, Marcus, could you let a Croat insult Rebecca, carry off Eddie to be an Austrian serf; and leave little Marcus bleeding in the dust? . . . If so, you are a Christian; you know I never pretended to be except in dabs and sparkles here and there."[28] Fuller's religion was eclectic, and the New Testament was but one of many books that shaped her self-image and sociopolitical thought.

A primary reason she responded as she did to Rossi's murder, and became an advocate of righteous violence, was that she viewed it through the lens of her reading in classical literature, which dominated her youth. Her first publication, an article written when she was twenty-four, was a defense of the character of Brutus, which drew heavily upon Plutarch's *Lives*,[29] and in Rome she assumed that task again. Like Plutarch and like Shakespeare in *Julius Caesar*, she imagined Brutus as the ideal patriot, motivated by a sense of duty and honor. In her Boston Conversations, Fuller and her students discussed whether a woman could ever perform Brutus's "great action" and show his moral courage and sense of duty, a "higher law," as the transcendentalists would call it. As Elizabeth Peabody put it in her transcription, "A great deal of talk arose here—and Margaret repelled the sentimentalism that took away woman's moral power of performing stern duty."[30] In her Roman diary, in an entry for February 1849, Fuller returned to the murder of Rossi, agreeing with a "young Frenchman" that "the act would have been heroic, if the murderer had stood firm and avowed it. It would indeed then have been the act of Brutus."[31] Of course, there are a number of other distinctions Fuller elides (Rossi was no powerful tyrant),[32] but this literary and historical treatment informed her perspective.

For some conservatives in the United States, though, the lens through which they viewed such an event was not the defense of the Roman Republic from Caesar's tyranny in 44 BC but, rather, the French Revolution of 1789. In antebellum American society, the nearness in time to the revolution's 1794 Reign of Terror gave terms such as "jacobinical," "bloody," and "revolutionary" powerful associations, now lost to us by the passage of time. The sensational reports about the horrors of the San Domingo slave revolt also provided terrifying images for those who pondered the relationship between abolitionist exhortation and slave violence. It was because of this alternative lens that Hawthorne, for one, viewed Fuller with ambivalence. James Russell Lowell in his "Ode to France" had described the two Liberties familiar to the public, one

> . . . a maiden mild and undefiled
> Like her who bore the world's redeeming child;

the other

> Vengeance, axe in hand, that stood
> Holding a tyrant's head up by the clotted hair.[33]

In her dispatches, Fuller assumed both personae. At times she became Liberty leading the people; at others, the Virgin Mary, especially the Mater Dolorosa, an image that had fascinated Fuller for years.

As Jeffrey Steele has pointed out, Fuller's finest poem, "Raphael's Deposition from the Cross" (1844), concerns itself with this image, perhaps inspired by a copy of the Raphael painting now known as *The Entombment*.[34] In Rome, her identification with the Virgin Mother recurs as she describes her activities in the hospital on Tiber Island, tending the revolution's wounded young men. "I was the Mater Dolorosa," she writes her sister Ellen, "and I remembered that the midwife who helped Angelino into the world came from the sign of the Mater Dolorosa."[35] The irony here, of course, is that Fuller had left Angelino in the countryside with a wet nurse for weeks at a time (a common practice) while she joined Ossoli in Rome during the fall, winter, and spring of 1848–49. In Rome, the childlike Ossoli, as well as the wounded young republicans, may have taken the place of Angelino for Fuller, evoking and fulfilling her maternal instincts.

Despite Fuller's attempts in Italy to keep her actual motherhood secret, rumors of her liaison with Ossoli and the existence of a love child circulated in the United States and affected responses to her dispatches. Moreover, by committing herself so wholeheartedly to the European revolutionary scene, by creating a fierce, public female persona speaking on behalf of the Italian people, by supporting the violent overthrow of the most powerful politico-religious leader in the world, she inspired both admiration and anxiety. Nathaniel Hawthorne's response contained a mixture of the two. In *The Scarlet Letter* (1850), he allows his heroine, Hester Prynne, to assume the role of Divine Maternity in the opening tableau of his novel, as she stands with the illegitimate Pearl on the scaffold, subjected to public humiliation, and he then presents her as the Mater Dolorosa in the final tableau, as she holds her lover, the dying Arthur Dimmesdale, in her arms. In the interval between these scenes, Hawthorne emphasizes the turmoil and wickedness Hester stirs up in her role as a revolutionary. Without the influence of Pearl, he writes, "she might, and not improbably would, have suffered death from the stern tribunals of the period, for attempting to undermine the foundations of the Puritan establishment."[36]

Throughout the summer of 1849, Hawthorne, like Pope Pius IX, had sought a political restoration, writing letters to friends, to be published in the newspapers, and later telling readers of "The Custom House" that he had been victimized by the bloodthirsty Whigs, who acting out of a "fierce and bitter spirit of malice and revenge"[37] had struck off his head with the political guillotine and ignominiously kicked it about. Hawthorne's association of Fuller with political assassination and revolutionary violence informed not only *The Scarlet Letter* but later works as well, as Thomas R. Mitchell points out in *Hawthorne's Fuller Mystery* (1998). In *The Blithedale Romance* (1852), for example, we learn that Zenobia, obviously based on Fuller, has the look of a woman about to plunge a dagger into her rival, an act of passion more likely "in Italy, instead of New England."[38] Some eight years later, in *The Marble Faun*, Hawthorne draws upon his knowledge of Fuller's sexual and political activities in Rome to create Miriam's relationships with the villainous un-named model and with her childlike friend Donatello, who murders the model at her bidding. As Mitchell points out, "In a parallel to Fuller's efforts to articulate an ideological justification for the republican in-surrection in Rome by linking it to democratic revolutions of the past, Miriam directs Donatello to Pompey's forum immediately after the mur-der and 'treading loftily past,' proclaims: 'For there was a great deed done here! . . . a deed of blood, like ours! Who knows, but we may meet the high and ever-sad fraternity of Caesar's murderers, and exchange a salutation?'"[39]

Obviously, Hawthorne understood Fuller's perspective on the revolu-tionary events of 1848–49, but by using the term "murderer" to denote Brutus and his co-conspirators, Hawthorne revealed his rejection of it. The notorious "defective and evil nature" Hawthorne attributed to Fuller in his Italian notebooks may stem from repressed political, as well as sex-ual, anxieties. In one of his last unfinished romances, "Septimius Felton," Hawthorne declared, "In times of Revolution and public disturbance, all absurdities are more unrestrained; the measure of calm sense, the habits, the orderly decency, are in a measure lost. More people become insane, I should suppose; offenses against public morality, female license, are more numerous; suicides, murders, all ungovernable outbreaks of men's thoughts, embodying themselves in wild acts, take place more frequently, and with less horror to the lookers-on."[40] This is Hawthorne's nightmare world, and Fuller is one of the ghosts who haunt it.

RADICAL ABOLITIONISTS

At the opposite end of the political spectrum from Hawthorne, a num-ber of ardent abolitionists responded with admiration to Fuller's revolutionary example and became active advocates of violent resistance to slavery in the United States. Samuel Gridley Howe, one of John Brown's Secret Six, was married to the popular poet Julia Ward Howe, who idolized John Brown and Fuller both. She had been a student of Fuller's in Boston and took her as her role model. Soon after Fuller's death, Howe went to Rome and socialized with Fuller's friends there and even took a lover, as Fuller had done. In her poem "From Newport to Rome, 1848" (published in 1854), Howe pays tribute to Fuller's revolutionary example by imagining herself witnessing the defeat of the Roman Republic:

> I hear the battle-thunder boom,
> Cannon to cannon answering loud;
> I hear the whizzing shots that fling
> Their handful to the stricken crowd.
> I see the bastions bravely manned,
> The patriots gathered in the breach;
> . . . The walls are stormed, the fort is ta'en,
> The city's heart with fainter throb
> Receives its death-stroke—all is lost,
> And matrons curse, and children sob.

Howe concludes the poem hopefully, punning on Fuller's name:

> With fuller power, let each avow
> The kinship of his human blood;
> With fuller pulse, let every heart
> Swell to high pangs of brotherhood.
> With fuller light, let women's eyes
> Earnest, beneath the Christ-like brow,
> Strike this deep question home to men,
> "Thy brothers perish—idlest thou?"[41]

Although Fuller died three years before *Passion Flowers* was published, she had read Howe's early poetry and told the young woman, "I admire the feeling of the prophetic spirit of the Old Testament as much as that of the purity and infinite love of Jesus. The parts all please me in various ways."[42] During the Civil War, when Howe penned the most famous lyrics of her career, "The Battle Hymn of the Republic," she not only recalled Fuller's power, pulse, and light but also assumed her apocalyptic discourse, creating a vision of righteous violence and destruction that echoes Isaiah's prophecy of the advent of Emmanuel. The words are no doubt familiar.

> Mine eyes have seen the glory of the coming of the Lord:
> He is trampling out the vintage where the grapes of wrath are stored;
> He hath loosed the fateful lightning of His terrible swift sword:
> His truth is marching on.

Notice that Howe barely alludes to events of the Civil War itself, but in the role of a female prophetess envisions regeneration through violence, inflicted upon the sinful. A later verse goes,

> In the beauty of the lilies Christ was born across the sea,
> With a glory in his bosom that transfigures you and me:
> As he died to make men holy, let us die to make men free,
> While God is marching on.[43]

As Edmund Wilson has pointed out, "Note that Christ is situated 'across the sea'; he is not present on the battlefield with His Father, yet, intent on our grisly work, we somehow still share in His 'glory.'"[44] The transatlantic connection Howe imagines, then, between God the angry father and Christ the glorious son, expresses the antebellum sense of the struggle for liberty as an international, rather than strictly national, project. Howe, like Emerson, wrote a biography of Margaret Fuller, and in her conclusion she suggested that the secret of Fuller's life was heroic nobility: "When all that could be known of Margaret was known, it became evident that there was nothing of her which was not heroic in intention." She was, Howe added, "an example of one who, gifted with great powers, aspired only to their noblest use."[45]

Perhaps the most heroically inclined of the radical abolitionists Howe and her husband knew was Thomas Wentworth Higginson. Like Julia Ward Howe, Higginson regarded Fuller as his role model and became one of her early biographers. As a boy, he knew Fuller as a fascinating friend of his older sister Louisa, and, as Barbara Miller Solomon has pointed out, he "drew strength from Fuller's call for an American hero. He identified his own striving with hers."[46] After graduating from

Harvard at age seventeen, Higginson became a Unitarian minister, radical abolitionist, journalist, woman's rights advocate, defender of John Brown, Civil War colonel, and later editor of the *Atlantic Monthly*. He thought of himself as a man of action, and Fuller's example persistently inspired him. At a women's rights meeting in 1853, he criticized the editors of Fuller's *Memoirs*—Emerson, James Freeman Clarke, and William Henry Channing—for failing to appreciate the obstacles Fuller had faced in her career as a woman of "genius." In his own biography of Fuller, published in 1884, he acknowledged her influence during his formative years. "Margaret Fuller," he declared, "had upon me, through her writings, a more immediate intellectual influence than any one except Emerson, and possibly Parker." Trying to correct the emphasis on self-culture that he felt the editors of the *Memoirs* had made, he declared that the goal of *his* biography was to keep before his readers "the fact that the best part of intellect is action, and that this was always her especial creed." In the final pages of the biography he compares her to Emerson and praises her for emphasizing action over thought. "In later years she had the fulfillment of her dreams. . . . She showed in great deeds. She was the counselor of great men, she had a husband who was a lover and she had a child."[47] Such a plotting of Fuller's life effectively transformed tragedy into triumph.

In the decade after Fuller's death, Higginson, as my introduction pointed out, sought to participate in "great deeds," with some success, including the unsuccessful attack on the Boston courthouse to free the fugitive Anthony Burns. Soon after that violent encounter, during which he received a cut to his chin leaving a lifelong scar, he delivered a sermon in which he defended himself by adopting the persona of a European revolutionary: "I am glad of the discovery . . . that I live under a despotism. . . . For myself, existence looks worthless under such circumstances; and I can only make life worth living for, by becoming a revolutionist. . . . I see now, that while Slavery is national, law and order must constantly be on the wrong side. I see that the case stands for me precisely as it stands for Kossuth and Mazzini, and I must take the consequences."[48] In 1856, like Fuller, he became a correspondent for Greeley's *Tribune*, traveling to "Bleeding Kansas," where he wrote dispatches describing events in revolutionary terms, casting free-state settlers as fighting for freedom against oppressive proslavery forces backed by a tyrannical U.S. government: "As Hungary, having successfully resisted her natural enemy, Austria, yielded at length to the added strength of Russia; so the Kossuths of Kansas, just as they had cleared her borders of Missourians are subdued by the troops of the United States."[49] The solution to slavery for Higginson was guerrilla warfare and slave insurrection. Even Fuller's gentle friend William Henry Channing agreed, writing Higginson, "the next thing to do is *guerrilla war* at every chance. They shall not sleep whether they pull down their caps or not."[50] Higginson met John Brown in Kansas and became his loyal backer. In fact, as Jeffery Rossbach has said, he "played a vital role, perhaps the key role, in coaxing the Secret Committee of Six to support John Brown's raid, and he provides the only example of unambivalent behavior for the entire group."[51]

Although the raid failed and Brown was hanged for treason, he "began the war that ended American slavery and made this a free Republic," as Frederick Douglass pointed out: "Until this blow was struck, the prospect of freedom was dim, shadowy and uncertain. The irrepressible conflict was one of words, votes and compromises. When John Brown stretched forth his arm the sky was cleared. The time for compromises was gone . . . and the clash of arms was at hand."[52] Brown acting on his own would not have had such an effect, of course. It was evidence of the conspiracy that alarmed the South by confirming its worst fears about the terrorist methods of northern abolitionists. As the historian James McPherson has pointed out, "Those Yankee fanatics would soon cause southern opinion to evolve into a third phase of unreasoning fury," making disunion seem inevitable. "Thousands joined military companies; state legislatures appropriated funds for the purchase of arms," and the attack on Fort Sumter soon followed.[53] John Brown's Secret Six, encouraged by Higginson's resolve and Fuller's example, had an impact far exceeding that suggested by their small number.

Throughout the twentieth century, American literary histories ignored the connection between the European revolutionary scene and the coming American Civil War, emphasizing American exceptionalism instead; however, many of Fuller's contemporaries recognized the connection and regarded it with pleasure or fear. In December 1851 John Brown wrote to his wife from Boston, "There is an unusual amount of very interesting things happening in this and other countries at present. . . . The great excitement produced by the coming of Kossuth, and the last news of a new revolution in France, with the prospect that all Europe will soon again be in a blaze seem to have taken all by surprise. I have only to say in regard to these things that I rejoice in them from the full belief that God is carrying out his eternal purpose in them all."[54] (In 1857 Brown would hire the English mercenary Hugh Forbes, who had fought under Garibaldi in Italy, to train recruits for Brown's "army.") At the conclusion of *Uncle Tom's Cabin* (1852), Stowe observes: "This is an age of the world when nations are trembling and convulsed," and she warns of a war that will take place on American soil. "And is America safe? Every nation that carries in its bosom great and unredressed injustice has in it the elements of this last convulsion."[55] Whereas Stowe urged emancipation and colonization to avoid such a convulsion, Fuller showed its heroic appeal. The revolutionary violence of John Brown, not the Christian pacifism of Uncle Tom, best represented Fuller's idea of how to respond to tyranny and oppression.

Sympathy with war is a juvenile and temporary
state. . . . [L]earning and art, and especially
religion weave ties that make war look like
fratricide, as it is.

  —EMERSON, "War," 1838

War civilizes: for it forces individuals & tribes to
combine; & act with larger views, & under the best
heads, & keeps populations together, producing
the effect of cities, for camps are wandering cities.

  —EMERSON, journal entry, 1862

CHAPTER TWO

Emerson, Guns, and Bloodlust

In the preceding chapter, I argued that Margaret Fuller's support of political violence in Europe in 1848–49 prefigured and influenced Ralph
Waldo Emerson's turn to righteous violence in the United States during
the 1850s. What I wish to examine more closely in this chapter are the
moral complexities this turn created for him and how he dealt with
them. Emerson's lifelong interest in the conversion of thought into practical power has recently dominated studies of transcendentalism, and a
number of scholars have extended our knowledge of Emerson's political
activism, especially his abolitionism.[1] The ways in which this activism ran
counter to his peace principles, however, have received little attention.
Len Gougeon, David Robinson, Albert von Frank, Robert Richardson,
and others have argued that Emerson's activism, even his support of
John Brown, was a natural outgrowth of his transcendental idealism.
As Gougeon puts it, Emerson played an "active role . . . throughout his
life in an effort to inculcate transcendental values in the 'real world' of

American society. The Civil War was the capstone of that quest."[2] When the values of freedom and justice are those under consideration, this argument rings true; however, when other Emersonian values, such as civility, love, and peace, are taken into account, internal contradictions in his thought become apparent. The most prominent rhetorical means he used to resolve these contradictions were elision, rejection, and rationalization, which were evoked by particular figures and events, most notably John Brown and the Civil War. In this chapter, I will focus on a series of Emerson's responses to the use of guns and other weapons in order to probe the contradictions in his political thought, without denying his success at helping rid the nation of slavery.

EMERSON'S DISARMING IDEALISM

Throughout the 1830s, Emerson consistently drew upon his idealism to advocate peaceful means to achieve social justice, and he did so using his rather unique notion of the relation between the individual and the world. In *Nature* (1836), he famously set out the way in which this relation functions. He argued that spirit acting through one's soul creates the world, a world that is perfect and not subject to the human will. The imperfections one sees, therefore, are appearances resulting from imperfections within the self, and this self has the power to change the world through spiritual regeneration, making Nature—that is, the material world—consonant with the influx of the divine. Emerson's most radical expression was the following: "As soon as you conform your life to the pure idea in your mind, that will unfold its great proportions. A correspondent revolution in things will attend the influx of the spirit. So fast will disagreeable appearances, swine, spiders, snakes, pests, madhouses, prisons, enemies, vanish; they are temporary and shall be no more seen."[3] Throughout his career, this idea would persist, even though he periodically seemed to accept and lament the obdurate and independent reality of a flawed material world, which he termed "fate."

Soon after he took up residence in Concord, Emerson contributed to the July 4, 1836, celebration of a "revolution in things," the commemoration of the engagement between American colonists and British troops at the North Bridge on April 19, 1775. In his poem "Concord Hymn," he elides the aggression of the colonists by omitting the immediate effect of "the shot heard round the world." The colonists' killing of three British soldiers goes unmentioned in the poem; instead, Emerson makes it seem as if the principle of freedom animated the "embattled farmers" and justified their actions. They chose "to die, or leave their children free," he writes, and he thus transforms their armed insurrection into a form of principled martyrdom.[4] He would later say the people were resisting "offensive usurpations, offensive taxes of the British Parliament."[5] Hawthorne's observation, that the colonists' killing of British soldiers seemed "so like murder," was one that Emerson chose not to make.

When writing about other violent events, Emerson often elided facts that ran counter to his arguments. Some sixteen months after the July 4 celebration, Emerson wrote about the November 7, 1837, shooting death of the abolitionist editor Elijah Lovejoy (discussed in my introduction), and he omitted the man's own use of guns. In his lecture "Heroism," delivered in January 1838 and later published in his *Essays, First Series* (1841), Emerson praises Lovejoy's heroism but does not mention his armed resistance, especially not the killing of Lyman Bishop. (Emerson would later use the technique of maintaining his idealism through elision in his speeches about John Brown.) Emerson's contemporaries were more explicit regarding Lovejoy's use of guns. In the *Liberator*, William Lloyd Garrison calls Lovejoy "a Martyr for Liberty," but he adds, "in the name of Jesus of Nazareth, who suffered himself to be unresistingly nailed to the cross, we solemnly protest against any of his professed followers resorting to carnal weapons under any pretext or in any extremity whatever."[6] Emerson's sometime mentor, the Reverend William Ellery Channing, likewise lamented that Lovejoy "fell with arms in his hands." "It is time for philanthropy to stop," he asserts, "when it can only advance by wading through blood."[7] Gougeon has quoted Channing and asserted, "Obviously, Emerson felt very differently about the matter," pointing out that Emerson "would provide funds to purchase Sharpe's rifles to aid John Brown and his followers in the Kansas land wars in the 1850s."[8]

One must question Gougeon's emphasis on Emerson's approval of armed resistance this early in his career, however, for Emerson fails to mention weapons in "Heroism," other than those of "truth" and "rectitude." Instead, he makes it seem as if Lovejoy stood defenseless before his enemies. He writes, "It is but the other day that the brave Lovejoy gave his breast to the bullets of a mob, for the rights of free speech and opinion, and died when it was better not to live."[9] Obviously, to give one's breast to bullets is far different from getting shot while aiming a gun at your adversaries. We can thus infer that Emerson's pacifism differed little from Garrison's and Channing's, except, unlike them, he chose to omit mention of Lovejoy's armed resistance. As for the possibility that Emerson found Lovejoy's use of guns irrelevant, the contemporary controversy about it argues otherwise.

Seven years later, in his 1844 "Address on the Emancipation of the Negroes in the British West Indies," Emerson similarly elides the fact of armed resistance. In the address, he calls upon the black man to engage in moral development and advance his own cause, peacefully, not through violent rebellion. Although Emerson celebrates "the arrival in the world of such men as Toussaint, and the Haytian heroes," he makes no mention of the horrific acts that attended their revolution, the "Santo Domingo Hour," as Stowe called it. He emphasizes, instead, their intellectual power: "Here is the anti-slave: here is man: and if you have man, black or white is an insignificance. The intellect,—that is miraculous!" (*AW* 31). Emerson also praises the peaceful ways the negroes within the British colonies greeted news of their emancipation in 1834. "I have never read anything in history more touching than the moderation of the negroes," he declares (*AW* 15). Similarly, when he tells of the reaction of the same group of blacks in 1838 when the apprentice system was abolished, he stresses their decorum and gratitude, claiming, "The manner in which the new festival was celebrated, brings tears to the eyes" (*AW* 18). For Emerson, such admirable restraint should have dispelled fears that free blacks would resort to violence against their former masters if given the opportunity, an argument used by southern slaveholders to justify maintaining their inhumane institution. To Emerson's mind, acts of kindness and goodwill engender kindness and goodwill in others.

A year later, in his August 1, 1845, address on the anniversary of West Indian emancipation, he concluded by declaring that one could solve the problem of slavery by bringing culture and civility to southern masters, who would then free their slaves: "Elevate, enlighten, civilize the semi-barbarous nations of South Carolina, Georgia, Alabama—take away from their debauched society the Bowie-knife, the rum-bowl, the dice-box, and the stews—take out the brute, and infuse a drop of civility and generosity, and you touch those selfish lords with thought and gentleness" (*AW* 38). Emerson viewed the removal of weapons, in this case the Bowie knife, as part of the civilizing process. When he criticized the annexation of Texas in 1845 and the start of the Mexican War in 1846, he characterized these events as the results of semi-barbaric and juvenile men. In his "Ode: Inscribed to W. H. Channing," he mocks those who do not see the degradation occurring in Texas:

> Go, blindworm, go,
> Behold the famous States,
> Harrying Mexico
> With rifle and with knife![10]

In a July 4, 1846, speech, Emerson attributes the eagerness to fight Mexico to "the war-party, a ferocious minority, which no civilization has yet caused to disappear in any country; that mob, which every nation holds within it, of young and violent persons craving strong drink, craving blood, craving coarse animal excitement, at any cost" (*AW* 42). These bloodthirsty men are spurred on by "profligate editors and orators, who find their selfish account in encouraging this brutal instinct" (*AW* 43). What one sees in such arguments is Emerson's rejection of political violence on the basis of peace principles he had long held.

REJECTION OF "MUSKET-WORSHIP"

The fullest exposition of Emerson's pacifism can be found in his 1838 lecture entitled "War," later published in Elizabeth Peabody's *Aesthetic Papers* (1849) and referred to in his later journals as "Peace." Because this important lecture has received little critical notice (it does not appear in most collections of his lectures and essays) and yet reveals much about Emerson's peace principles, I want to summarize it carefully. He gave the lecture on March 12, 1838, as part of a winter series of lectures sponsored by the American Peace Society, a "union of the friends of peace," founded in 1828, that traced its origins to the Sermon on the Mount and Noah Worcester's *Solemn Review of the Custom of War* (1814). The Reverend Channing, Amasa Walker, William Ladd, and Samuel J. May also participated in the series. In his lecture, Emerson drew upon his idealism to argue that the use of arms was a barbaric practice that was disappearing as civilization advanced and that the power of "the pure idea" in one's mind could bring about universal peace. In his opening passages, he traces the residual evidence of man's impure state. Referring perhaps to civil war in Spain, an international war in South America, and hostilities against the Indians in Florida, all occurring at the time, he declares that "to sane men at the present day" war "begins to look like an epidemic insanity, breaking out here and there like the cholera or influenza, infecting men's brains instead of their bowels."[11] He claims that the warfare of savage tribes was almost inevitable and necessary: "It is not easy to see how war could be avoided by such wild, passionate, needy, ungoverned, strong-bodied creatures" (151). The instinct of self-help, he observes, "very early unfolded in the coarse and merely brute form of war. . . . It is the ignorant and childish part of mankind that is the fighting part. Idle and vacant minds want excitement, as all boys kill cats" (155).

In the contemporary world, he observes, "we read with astonishment of the beastly fighting of the old times" (158). He cites the example of Elizabethan buccaneers and points out the irony that Thomas Cavendish, "a good Christian man," bragged about burning villages and sinking ships on the coast of South America and claimed, "'It hath pleased Almighty God'" (158–59). (With no sense of irony, Emerson himself would make the same claim following the North's defeat of the South in the Civil War.) In "War," he acknowledges that for "[a]ll that society has yet gained is mitigation: the doctrine of the right of war still remains" (159). In the future, though, this doctrine too will give way because peace represents a natural advancement: "War is on its last legs; and a universal peace is as sure as is the prevalence of civilization over barbarism, of liberal governments over feudal forms" (161). He dismisses the objection that universal peace is a fantasy by pointing out that "There is no good now enjoyed by society that was not once as problematic and visionary as this" (163).

As for the question of how peace will spread, Emerson turns to the idea of the enlightened individual. As long as mankind remains undeveloped, then the phenomena of frigates, navy yards, armed forts, arsenals, and militia are the degraded appearances taken for reality. At present, "We are daunted by the appearances; not seeing that their whole value lies at bottom in the state of mind. It is really a thought that built this portentous war-establishment, and a thought shall also melt it away" (163–64). The individual, "inspired with a tender kindness to the souls of men," will alter the world, for "every degree of the ascendency of this feeling would cause the most striking changes of external things: the tents would be struck; the men-of-war would rot ashore; the arms rust; the cannon would become street-posts" (166). All of the articles of war, in other words, would go to the "museums of the curious, as poisoning and torturing tools are at this day" (166). As for the national consequences of turning the other cheek when attacked, they include increased respect and security, according to Emerson: "Whenever we see the doctrine of peace embraced by a nation, we may be assured it will not be one that invites injury; but one, on the contrary, which has a friend in the bottom of the heart of every man, even of the violent and the base" (169). The commitment to peace, he insists, is a sign not of weakness but courage, for "[i]f peace is to be maintained, it must be by brave men, who have come up to the same height as the hero, namely, the will to carry their life in their hand, and stake it at any instant for their principle, but who have gone one step beyond the hero, and will not seek another man's life" (174).

This last point deserves emphasis, for not all readers have appreciated the fact that in Emerson's value system, the "hero" does not garner his highest admiration. Those men of thought who reject killing do. They have gone "one step beyond the hero." In a little-known lecture titled "Celebration of Intellect," delivered at Tufts College on July 10, 1861, near the start of the Civil War, he begins by observing that "the brute noise of cannon has . . . a most poetic echo in these days, when it is an instrument of freedom and the primal sentiments of humanity," yet he goes on to declare that "it were a compounding of all gradation and reverence to suffer the clash of swords, and the boyish strife of passion, and the feebleness of military strength to intrude on this sanctity and omnipotence of Intellectual Law. Against the heroism of soldiers I set the heroism of scholars, which consists in ignoring the other. You shall not put up in your Academy the statue of Caesar or Pompey, of Nelson or Wellington, of Washington or Napoleon, or Garibaldi, but of Archimedes, of Milton, of Newton."[12] He points out that Archimedes "conducted the defence of Syracuse against the Romans" but later, "when the Roman soldier, at the sack of Syracuse, broke into his study, the philosopher could not rise from his chair and his diagram, and took his death without resistance."[13] (Archimedes supposedly chose to continue his mathematical work and ignore the soldier's command.)

When Emerson traveled in Europe during 1847–48, he persisted in rejecting the notion that political violence could achieve any lasting good for mankind. The two main ideas he took with him on his trip were that the detached scholar wields more power than any warrior, past or present, and that it is the scholar's pure ideas, not weapons or force, that alter the world for the better. Most of the lectures he delivered during his eighteen months were from his "Representative Men" series, and in his essay "Napoleon," delivered fourteen times, he concludes: "Never was such a leader so endowed, and so weaponed; never leader found such aids and followers. And what was the result of this vast talent and power, of these immense armies, burned cities, squandered treasures, immolated millions of men, of this demoralized Europe? It came to no result. . . . He left France smaller, poorer, feebler, than he found it; and the whole contest for freedom was to be begun again."[14] His new lectures made the same argument, that the advance of principles such as freedom depended upon the power of ideas, not arms. In "Tendencies and Duties of Men of Thought," given in London in June 1848, Emerson addressed the struggles of English Chartists and French workers to better their lot through the use of force and declared that each needed "creative supplying power. He must be armed, not necessarily with musket and pike. Better, if seeing these, he can feel that he has better muskets and pikes in his energy and constancy. . . . The way to mend the bad world is to create the right world."[15]

Emerson's months in Europe during 1847 and 1848 strengthened his transcendental idealism and provoked him to argue on behalf of the inspired individual aloof from the political strife of the times.[16] In his new lecture, "The Powers and Laws of Thought," he asserted, "Thought, while it lasts, is the only thing of value, and appears of universal and eternal value. Whatever addresses itself to the Intellect, subordinates the senses. The intellect absorbs so much vital power, that it kills or suspends the senses."[17] As for the European revolutions, he dismissed them as childish and pointless. "All spiritual or real power makes its own place," he declared in his journal. "Revolutions of violence then are scrambles merely" (*JMN* 10: 318).

During his stays in England and France, Emerson witnessed first-hand the importance of guns to the workers who tried to seize power in England and actually did so in France. At a Chartist meeting in London in March 1848, he reacted to the spirit of rebellion among the workers and noticed that "the great body of the meeting liked best the sentiment, 'Every man a ballot & every man a musket'" (*JMN* 10: 239). When he visited the clubs of Paris two months later, he found everyone "in some kind of uniform[—]red sash, red cap, blouse perhaps bound by red sash, brass helmet, & sword, and every body supposed to have a pistol in his pocket." The "fire & fury" of the speakers impressed him, as well as their desire "to secure a fair share of bread to every man, and to get the God's justice done through the land."[18] Though he appreciated the goals of European political radicals, he rejected their violent activities as superficial and ineffective. In *English Traits*, he applauded the conservative London *Times* for turning public opinion against them: the *Times*, he declared, "denounced and discredited the French Republic of 1848, and checked every sympathy with it in England, until it had enrolled 200,000 special constables to watch the Chartists and make them ridiculous in the 10 April" (the date of the Chartists' mass demonstration).[19]

Although Emerson sympathized with the goals of the socialists and communists, he remained a gentleman who preferred to see guns in the hands of the civilized and well-bred. In a journal entry of 1847, Emerson wrote the single sentence, "a gun is a liberalizer" (*JMN* 10: 374), which seems to express sympathy toward the use of armed force to overthrow oppressive rulers or masters. The entry refers not to pistols or muskets in the hands of the "people" or of slaves, however, but rather to guns used for sport among young gentlemen of means. In his essay "Culture," published in *The Conduct of Life* (1860), he explains: "Archery, cricket, gun and fishing-rod, horse and boat, are all educators, liberalizers." These, along with other activities such as chess, whist, and dancing, become "lessons in the art of power" and prepare young men to enter a society of the privileged and powerful. "The gun, fishing-rod, boat, and horse, constitute, among all who use them, secret free-masonries. They are as if they belonged to one club."[20] A fondness for social clubs was a dominant feature of Emerson's personality.

At his famous parting with Carlyle at Stonehenge before returning to the United States in 1848, Emerson rejected Carlyle's arguments on behalf of ruthless warriors, skilled in the use of weapons. Carlyle had essayed this argument in *Heroes and Hero-Worship* (1841), in which he celebrated the use of brute force by Cromwell and Napoleon. In his third edition of *Oliver Cromwell's Letters and Speeches* (1849), which he had recently completed before Emerson's arrival, Carlyle lauded the fact that Cromwell and his age "declared war to the death" with "knaves and quacks" and "would have neither truce nor treaty with these; and went forth, flame-crowned, as with bared sword, and called the Most High to witness that it would not endure these!"[21] Carlyle's edition would help create the "cult of Cromwell" in the United States, which John Brown made use of. Emerson, who had yet to meet Brown, responded to Carlyle's bellicosity with arguments on behalf of pacifism. He informed his friend Samuel Gray Ward, in a letter written during his voyage home, that Carlyle and Arthur Helps had asked him "if there were any Americans, if there were any who had an American idea? Or what is it that thoughtful & superior men with us would have? . . . So I sketched the Boston fanaticism of right & might without bayonets or bishops, every man his own king, & all cooperation necessary & extemporaneous. Of course, men went wild at the denying to society the beautiful right to kill & imprison. But we stood fast for milk & acorns, told them that musket-worship was perfectly well known to us, that it was an old bankrupt."[22] For Emerson, who seems to be referencing members of the Peace Society, America's claim to national superiority resided in its freedom from England's history of warfare, which had left it burdened with debt.

In *English Traits* (1856), Emerson draws upon his letter to Ward and adds an implicit compliment to Carlyle as a great man: "I can easily see the bankruptcy of the vulgar musket-worship,—though great men be musket-worshippers;—and 'tis certain as God liveth, the gun that does not need another gun, the law of love and justice alone, can effect a clean revolution."[23] Five months after Emerson left England, Carlyle wrote him: "Of one impression we fail not here: admiration of your pacific virtues, of gentle and noble tolerance, often *sorely* tried in this place! Forgive me my ferocities."[24] Emerson not only forgave those ferocities, but during the Civil War, emulated them.

REJECTING CALLS TO ARMS

Len Gougeon has argued that the example of the Chartists and French radicals inspired Emerson to become an enthusiastic social reformer upon his return home.[25] While this is in part the case, he also gained a stronger sense that unruly masses, as well as unprincipled governments, posed threats to the power of the enlightened individual. The "Bloody June Days" in France in the summer of 1848 confirmed his sense that the French citizens' violent means of altering their government failed to enhance the lives of anyone. "Perhaps the French Revolution of 1848," he grumbled, "was not worth the trees it cut down on the Boulevards of Paris" (*JMN* 11: 74). Phyllis Cole has discussed the emergence of Emerson's concept of fate during his months in England, and she points out that for him "the remedy to tyrannous circumstances remains the same: individual assertion of visionary power."[26] In his essay "Fate," Emerson puts it this way: "Every solid in the universe is ready to become fluid on the approach of the mind, and the power to flux it is the measure of the mind. If the wall remain adamant, it accuses the want of thought."[27]

The Fugitive Slave Act of 1850 added to Emerson's sense of limitation that he identified with fate, and in his May 3, 1851, speech on the subject, he delivered what Cole calls "the most enraged and most partisan address of his career."[28] Yet while Emerson called for civil disobedience in the lecture, he stopped short of advocating violence against the state, as Higginson and Parker did. On the contrary, he suggested that the authors of the "immoral" Fugitive Slave Law had engaged in terrorist activities: "[H]e who writes a crime into the statute-book, digs under the foundations of the capitol to plant there a powder magazine, and lays a train [i.e., a combustible fuse]" (*AW* 68).

Beginning in 1850, Emerson became more involved in abolitionism, but not to the extent of Parker, Thoreau, or even Bronson Alcott, all of whom endorsed the attack on the Boston courthouse to free Anthony Burns. He only reluctantly abandoned his peace principles, and his acceptance of violent means remained covert until the Civil War, even then evoking from him various forms of rationalization. As John Carlos Rowe has pointed out, "Emersonian transcendentalism and political activism in mid-nineteenth-century America were inherently incompatible."[29] David Reynolds has observed the turn to violence by a number of transcendentalists as a result of the Fugitive Slave Act and observed that "[f]irst they promoted the *idea* of righteous violence. Then they boldly promoted John Brown, the most violent anarchist of the era. Finally, they promoted his principles during the war."[30] Yet such a sweeping narrative, as Reynolds acknowledges, elides the qualifications and reversals in Emerson's thought. When he became most distressed by the social injustice in his state and nation, he maintained a sense that his "sanity," as he called it, had been lost. For example, in the spring of 1852, he confided to his journal, "I waked at night, & bemoaned myself, because I had not thrown myself into this deplorable question of Slavery, which seems to want nothing so much as a few assured voices. But then, in hours of sanity, I recover myself. . . . I have quite other slaves to free than those negroes, to wit, imprisoned spirits, imprisoned thoughts . . . which, important to the republic of Man, have no watchman, or lover, or defender, but I" (*JMN* 13: 80). As a "man of thought," Emerson tried to stay true to his belief in the power of ideas. Whereas Emerson's fellow transcendentalist Parker kept a loaded pistol in his desk and a drawn sword within reach of his right hand, Emerson, of course, did not. Private thought and public words were his weapons of choice.

Even during the turbulent years of 1854–56, Emerson continued to reject violence as a legitimate political means. In the spring of 1854, when the Kansas-Nebraska Act and the remission of Anthony Burns led to Higginson's attack on the courthouse, Emerson responded sympathetically, but not ardently. In a June 9, 1854, letter to Charles Sumner, who had been attacking the Kansas-Nebraska Bill in the Senate, Emerson wrote: "My dear Sumner, I thank you heartily for your brave temperate & sound Speeches,—all rooted in principles, and, what is less to my purpose, but grateful also to me,—rooted in history."[31] The beating inflicted on Sumner on the Senate floor two years later, in the spring of 1856, outraged Emerson, yet in his address on the assault, Emerson resisted the impulse to argue for revenge. Instead, he made the point that the use of brute force was a southern trait, not a northern one. Civilized men rose above such behavior. In the South, he declared, "life is a fever; man is an animal, given to pleasure, frivolous, irritable, spending his days on hunting and practicing with deadly weapons to defend himself against his slaves, and against his companions brought up in the same idle and dangerous way" (AW 107). As he had in his 1838 lecture "War," he associated fighting with ignorance: "Now as men's bodily strength, or skill with knives and guns is not usually in proportion to their knowledge and mother wit, but oftener in the inverse ratio, it will only do to send foolish persons to Washington, if you wish them to be safe" (AW 108).

Even if Emerson wished someone would physically attack Sumner's assailant, Congressman Preston Brooks, he could not publicly express such a wish. In his speech on affairs in Kansas, though, he fantasized about a time in the past when "Massachusetts, in its heroic day, had no government—was an anarchy. . . . Every man throughout the country was armed with knife and revolver, and it was known that instant justice would be administered to each offence, and perfect peace reigned" (AW 115). In Kansas, four months before Emerson's speech, Brown took it upon himself to administer such justice, committing the Pottawatomie massacre apparently after learning about Sumner's beating. Brown's son Salmon recalled that he and his father and brothers "went crazy—*crazy*" when they heard the news. "It seemed to be the finishing, decisive touch."[32] After the killings and battles throughout the summer of 1856, Brown came east in the winter of 1856, visited Sumner, held his bloody shirt, and evidenced desire for more revenge.

Emerson was deeply moved by newspaper reports of the distress suffered by New England emigrants to Kansas in 1856. Higginson's pieces in the *Tribune* and reports by Reverend Nute in the *Boston Transcript* told of the theft, torture, and murder of the Free State men in Kansas by Border Ruffians. An incendiary pamphlet published in Boston in 1856 that Emerson may have read was titled *The Reign of Terror in Kanzas: As*

Encouraged by President Pierce, and Carried out by the Southern Slave Power: by Which Men have been Murdered and Scalped! Women dragged from their Homes and Violated! Printing Offices and Private Houses burned! Ministers of the Gospel tarred and feathered! Citizens robbed and driven from their Homes! And Other Enormities Inflicted on Free Settlers by Border Ruffians as Related by Eye witnesses of the Events.[33] In his September 10, 1856, address at a Kansas relief meeting, Emerson asserted that "all the right is on one side. We hear the screams of hunted wives and children answered by the howl of the butchers" (*AW* 111). Emigrants from Massachusetts, he asserted, are "set on by highwaymen, driven from their new homes, pillaged, and numbers of them killed and scalped, and the whole world knows that this is no accidental brawl, but a systematic war to the knife, and in loud defiance of all laws and liberties" (*AW* 112).

Emerson's solution to this state of affairs, however, was not the use of force but, rather, organization like that used by the colonists before the Revolution and by free-staters in Kansas; he concluded, "I think the towns should hold town meetings, and resolve themselves into Committees of Safety, go into permanent sessions, adjourning from week to week, from month to month" (*AW* 115). Although he knew that Sharps rifles were at the heart of the "relief" Brown and the free-state settlers sought, he buried this deadly fact among other items: "The people of Kansas ask for bread, clothes, arms, and men, to save them alive, and enable them to stand against these enemies of the human race" (*AW* 112). These enemies included the United States government as well as Missouri Ruffians, which, from a legal point of view, would have made Emerson's victimized New England emigrants seem armed insurgents. By calling them "the people of Kansas" and emphasizing their victimization, Emerson places them on the high moral ground, peaceful and outgunned.

BLOODLUST AND THE KILLING OF ANIMALS AND MEN

Given Emerson's perspective on the troubles in Kansas, it is not surprising that when John Brown came to Concord in the spring of 1857, seeking additional donations to reimburse him for his losses and to continue his independent war against proslavery forces, he persuaded Emerson to reconsider his peace principles. Brown's March 15, 1857, speech to the people of Concord was exciting and spectacular. As he had done at

Hartford and Boston, he told of the false arrest of his sons Jason and John Jr. by government troops who beat them, chained them, and drove them on foot to a U.S. cavalry camp where they were kept in irons. Brown dramatized his account by holding up one of the chains. A version of his speech goes as follows: "On or about the 30th of May last two of my sons, with several others, were imprisoned without other crime than opposition to bogus enactments, and most barbarously treated for a time,—one being held about one month, the other about four months. Both had their families in Kansas, and destitute of homes, being burned out after they were imprisoned. In this burning all the eight were sufferers, as we all had our effects at the time, and never recovered them. Here is the chain with which one of them was confined, after the cruelty, sufferings, and anxiety he underwent had rendered him a maniac,—yes, a maniac."[34] Practicing his own brand of elision, Brown failed to mention that this occurred soon after the Pottawatomie killings, which had stirred outrage throughout southeastern Kansas, and that the soldiers who subjected John Jr. and Jason to such treatment did so because they thought they were among "the Browns" who had murdered proslavery settlers. He also failed to mention that these two sons had been appalled to learn what their father and brothers had done, and that John Jr. was driven to distraction by the news and by the anger of their free-state friends, who knew retaliation would follow.[35]

Brown's speech stirred Emerson considerably, and soon afterward he recorded in his journal: "Captain John Brown of Kansas gave a good account of himself in the Town Hall, last night, to a meeting of Citizens. One of his good points was, the folly of the peace party in Kansas, who believed, that their strength lay in the greatness of their wrongs, & so discountenanced resistance. . . . The first man who went in to Kansas from Missouri to interfere in the elections, he thought, had a perfect right to be shot" (*JMN* 14: 125). Even though the fighting in Kansas was subsiding in 1857, which made it difficult for Brown to raise money for his plans, his speech obviously undermined Emerson's respect for "the peace party in Kansas" and evoked a new anger in Emerson toward the South.

For a number of years, Emerson had regarded slaves and slaveowners alike as brutelike creatures. In a journal entry of 1853, he wrote that

the "secret" which abolitionists had yet to discover "is, that the negro
& the negro-holder are really of one party, & that, when the apostle
of freedom has gained his first point of repealing the negro laws, he
will find the free negro is the type & exponent of that very animal law;
standing as he does in nature below the series of thought, & in the plane
of vegetable & animal existence, whose law is to prey on one another,
and the strongest has it" (*JMN* 13: 35). In 1857, several months after
listening to John Brown speak, Emerson went one step farther in his
animosity toward southerners and declared, "The shooting complexion,
like the cobra capello & scorpion, grows in the South. It has no wisdom,
no capacity of improvement. . . . With such a nation or a nation with a
predominance of this complexion, war is the safest terms. That marks
them, &, if they cross the lines, they can be dealt with as all fanged animals must be" (*JMN* 14: 170). By regarding southerners as dangerous
animals, Emerson tried to convince himself that killing them was natural
and justified.

Despite his peace principles, Emerson began to rationalize warfare
and killing under the influence of John Brown's rhetoric. In the summer
of 1858, he even bought himself a gun, not to shoot Missouri Ruffians,
but other kinds of animals. When William J. Stillman, the artist and journalist, organized a hunting trip in the Adirondacks with fellow members
of the Saturday Club, he offered to let Emerson choose from a number
of guns he owned, but Emerson bought his own doubled-barreled one.
Upon learning of this, Thoreau satirically wrote in his journal, "the story
on the Mill-Dam is that he has taken a gun which throws shot from
one end and ball from the other!"[36] Longfellow, a fellow member of
the Saturday Club, when he heard that Emerson would be armed, "respectfully declined joining the party."[37] Though the image of Emerson
as hunter may seem comic, his experiences on the trip provide a glimpse
of his subsequent bloodlust.

Stillman painted an outdoors portrait of the group that now hangs
in the Concord Free Public Library, and Emerson wrote a long narrative poem about the experience titled "The Adirondacs," published in
May Day and Other Poems (1867), but perhaps the most accurate representation of the trip appears in Stillman's 1893 *Century Magazine* piece
titled "The Philosophers' Camp. Emerson, Agazziz, Lowell, and Others

in the Adirondacks." At the camp, located at Follansbee Pond, the group hunted deer, fished for trout, and explored the natural flora and fauna in the area, with Louis Agassiz, a leading scientist at Harvard, taking charge and lecturing the others on the fine points of natural science. The hunting lacked a high degree of sportsmanship. As Judge Hoar explained to his wife, "In the day-time, we went out in our boats, and scattered to different points on the lake, to look out for the deer when he should take to the water. Then one of the guides took a hound into the woods and looked out for a fresh deer-track, and put him on it, and the dog followed it up till he found the deer, which he then chased perhaps for an hour or two, till the deer would take to the water to escape the dog, and attempt to swim across the lake. The boats would pursue him and shoot him while swimming." The other method of hunting, just as unsportsmanlike, involved going out in boats at night with a bright light in the bow, which mesmerized the deer feeding on the lily pads, allowing the hunter to shoot them as they stood stock still just yards away. As Hoar explained it to his wife, "One man paddles in the stern, and another with a gun sits just behind the light in the bow; and as the light noiselessly approaches the shore, the deer stand and gaze on it, seeming to be fascinated, until you can sometimes get within two rods of them."[38]

At first Emerson chose not to hunt, preferring instead to observe and meditate, as depicted in Stillman's painting, where he stands in the very middle, apart from the other two groups of campers, one of which is listening to a lecture by Agassiz, the other shooting at a target (see figure 2). On one particular Sunday morning, however, when Stillman took Emerson to a quiet part of the lake for meditation while the guides staged a hunt, the sound of the baying hounds excited Emerson, and according to Stillman, he exclaimed, "'Let us go after the deer!' . . . and though, having come out for meditation, we had no gun with us, we were soon flying down the lake from our remotest corner to where the baying led to the shore." But they were too late: "Lowell had already killed the deer before we got there."[39] From that moment, Emerson, according to Stillman, "caught the temper of the occasion, and began to desire to kill his deer." The accommodating Stillman took him out on a night hunt, and though they glided near a deer feeding near shore, "Emerson could distinguish nothing. 'Shoot!' finally whispered the guide in the faintest

FIGURE 2. William James Stillman, *The Philosophers' Camp in the Adirondacks, 1858*. Oil on canvas. Courtesy of Concord Free Public Library.

breath. 'Shoot!' I repeated nearer. But the deer was invisible to him, and we drifted to a boat's length from him before the animal took fright, and bolted for the woods, undisturbed by a hasty shot I sent after him, and we heard his triumphant whistle and gallop dying away in the forest depths. Emerson was stupefied" (602).

In his poem, Emerson recorded the scene, adding high drama and eliding its embarrassing features:

> In the boat's bows, a silent night-hunter
> Stealing with paddle to the feeding-grounds
> Of the red deer, to aim at a square mist.
> Hark to that muffled roar! It has not scared the buck,
> Who stands astonished at the meteor light,
> Then turns to bound away,—is it too late?[40]

Apparently it was too late, but Stillman recalls:

> Each disappointment . . . plunged him more deeply into the excitement of the chase, and he was most anxious to kill his deer before he went home,

unable to resist the contagion of the passion for it. He said to me one day, "I must kill a deer before we go home, even if the guide has to hold him by the tail." At that season of the year, when the deer are in their short coat, the body sinks at once if shot in the deep water; and on overtaking the quarry in the lake, if the deerslayer was not sure of his shot, the guide used to run the boat alongside of it, and catch it by the tail, when the shot became a sure one. . . . Emerson never had the gratification of his desire; the deer never came to him on the drive, and his repetition of the night-hunt was no more successful. (602)

According to Thoreau, Emerson did make a kill on the hunt, a peet-weet, a small shore bird that goes unmentioned in his poem. The un-likeliness of Emerson as sportsman makes Thoreau exclaim, "Emerson says that he and Agassiz and Company broke some dozens of ale-bottles, one after another, with their bullets, in the Adirondack country, using them for marks! It sounds rather Cockneyish. He says that he shot a peetweet for Agassiz, and this, I think he said, was the first game he ever bagged. . . . Think of Emerson shooting a peetweet (with shot) for Agassiz, and cracking an ale-bottle (after emptying it) with his rifle at six rods!"[41]

Several key understandings emerge from Emerson's participation in this outing. First of all, his tendency to elide unpleasant facts, converting his actual poor vision into a soft-focus representation of what lies before him. Second, his class consciousness, even while satirizing it:

> Look to yourselves, ye polished gentlemen!
> No city airs or arts pass current here.
> Your rank is all reversed: let men of cloth
> Bow to the stalwart churls in overalls:[42]

The ten veteran guides on this trip ("stalwart churls"), who accompanied the ten club members, remain nameless types. As John McAleer has pointed out, they assumed the burdens of portage, prepared meals, cleaned the game, and managed the hunts.[43] Third, and perhaps most important, Emerson's tendency to become caught up in the thrill of violent action, the use of guns to assert power, bond with others, and demonstrate masculinity. In his essay "Circles" (1844), he had discussed how men are attracted to the "abandonment" of dreams and drugs that mimic the effects of genius, and observed that "[f]or the like reason, they ask the aid of wild passions, as in gaming and war, to ape in some manner these flames and generosities of the heart."[44] At the beginning of the Civil War, Emerson's inability to resist the "contagion" of passion, to use Stillman's term, reappeared in his response to the "whirlwind of patriotism" of his fellow New Englanders that swept him up in it.

As I have pointed out previously, a key event leading to the Civil War was John Brown's 1859 raid on Harpers Ferry. Emerson's response to the raid and his defense of Brown reveal his growing willingness to rationalize political violence. One way he did this was to conceptualize the deed as an outcome of idealism. Another way, as with his praise of Lovejoy, was to elide the use of weapons by the martyred hero. Soon after Brown's raid, Emerson wrote to his brother William that Brown "is a true hero, but he lost his head there."[45] In a letter drafted to Governor Wise, in an apparent attempt to persuade him not to execute Brown, Emerson similarly declared that Brown was "the rarest of heroes[,] a pure idealist, with no by-ends of his own. He is therefore precisely what lawyers call crazy, being governed by ideas, & not by external circumstance. He has afforded them the first trait marked in the books as betraying insanity, namely, disproportion between means & ends" (*JMN* 14: 334). In his speech in aid of Brown's family, Emerson elided the bloodshed inherent in Brown's plan, which the weapons Brown took with him surely implied. Instead, Emerson calls the raid an "enterprise," and says Brown intended "to go into Virginia and run off five hundred or a thousand slaves." This statement seems disingenuous, as does his attempt to link Brown with the class of people Emerson most admired: "All gentlemen, of course, are on his side," he declared. "For what is the oath of gentle blood and knighthood? What but to protect the weak and lowly against the strong oppressor?" (*AW* 123). When he compared Brown to Christ, saying his death would "make the gallows glorious like the cross," he was rebuked about it, by Hawthorne, in particular, and he later removed the comparison from the published piece, perhaps recognizing its absurdity, given the Sermon on the Mount.

In one of the final essays in Emerson's *The Conduct of Life* (1860), one perceives the influence of Brown's ferocity in a passage devoted to the benefits of bloodshed and violence, marking a major shift in Emerson's thinking. The innocuous-sounding "Considerations by the Way" (which draws from journal entries of 1856 and later) offers Emerson's rationalization of violence and his most outrageous thoughts on "the good of evil," as he puts it. He argues, "Wars, fires, plagues, break up immovable routine, clear the ground of rotten races and dens of distemper, and open a fair field to new men. There is a tendency in things to right themselves, and the war or revolution or bankruptcy that shatters a rotten system, allows things to take a new and natural order. . . . Passions, resistance, danger, are educators. We acquire the strength we have overcome. Without war, no soldier; without enemies, no hero."[46] Michael Lopez has called Emerson's notion that "War is the father of all things" "the cornerstone of his philosophy of power,"[47] yet this philosophy now locates power not in "the law of love and justice alone," as he told Carlyle it did, but in the purifying forces of death and destruction. Disdain for war has given way to enthusiasm for it.

THE SIREN VOICES OF THE CANNON

As the Civil War began, Emerson procured thirty rifles for young volunteers in Concord to drill with and justified his eagerness for war by privileging passion over reason. On April 16, 1861, he acknowledged in a letter to Arthur Clough in England that he had been swept up in the war fever: "We are quite too busy here with our mad war,—the most wanton piece of mischief that bad boys ever devised."[48] A week later, he gave the lecture "Civilization at a Pinch" and declared that the war was "an affair of instincts," which "we did not know we had." He continued, "we valued ourselves as cool calculators; we were very fine with our learning and culture . . . and our religion of peace;—and now a sentiment mightier than logic, wide as light, strong as gravity, reaches into the college, the bank, the farm-house, and the church."[49] The lecture abandoned his famous argument for self-reliance and declared, "It is the day of the populace; they are wiser than their teachers. . . . We are wafted into a revolution which, though at first sight a calamity of the human race, finds all men in good heart, in courage, in a generosity of mutual and patriotic support" (600). Referencing compromises the North had made with slavery, beginning in 1850, he conflated political tension with actual killing, declaring: "It was war then, and it is war now; but declared war is vastly safer than war undeclared" (601). The deaths of thousands of young men soon undermined this sophistry. Yet as Ralph Rusk accurately discerned long ago, for Emerson the Civil War became "a disease in his own system as well as in the body politic," and he "found it hard to get the poison of hate out of his blood."[50]

Enthusiasm in the North for the war quickly dissipated after the humiliating defeat at the First Battle of Bull Run. In July 1861 Emerson, like everyone else in the North, became depressed, but he did not relinquish his notion of southerners as fanged creatures (some early rebel flags featured a rattlesnake, in imitation of the colonial Gadsden flag, a snake with the motto "don't tread on me"). Emerson told his friend Conway, "We need a more scientific knowledge of the nature of a rattlesnake, and may be taught by this defeat."[51] On August 4, 1861, he wrote James Elliot Cabot saying that he had long admired the "suave, cool, & picturesque manners" of the southerner, yet "a long experience only varying from bad to worse has shown us, I think finally, what a noxious reptile the green & gold thing was."[52] When it became clear that emancipation was not a priority of the Lincoln administration, Emerson lost his enthusiasm for killing. At a meeting of the Saturday Club, Emerson said, "If the Union is incapable of securing universal freedom, its disruption were as the breaking up of a frog pond. Until justice is the aim of war one may naturally rather be shot than shoot."[53] In other words, the principle of peace, along with the martyrdom that accompanied it, could only be superseded by the principles of freedom and justice.

Faced with surprising victories by the rebel army, Emerson returned to his thesis that the man of thought needed to rise above the political turmoil of the times. In his lecture "Truth," given on October 27, 1861, before the Twenty-Eighth Congregational Society in Boston, he confessed:

> In the noise of war, in the shifting rumors of advance and retreat, in the alarms of conflict and the joy and pain of friends at home who listen with trembling interest for every syllable of tidings of the combatants, it is difficult to draw attention to the thoughts and teachings that belong to the

house of worship. . . . We come up to the house of social worship to oper-
ate a right diversion of an attention and affection too anxiously strained
on private details: to school our affections drenched in personal and patriotic hopes and fears, by lifting them out of the blinding tumult into a
region where the air is pure and serene; to still our passions, by calling
into action our reason; to stop the craving for exciting events, by the consideration of eternal laws, which hold on their beneficent way through all
temporary and partial suffering, and so assure not only the general good,
but the welfare of all the suffering individuals.[54]

While not explicitly protesting the war effort or arguing on behalf
of peace, Emerson clearly in "Truth" sought to regain the equanim-
ity he had lost. Contributing to his distress, as Robert Richardson has
pointed out, is that Emerson and his wife "both regarded the preservation of the Union as insufficient reason for war. Only if the North
would fight the war explicitly to free the slaves would they regard it as
moral."[55]

In his January 31, 1862, lecture "American Civilization" given at the
Smithsonian Institution in Washington, D.C., Emerson delivered a strong
plea for emancipation and returned to his argument that war was more
suited to a barbarous people, even if they pretended to be civilized: "War
is welcome to the Southerner: a chivalrous sport to him, like hunting,
and suits his semi-civilized condition. On the climbing scale of progress,
he is just up to war, and has never appeared to such advantage as in the
last twelve-month. It does not suit us. We are advanced some ages on the
war-state,—to trade, art, and general cultivation."[56] When the war started
turning in favor of the Union forces, beginning in the summer of 1863,
he had to reverse himself once more, but even before it did, he found
himself in an ambivalent situation and realized that if peace came too
soon, before Lincoln freed the slaves in the South, there would be no
emancipation and all the lives lost up to that moment would have been
for a cause that was not his. Thus, he felt compelled to support the war
effort and urge the total subjugation of the South.

At the start of 1862, he began a journal he titled "War" and also began devising multiple ways of rationalizing war. Here are two of them:
(1) "Well, this is the task before us, to accept the benefit of the War: it

has not created our false relations, they have created it. It simply demonstrates the rottenness it found" (*JMN* 15: 300); (2) "Let it search, let it grind, let it overturn, &, like the fire when it finds no more fuel, it burns out. The war will show, as all wars do, what wrong is intolerable, what wrong makes & breeds all this bad blood" (*JMN* 15: 300). His insistence on the benefits of war shows not just the urgency of the topic to him but perhaps anxiety about denying the death, suffering, and destruction it brought with it. Surely he knew that his views now betrayed a key principle of his own idealism, the principle of peace that rings so strongly and persuasively in the early essays. As Rusk observes, his new position on war "was essentially false to his character and philosophy."[57] In Emerson's eyes, consistency had to be sacrificed to necessity.

In the summer of 1862, after the Union victory of sorts at Antietam, Lincoln made known his plans to free the slaves in the states in rebellion, and Emerson was elated. In a speech celebrating the Emancipation Proclamation given October 12, 1862, Emerson declares, "This act makes that the lives of our heroes have not been sacrificed in vain. It makes a victory of our defeats" (*AW* 131). He also claims, "It is wonderful to see the unseasonable senility of what is called the Peace party, through all its masks blinding their eyes to the main features of the war, its inevitableness" (*AW* 133). Emerson thus began venturing the idea that victory would mean that freedom for slaves was part of God's plan, that the war was righteous. Whereas in his 1838 lecture "War" he had written satirically of those in the past, such as Cavendish, who had claimed God was on their side, he now proceeded to express the same idea.

After Lincoln's emancipation proclamation went into effect on January 1, 1863, Emerson's enthusiasm for the war soared. He started to argue that the war showed that God exists, that right makes might. With the Emancipation Proclamation, the war became moral in his eyes, and the principles of justice and freedom were elevated to preeminence in his thought. During the summer of 1863, he visited West Point as a member of the visitation committee appointed by the secretary of war, and in this role he "saw flying artillery drill, watched a mortar practice with eight-to-ten-inch shells, witnessed a siege battery in action against a target over five thousand yards away."[58] He found the experience heady and started to speak like a recruiting officer. In an address at Waterville College several weeks later, he told the gentlemen of the literary societies there:

> All of us have shared the new enthusiasm of country and of liberty which swept like a whirlwind through all souls at the outbreak of war, and brought, by ennobling us, an offset for its calamity. . . . The war uplifted us into generous sentiments. War ennobles the age. . . . Slavery is broken, and, if we use our advantage, irretrievably. For such a gain, to end once for all that pest of all our free institutions, one generation might well be sacrificed; perhaps it will. . . . Who would not, if it could be made certain that the new morning of universal liberty should rise on our race by the perishing of one generation,—who would not consent to die?[59]

One imagines some in his audience silently answered "me." Not all of these young men could have shared Emerson's newfound enthusiasm for dying.

His own son Edward, a nineteen-year-old student at Harvard, was eager to enlist, but in October 1863, when Colonel E. N. Hallowell asked Emerson for leave to recruit Edward, the father replied, "He is not quite yet worth the sending as a soldier. With a taste for rough life, he is of a delicate health, & very easily disordered. . . . I hope you will not make any proposition to him at this moment, since I fear the proposition would make his stay in college useless, if it did not take him out of college."[60] Hallowell commanded the 54th Massachusetts Volunteers, an all-black regiment led by white officers, and its casualty rate was horrendous, as Emerson well knew. Also, as Jessie Bray has pointed out, prisoners of war from this unit suffered inhumane treatment at the hands of their captors.[61]

In the poem "Voluntaries," which Emerson wrote as a dirge for Colonel Robert Shaw and the black soldiers of the Massachusetts 54th who died in the doomed attack on Fort Wagner in mid-July 1863, the deaths of the young soldiers raise them in God's eyes:

> Whoever fights, whoever falls,
> Justice conquers evermore,
> Justice after as before—

And he who battles on her side,
God, though he were ten times slain,
Crowns him victor glorified,
Victor over death and pain;[62]

The Union victories at Vicksburg and Gettysburg in the summer of 1863, despite the massive casualties (a total of some sixty thousand), also evoked Emerson's enthusiasm for the war effort. In a journal entry made in September 1863, he expressed appreciation of "the new Parrott guns" used by the Union army to bombard Vicksburg and more famously Charleston, South Carolina, in August: "There were always guns & powder. But here today are latest experiments & a success which exceeds all previous performance in throwing far, & in crushing effect" (*JMN* 15: 363). The gun, invented and manufactured by Robert Parker Parrott, was a cannon made of iron, weighing some twenty-four thousand pounds, that could send shells over four miles with deadly accuracy (see figure 3).

FIGURE 3. *The Pet Parrott on the United States Steamer 'Richmond' in a Storm.* From *Harper's Weekly* 8 (May 14, 1864): 312.

The Parrot gun that bombarded Charleston with incendiary shells in the summer of 1863 was known as the "Swamp Angel," and Melville, in his poem of that title, provided a dramatic description of its effects:

> By night there is fear in the City,
> Through the darkness a star soareth on;
> There's a scream that screams up to the zenith,
> Then the poise of a meteor lone—
> Lighting far the pale fright of the faces,
> And downward the coming is seen;
> Then the rush, and the burst, and the havoc,
> And wails and shrieks between.

Melville ends the poem with his characteristic religious compassion:

> Who weeps for the woeful City
> Let him weep for our guilty kind;
> Who joys at her wild despairing—
> Christ, the Forgiver, convert his mind.[63]

Emerson's comment on the "crushing effect" of the Parrott gun reads: "Much is sacrificed for this, but this is done" (*JMN* 15: 363). Obviously, Emerson's war fervor ran counter to his creative capacity to empathize.

In his lecture "Fortune of the Republic" given in December 1863, Emerson may have had the Parrott gun in mind when he asserted, with notable righteousness: "When the cannon is aimed by ideas, then gods join in the combat, then poets are born. . . . When men die for what they live for, . . . then the cannon articulates its explosions with the voice of a man. Then the rifle seconds the cannon, and the fowling-piece the rifle, and the women make cartridges, and all shoot at one mark, and the better code of laws at last records the victory" (*AW* 142–43). Here Emerson personifies weapons—cannon, rifle, fowling-piece—as if they are eloquent speakers sharing a platform with him, articulating the ideas he has formulated, effecting legislation he desires. The moral absolutism at work in the lecture, rationalizing the terrible carnage of the war, echoes that of his Puritan ancestors. Having abandoned his peace principles, Emerson justified the war with remarkable righteousness: "'Tis vain to say that the war was avoidable by us, or, that both are in the wrong. The difference between the parties is eternal,—it is the difference of moral and immoral motive" (*AW* 148–49). "The war has made the Divine Providence credible to a good many people," Emerson wrote in his journal. "They did not believe that Heaven was quite honest" (*JMN* 15: 65). He incorporated this line into his speech at the dedication for the Concord "Soldiers' Monument" honoring the men who died in the war.

In the last years of the war, he maintained his enthusiasm for it. In a letter of September 26, 1864, to Carlyle, he declared: "I shall always respect War hereafter. The cost of life, the dreary havoc of comfort & time are overpaid by the Vistas it opens of Eternal Life, Eternal Law, . . . reconstructing & uplifting Society."[64] Within a year of the war's end, however, the setback to "reconstructing and uplifting" started to make Emerson reconsider the "Vistas" he saw. The prevalent failure to protect the freedom and safety of blacks foreshadowed even greater hardships for freedmen in the future. While Congress was out of session during 1865, President Johnson pardoned thousands of former Confederates, allowing them to regain power over state governments, which in turn passed the notorious Black Codes that limited the freedom of former slaves, prohibiting them, for example, from owning or renting land, carrying firearms, and attending state-supported schools. In February 1866 Johnson vetoed legislation intended to strengthen the Freedmen's Bureau, and in April he vetoed the Civil Rights Act of 1866, which granted citizenship to all persons born in the United States (except Native Americans). (Congress subsequently passed the act over Johnson's veto, but southern state governments devised various ways of vitiating the act.)

The failure of Reconstruction was foreshadowed early. In a letter to Carlyle at the beginning of 1866, Emerson lamented: "We were proud of the people & believed they would not go down from this height[.] But Peace came, & everyone ran back into his shop again, & can hardly be won to patriotism more, even to the point of chasing away the thieves that are stealing not only the public gold, but the newly won rights of the slave, & the new measures we had contrived to keep the planter from sucking his blood."[65] As Emerson's passions cooled, his sight cleared, and he recognized that the ideals of freedom and justice remained far distant goals. The Civil War, rather than being the capstone of his quest to inculcate transcendental values, became, at last, the event that shattered his peace principles and his transparent vision as well, which he never fully regained.

I love the pure, peaceable, and impartial
Christianity of Christ.

    —DOUGLASS, *Narrative,* 1845

I am a peace man yet would greet with joy
glad news of slave insurrection.

    —DOUGLASS, speech, April 23, 1849

CHAPTER THREE

Douglass, Insurrection, and *The Heroic Slave*

Frederick Douglass and Ralph Waldo Emerson knew and admired each other, yet their perspectives on political violence, while similar, arose from different experiences.[1] Unlike Emerson, Douglass understood slavery as a bloody and bodily reality; he had been whipped, beaten, and terrorized as a slave, and he had witnessed much worse inflicted upon others, as his *Narrative* (1845) reveals. Such experiential knowledge, rather than philosophical adherence to a "higher law," led to Douglass's alliance with John Brown. It also informed his decision not to join the armed insurrection at Harpers Ferry. In 1859 Douglass, age forty-one, despite his anger and courage, was not ready to kill slaveowners or to die; Brown, at fifty-nine, apparently was. As Douglass admitted in his *Life and Times* (1881; rev. 1892), Brown said to him, "'When I strike, the bees will begin to swarm, and I shall want you to help hive them.' But my discretion or my cowardice made me proof against the dear old man's eloquence—perhaps it was something of both which determined my course."[2] Douglass's "discretion" (he was no coward) resulted from his wealth of knowledge and understanding, which few in the antislavery movement, including Brown, could match.

The development of Douglass's complex attitude toward political violence, which this chapter will trace, roughly paralleled Emerson's in a number of ways, because in the 1840s Douglass called himself "a peace man" and advocated the use of moral suasion to address the slavery issue, yet in the 1850s he reluctantly became more committed to the use of violence, in part due to John Brown's influence.[3] During the Civil War, he recruited for the Union Army, as did Emerson, and advocated all-out war against slaveholders. Unlike Emerson, however, Douglass was willing for his sons, Charles (his youngest) and Lewis (his oldest), to join the Massachusetts 54th, even knowing the dangers they faced. Both survived the war.

Although Douglass charged himself with cowardice for not joining Brown at Harpers Ferry, his set of values and beliefs differed markedly from the older man's, having been shaped more by the New Testament than by the Old.[4] He was no would-be Cromwell. Moreover, unlike Brown, he knew a number of white southerners personally, some even as blood relatives and friends.[5] Early in his career as an agent of Garrison's American Anti-Slavery Society, Douglass argued on behalf of Christian pacifism, not merely because Garrison advocated it, but also because he believed in it. As a youth in Baltimore, Douglass had undergone a religious conversion experience under the influence of black lay preacher Charles Johnson and an old free black named Charles Lawson. The result was love for "the pure, peaceable, and impartial Christianity of Christ" (*A* 97). In *My Bondage and My Freedom* (1855), Douglass relates, "I finally found that change of heart which comes by 'casting all one's care' upon God, and by having faith in Jesus Christ, as the Redeemer, Friend, and Savior of those who diligently seek Him" (*A* 231). Despite his Christianity, Douglass, as David Blight has observed, harbored an enduring hatred of slaveholders and a desire for revenge.[6] As a fugitive and later a free man, he found the prospect of slave insurrection appealing, and he employed various rhetorical strategies to make such a desire accord with his pacifism. After Brown's execution, for example, he called southern slaveholders "an armed band of insurgents" and claimed that "John Brown merely stepped in to interrupt and arrest this insurrection against the rights and liberties of mankind; and he did right" (*FDP* 3: 317). By calling slavery an insurrection, Douglass sought to deflect the main charge against Brown, yet it was a questionable rhetorical ploy, unusual for Douglass. More often, he made powerful forthright arguments against slavery and racism (his two major targets), using firsthand experience, humor, sarcasm, mimicry, pathos, and gruesome facts.

As is well known, Douglass gained fame as an abolitionist orator and as author of his first autobiography, *Narrative of the Life of Frederick Douglass, an American Slave, Written by Himself* (1845). Recently, his one work of fiction, *The Heroic Slave* (1853), has gained critical attention, as scholars have examined Douglass's methods of using the American Revolution (and the founding fathers) to defend the idea of slave insurrection.[7] Because of its unusual treatment of insurrection and race relations, the novella is one of the most internally conflicted yet thematically rich antislavery texts written during the antebellum period. One goal of this chapter will be to locate its composition within the trajectory of Douglass's career as an abolitionist and show how it combines his early pacifism with his growing belief in the justice of black slaves killing their white masters.[8] Douglass wrote the novella for the collection *Autographs of Freedom* (1853), a fund-raising project for his *Frederick Douglass' Paper* sponsored by the Rochester Ladies' Anti-Slavery Society and organized by his friend and editorial assistant, Julia Griffiths. Emerson contributed his poem "Freedom" to the collection, which counsels the reader: "Loiter not for cloak or food; Right thou feelest, rush to do,"[9] and Douglass's novella similarly calls for action, not supplication. His "heroic slave" stands as an exemplar for slaves and abolitionists alike.

Douglass's fictional portrayal of the 1841 revolt on the *Creole* obscures its violence by having events related after the fact by a fictional white first mate who was unconscious when the killings onboard occurred. The mate's narrative comprises the last section of the novella; the three sections that precede it focus on Madison Washington's relations with another white man, a traveler from Ohio with the suggestive name Listwell, who becomes a convert to abolitionism after listening to the slave Washington "pouring out his thoughts and feelings, his hopes and resolutions"[10] deep in a Virginia forest. Five years later, Listwell harbors

Washington during his flight to Canada as a fugitive, and one year after that, when Washington is captured in Virginia trying to rescue his wife, Listwell slips him files to help him escape from his shackles on a slave ship bound for New Orleans. The revolt thus emerges literally and literarily from the friendship between a black rebel slave and his white sympathizer. Race and moral conduct do not fall into a predictable binary here, even though melodrama powers Washington's speeches.

William McFeely has called the novella Douglass's "fantasy of his own heroism,"[11] and the protagonist indeed excels as a persuasive orator whose strength lies in his words rather than his deeds: "His voice, that unfailing index of the soul, though full and melodious, had that in it which could terrify as well as charm" (134). In many ways, Listwell, too, occupies a subject position Douglass knew as his own, the abolitionist enthralled by a bold rebel leader more violent than he could ever be. Douglass represents the killings of the two whites (the captain and the slaves' owner) by black rebels on the fictional *Creole* as acts of patriotism (only one white was killed on the actual *Creole*), and Washington is represented as heroic; nevertheless, Douglass's layered narrative technique reveals his reservations about the violence of the revolt itself. As Ronald Takaki indicated many years ago, "Violence against the oppressor was a question Frederick Douglass faced with profound ambivalence."[12] This ambivalence underwent significant change during Douglass's career in response to contemporary events. By the Civil War, it had disappeared altogether, replaced by relentless warmongering. As Carolyn Karcher has pointed out, Douglass interpreted the Civil War "as divine retribution for the sin of slavery," and he "deliberately demonized southern slaveholders," calling for their slaughter.[13] His Christian pacifism disappeared from view.

DOUGLASS'S PACIFISM

Douglass escaped from slavery in 1838 and began his career as an antislavery activist in 1841, working as a general agent for Garrison's struggling Massachusetts Anti-Slavery Society. At the time, he told audiences that a primary benefit of abolitionist activities was the prevention of bloody slave uprisings. He was well aware that Garrison had been blamed for Nat

Turner's 1831 slave revolt and that the abolitionists were being accused of encouraging a race war. During a speech in Lynn, Massachusetts, in October 1841 he declared, "There will be no outbreaks, no insurrections, whilst you continue this excitement [antislavery agitation]: let it cease, and the crimes that follow cannot be told. . . . Emancipation . . . alone will give the south peace and quietness" (*FDP* 1: 4). His rationale was that as long as slaves had hope that abolitionists were working to end slavery peacefully, they would not take the risks that Nat Turner took before the abolitionist movement made itself felt in the nation. It is an argument obviously flattering to the American Anti-Slavery Society that paid his salary and to the current or prospective members of this organization in his audience.

He apparently meant what he said, because he testified several other times to the beneficent effects of abolitionism upon him. In an October 1847 speech in New York City, he declared, "I am not a man of war. The time was when I was. I was then a slave: I had dreams, horrid dreams of freedom through a sea of blood. But when I heard of the Anti-Slavery movement, light broke in upon my dark mind. Bloody visions fled away, and I saw the star of liberty peering above the horizon. Hope then took the place of desperation, and I was led to repose in the arms of Slavery. I said, I would suffer rather than do any act of violence—rather than that the glorious day of liberty might be postponed" (*LW* 1: 277). This speech and many others Douglass made in the 1840s confirmed his loyalty to the nonresistance principles of Garrison and the American Anti-Slavery Society, although his "bloody visions" (surely indebted to Nat Turner) remained active in his subconscious.[14]

During his early years as a fugitive and a Garrisonian, he attended the August 1843 National Convention of Colored Citizens, held in Buffalo, New York, and heard the radical black minister Henry Highland Garnet give his infamous speech, "Call to Rebellion," addressed to slaves. "Brethren, arise, arise!" Garnet declared. "Strike for your lives and liberties. Now is the day and the hour. Let every slave throughout the land do this and the days of slavery are numbered. You cannot be more oppressed than you have been—you cannot suffer greater cruelties than you have already. *Rather die freemen than live to be slaves.* Remember that you are 4 millions!"[15] Garnet also moved that a "motto of resistance" be adopted by the convention, which Douglass opposed. According to the minutes of the meeting (no transcript of Douglass's speech exists), Douglass declared that "there was too much physical force both in the address and remarks of Garnet."[16] Several years later, Douglass in the *North Star* again challenged Garnet by declaring, "We should like to hear a sermon from this Reverend of blood and pretended disciple of the Lord Jesus Christ, of the following passages of scripture: 'Ye have heard that it hath been said, an eye for an eye . . . *but I say unto you, that ye resist not evil; but whosoever shall smite thee on the right cheek, turn to him the other also*' [Matthew 5:38–39]" (*LW* 5: 145–460). By 1857, however, Douglass was calling Garnet "my loved, and honored and much respected friend" (*FDP* 3: 187). Their perspectives on slave rebellion converged as the slavery controversy became more and more violent.

Even during his early years as a Garrisonian nonresistant, Douglass at times felt the need to respond to violence with violence, at least in the heat of the moment. During his 1843 western lecture tour, he was attacked by an anti-abolitionist mob in Pendleton, Indiana, and he fought back, picking up a board to strike out at his attackers, before they pummeled him to the ground. His companion William A. White reported to the *Liberator:*

> Frederick Douglass who, at the time, was safe among the friends, not seeing me, thought I was knocked down, and seizing a club, rushed into the crowd. His weapon was immediately snatched from him, and he, finding he had attracted their anger against himself, fled for his life, and ten or more of the mob followed, crying, "Kill the nigger, kill the damn nigger." I hope never to look upon so fearful a sight, as poor Frederick flying before these hell-hounds, panting for his blood. . . . The leader of the mob soon overtook him, and knocked him down and struck him once with his club, and was raising it the second time to level a blow which must have been fatal had it fallen, but I, by dint of hard running, came up in time to throw myself upon him, and stop him in his murderous purpose.[17]

Douglass's right hand was broken in this assault and never healed properly. Local Quakers, Mr. and Mrs. Neal Hardy, assisted Douglass and White after the attack, bandaging their wounds. According to Philip Foner, Douglass "never forgot the experience. Three years later he wrote to White that it still 'haunted his dreams'" (*LW* 1: 57). It was one of several times in his life when he thought he might be killed.

In the months that followed the mob scene in Pendleton, Douglass's rhetoric understandably became more angry and bellicose. In a letter written late in his life, Douglass recalled, "I was a Non-Resistant til I got to fighting with a mob at Pendleton, Ind: in 1843 . . . fell never to rise again, and yet I cannot feel I did wrong."[18] In February 1844 Nathaniel P. Rogers, editor of *Herald of Freedom*, described one of Douglass's "volcanic" speeches, given in Concord, New Hampshire: "It was the storm of insurrection—and I could not but think, as he stalked to and fro on the platform, roused up like the Numidian Lion—how that terrible voice of his would ring through the pine glades of the South, in the day of her visitation—calling the insurgents to battle and striking terror to the hearts of the dismayed and despairing mastery. He reminded me of Toussaint among the plantations of Haiti. . . . He was not up as a speaker—performing. He was an insurgent slave taking hold on the right of speech, and charging on his tyrants the bondage of his race" (*FDP* 1: 26–27).[19]

Rogers's active imagination conflates Douglass with Toussaint; Douglass in his more ardent moments probably made the same identification. As Robert Levine has pointed out, Douglass "saw in the Haitian Revolution a model for blacks who were fighting a war against slavery in the United States."[20] In the months following the "volcanic" speech that Rogers witnessed, Douglass continued to lecture and wrote his *Narrative of the Life of Frederick Douglass*, published in May 1845. The defiant spirit running through that book, I suspect, gained intensity from the violence he had recently encountered as an antislavery activist. As is well known, in the *Narrative*, he made his fight with Covey the dramatic turning point of his life as a slave, and, as a number of scholars have discussed, violence and manhood became linked as he describes his transformation from slave to man: "This battle with Mr. Covey was the turning-point in my career as a slave. It rekindled the few expiring embers of freedom, and revived within me a sense of my own manhood" (*A* 65).[21] Such an assertion provided a counterpoint to his recent publicized beating in Pendleton. He warned in the *Narrative* that in the future, "the white man who expected to succeed in whipping, must also succeed in killing me" (*A* 65).

During his years in the North in the early 1840s, Douglass became familiar with the charge that slaves were too cowardly and submissive to rebel, a charge he found insulting. Several days before the *Narrative* appeared, he asked a New York audience, "Who are these that are asking for manhood in the slave, and who say that he has it not, because he does not rise?" He then answered his own question, shifting from the third person to the first: they are the "very men who are ready by the Constitution to bring the strength of the nation to put us down. . . . We know that we are unable to cope with you in numbers; you are numerically stronger, politically stronger, than we are." (*FDP* 1: 32–33). (When John Brown proposed the Harpers Ferry raid, the odds had not altered, as Douglass well knew.) Despite conceding the futility of taking on the United States government, Douglass asserted, as he had in his *Narrative:* "You may put the chains upon me and fetter me, but I am not a slave, for my master who puts the chains upon me, shall stand in as much dread of me as I do of him" (*FDP* 1: 33). This is the rhetoric of defiance he encountered in Caleb Bingham's *The Columbian Orator* (1797; Boston 1832), a collection of patriotic speeches for young schoolboys, which Douglass studied and memorized as a slave in Baltimore.

One speech in that collection, "Dialogue Between a Master and Slave," written by the English dissenter John Aikin (1747–1822), shaped his conception of the unspoken relation between master and slave. As Douglass explains in his *Narrative*, it "gave tongue to interesting thoughts of my own soul, which had frequently flashed through my mind, and died away for want of utterance. The moral which I gained from the dialogue was the power of truth over the conscience of even a slaveholder" (*A* 42). In the dialogue, the master claims to be humane and says he did not take away the slave's liberty because it had already been lost when the slave was purchased, to which the slave replies: "I had lost the power, but how the right? I was treacherously kidnapped in my own country, when following an honest occupation. I was put in chains, sold to one of your countrymen, carried by force on board his ship, brought hither, and exposed to sale like a beast in the market, where you bought me.

What step in all this progress of violence and injustice can give a *right?*"
When the master claims that throughout human history, "the order of
Providence" has given one man power over another, the slave responds,
"You cannot but be sensible, that the robber who puts a pistol to your
breast may make just the same pleas," and he then asks, "What should
restrain me from retaliating the wrongs I have suffered, if a favourable
occasion should offer?" Moved by the slave's arguments, the master restores his liberty and, in return, learns the truth of his situation. His
former slave tells him,

> You are surrounded with implacable foes, who long for a safe opportunity
> to revenge upon you and the other planters all the miseries they have
> endured. The more generous their natures, the more indignant they feel
> against that cruel injustice which has dragged them hither, and doomed
> them to perpetual servitude. You can rely on no kindness on your part, to
> soften the obduracy of their resentment. You have reduced them to the
> state of brute beasts; and if they have not the stupidity of beasts of burden,
> they must have the ferocity of beasts of prey. Superior force alone can give
> you security. As soon as that fails, you are at the mercy of the merciless.[22]

The threat of violence captured in this dialogue would become part
of the rhetorical arsenal Douglass would eventually use in his antislavery
addresses. Garrison, despite his pacifism, had indulged in the same kind
of rhetoric, warning of the time when "[b]lood will flow like water—the
blood of guilty men, and of innocent women and children."[23] Obviously,
Douglass did not speak in Garrisonian extremes, which repelled many
in the antislavery movement. As a former slave, he did not need to. His
scarred back, which he occasionally revealed to skeptical audiences, also
spoke loudly, if silently, for his cause. Margaret Fuller, in her 1845 review
of the *Narrative*, calls Douglass's writing "very just and temperate" in
comparison to Garrison, "who has indulged in violent invective and denunciation till he has spoiled the temper of his mind."[24] In the *Narrative*,
Douglass confesses that reading the *Columbian Orator* led him "to abhor
and detest my enslavers" (*A* 42), yet when he expressed these feelings,
he kept his spirit of revenge in check.

When Douglass's *Narrative* appeared in mid-May 1845, citing names
and places on Maryland's Eastern Shore and essentially identifying him-

self as the runaway Frederick Bailey, he risked being hunted down and returned to his enslavers to do with as they would. This danger led to his eighteen-month lecture tour of Ireland, Scotland, and England in 1845–47, where Douglass muted his militancy and emphasized instead his pacifism (he and Garrison remained allied at this time). He expressed strong antiwar sentiments to his British audiences, due in part to his pacifism and in part to the growing prospect of war between the United States and Britain over the Oregon boundary question. When he spoke before the Peace Society in Scotland on March 19, 1846, he observed that "if a foreign enemy were to land in America and plant the standard of freedom the slaves would rise to a man . . . they would not spare the guilty traders in human blood. But you are not to infer from this that I am an advocate for war, no, I hate war. I have no weapon but that which is consistent with morality, I am engaged in a holy war; I ask not the aid of the sword, I appeal to the understanding and the hearts of men — we use these weapons, and hope that God will give us the victory" (*FDP* 1: 187). Similarly, when he spoke before the London Peace Society on May 19, 1846, he titled his lecture "My Opposition to War" and declared, "Were I to be asked the question as to whether I would have my emancipation by the shedding of one single drop of blood, my answer would be in the negative (*Loud cheers*)" (*FDP* 1: 261). To explain his answer, he relates that after his escape he experienced the "first glare of Christian truth . . . a spirit of love," and he may be referring to those people, black and white, who helped him during his journey to the North and freedom.

When Douglass returned as a celebrity to the United States from England in 1847, the famous split between him and Garrison occurred. The main reasons usually cited are Douglass's decision to start his own antislavery newspaper, *North Star*, which would compete directly with the *Liberator*, and his newfound belief that participation in politics was a legitimate means to combat slavery. Under the influence of Gerrit Smith, he began to argue that the Constitution was not, as Garrison claimed, a "Compact with the Devil," but a founding document whose emphasis upon liberty could prove useful in the antislavery cause. A third underlying cause of the widening gulf between the two may have been Douglass's suppressed militancy.[25] Although he and Garrison would both support the war against the South, Garrison clung to his pacifism years longer than did Douglass.

Gerrit Smith, the wealthy upstate New York landowner, abolitionist, and philanthropist, helped Douglass establish his independence from Garrison by providing financial support for the *North Star* and encouraging Douglass's interest in politics. Smith also became Douglass's close friend. The two shared ambivalent feelings toward the idea of slave insurrection, but Smith's ambivalence could more accurately be described as instability. On the one hand, he told an abolitionist convention in New York City in 1856 that he was ready to have slavery "repulsed by violence" and "pursued even unto death by violence."[26] On the other hand, as Rossbach has pointed out, Smith's "fierce denunciation of the Slave Power and emotional outbursts in defense of violence were occasionally contradicted by his actions."[27] Smith became one of John Brown's "Secret Six" and supported Brown's Harpers Ferry raid, yet after Brown's capture, he became distraught about his complicity. He checked himself into the New York State Lunatic Asylum at Utica and later swore he knew nothing about Brown's plans, which the *New-York Tribune* exposed as a lie.

Smith's support of Douglass was generous, consistent, and friendly. He thus may have served as one model for the character Listwell in *The Heroic Slave*. Smith and his wife socialized with Douglass and his wife, Anna, and as John McKivigan has pointed out, "Even in Rochester, close interracial friendships were quite rare, and the emotional bond between the Douglass and Smith families in these years was a remarkable occurrence and goes far to explain the strength of the political alliance between the two men during the rest of the decade."[28] Douglass extended a compliment to Smith by name in *The Heroic Slave*. Listwell tells Washington about "a conversation with Gerrit Smith (a man, by the way, that I wish you could see, for he is a devoted friend of your race . . .)" (142). In 1855 Douglass dedicated *My Bondage and My Freedom* "To Honorable Gerrit Smith, as a slight token of esteem for his character, admiration for his genius and benevolence, affection for his person, and gratitude for his friendship, as a small but most sincere acknowledgement of his pre-eminent services in behalf of the rights and liberties of an afflicted, despised and deeply outraged people, by ranking slavery with piracy and murder, and by denying it either a legal or constitutional existence, this volume is respectfully dedicated, by his faithful and firmly attached friend, Frederick Douglass" (*A* 104).[29] Douglass's and Smith's mutual acquaintance with John Brown strengthened their friendship with each other and took them farther down a more radical path than they wanted to go at the time.

MORAL SUASION VERSUS VIOLENT MEANS

Douglass and Brown first met in 1847, and the older man's outlook seems to have had a profound effect on Douglass's thinking about violence. In his *Life and Times*, he tells of meeting and talking with John Brown in Springfield, Massachusetts, in February 1847 and relates that later, in Salem, Ohio, he spoke, like Brown, of shedding blood. Sojourner Truth, when she heard his speech, asked, "Frederick, is God dead?" and Douglass reportedly replied, "No, . . . and because God is not dead Slavery can only end in blood." He relates, "My quaint old sister was of the Garrison school of non-resistants, and was shocked at my sanguinary doctrine, but she too became an advocate of the sword, when the war of the maintenance of the Union was declared." He admits that after meeting with Brown, "My utterances became more and more tinged by the color of this man's strong impressions" (*A* 719). Ten years after they first met, Brown's influence grew stronger, especially during the several weeks in 1858 that he stayed with Douglass at his home in Rochester.[30] At the time Brown was writing the constitution for the nation he hoped to establish with runaway slaves in the mountains of western Virginia.

The European revolutions of 1848–49 also encouraged a shift in Douglass's attitude toward political violence, as they did for a number of abolitionists. We do not know for sure if Douglass was among those influenced by Fuller's political radicalism in Italy, but we do know he was familiar with and admired her writings.[31] Newspaper coverage of the European revolutions and the response to them in the United States informed his indictment of American hypocrisy about liberty. On May 30, 1848, soon after the uprising of workers in Paris, he gave the lecture "The Slave's Right to Revolt," in which he praises Madison Washington and Nat Turner as noble, brave, generous, patient, disinterested, and fearless (*FDP* 2: 131). A year later, on June 8, 1849, he delivered in Boston's Faneuil Hall a lecture that shocked his audience:

> I should welcome the intelligence to-morrow, should it come, that the slaves had risen in the South, and that the sable arms which had been engaged in beautifying and adorning the South, were engaged in spreading death and devastation there. (*Marked sensation.*) . . . Why, you welcomed the intelligence from France, that Louis Philippe had been barricaded in Paris—you threw up your caps in honor of the victory achieved by Republicanism over Royalty . . . and joined heartily in the watchword of "Liberty, Equality, Fraternity"—and should you not hail, with equal pleasure, the tidings from the South, that the slave had risen, and achieved for himself, against the iron-hearted slave-holder, what the republicans of France achieved against the royalists of France? (*Great applause, and some hissing.*) (*FDP* 2: 216–17)

Throughout the North in the spring of 1848, news of the European revolutions was greeted with excitement and enthusiasm, and abolitionists in particular celebrated France's emancipation of slaves in its colonies. Southerners, of course, were appalled by the news.[32]

Even though his relations with John Brown and the example of European revolutions drew Douglass toward a new appreciation of violence as a means to effect political change, one thing Douglass knew that Brown did not was that moral suasion alone could also be effective, that rhetoric could effect change. His own master, Thomas Auld, had been shamed by Douglass's *Narrative* and had acted upon it. This little-known fact can be found in the public letter to Auld that Douglass published in the *North Star* on September 3, 1849. His 1848 letter to Auld is famous because he included it as an appendix in *My Bondage and My Freedom* (1855). There he warns Auld, "I intend to make use of you as a weapon with which to assail the system of slavery—as a means of concentrating public attention on the system, and deepening the horror of trafficking in the souls and bodies of men" (*A* 418). Douglass's second, 1849, letter to Auld is seldom discussed (it goes unmentioned in McFeely's biography); nevertheless, it was one of the most revelatory communications of his entire life. (Ironically, Auld, no reader of the *North Star*, remained ignorant of its contents until Douglass visited him some twenty-eight years later.) The letter reveals why Douglass was reluctant to argue that slaveholders were impervious to moral suasion. Douglass tells Auld,

> Information concerning you and your household, lately received, makes it unjust and unkind for me to continue the style of remark, in regard to your character, which I primarily adopted. I have been told by a person intimately acquainted with your affairs . . . that you have ceased to be a slaveholder, and have emancipated all your slaves, except my poor old grandmother, who is now too old to sustain herself in freedom; and that you have taken her from the desolate hut in which she formerly lived, into your own kitchen, and are now providing for her in a manner becoming a man and a Christian.[33]

In his earlier letter, Douglass accused Auld of turning his grandmother "out like an old horse to die in the woods" (*A* 417).

Apparently, there existed a residual affection between Douglass and Auld, for Auld had more than once protected Douglass and expressed concern about his future,[34] especially when he sent him back to Sophia and Hugh Auld in Baltimore after the failed escape attempt Douglass planned with others. McFeely has gone so far as to declare that "Frederick loved Thomas, and that love was returned."[35] Yet only in the *Life and Times* does Douglass give any indication of this, as he describes his emotional 1878 visit to the aged "Captain Auld," stricken with palsy. "[A]ll the circumstances of his condition affected me deeply," Douglass writes, "and for a time choked my voice and made me speechless. We both, however, got the better of our feelings, and conversed freely about the past" (*A* 876–77).

In 1849, as radical abolitionists such as Higginson, Parker, Sanborn, and John Brown were becoming convinced that moral suasion was ineffective and that slaveowners would only respond to brute force, Douglass was discovering otherwise. Douglas concludes his 1849 letter to Auld, by telling him, "You . . . have added another striking proof to those already existing, that the heart of the slaveholder is still within the reach of the truth, and that to him the duty of letting 'the oppressed go free,' is not in vain. I shall no longer regard you as an enemy to freedom nor to myself—but shall hail you as a friend to both."[36] Later he would learn

that Auld was not even Douglass's grandmother's master, as he had assumed he was. In *Life and Times*, Douglass quotes "Capt. Auld" saying,
"Ah! that was a mistake, I never owned your grandmother; she in the
division of the slaves was awarded to my brother-in-law, Andrew Anthony;
but, I brought her down here and took care of her as long as she lived"
(*A* 877).

THE HEROIC SLAVE

In 1853, when Douglass wrote about Madison Washington's slave revolt on the *Creole*, he was not certain, as he would later claim to be in
1859, that moral suasion was a futile means of ending slavery. By choos-
ing Washington as his hero, he made certain that a slave insurrection
would form part of his narrative, contributing to the stature of his hero.
Nevertheless, he handled the event gingerly and employed a number of
means to make it seem righteous and restrained.[37] Madison Washington's
name lent itself to Douglass's decision in the novella to compare him to
those Virginians who led the American Revolution. His opening paragraph proclaims that "a man who loved liberty as well as did Patrick
Henry, — who deserved it as much as Thomas Jefferson, — and who
fought for it with a valor as high, an arm as strong, and against odds as
great, as he who led all the armies of the American colonies through the
great war for freedom and independence, lives now only in the chattel
records of his native State" (132). The soliloquy that the Ohio traveler
Listwell overhears in part 1 of the work becomes Washington's liberty-
or-death speech, delivered in high rhetorical style. "*Liberty* I will have,"
he declares at one point, "or die in the attempt to gain it" (133). His
solitary lament in the Virginia forest fascinates and disturbs the listening
traveler.

Douglass's description of Washington resembles others' descriptions
of Douglass himself (see figure 4). His "manly form" is "tall, symmetrical,
round, and strong. In his movements he seemed to combine, with the
strength of a lion, a lion's elasticity. His torn sleeves disclosed arms like
polished iron" (134). Both Listwell and the reader are encouraged to
admire this spectacular lionlike figure viewed unawares, and Douglass
enhances his mystery by writing that "As our traveler gazed upon him,

he almost trembled at the thought of his dangerous intrusion" (134). In this opening scene, Douglass not only introduces Washington as an imposing figure who shares the intelligence, eloquence, and spirit of the leaders of the American Revolution but also emphasizes the two sides of his character, namely, his kindness and his controlled fury: "His eye, lit with emotion, kept guard under a brow as dark and as glossy as the raven's wing. His whole appearance betokened Herculean strength; yet there was nothing savage or forbidding in his aspect. A child might play in his arms, or dance on his shoulders." His voice is said to "terrify as well as charm," and he "was one to be sought as a friend, but to be dreaded as an enemy" (134). His role as the leader of a violent revolt is foreshadowed, but the shadows are lightened by the classical Greek hue Douglass gives him. All in his audience were familiar with representations of Hercules in painting and sculpture.

Obviously, Listwell stands in for those well-meaning whites Douglass wishes to enlist in the antislavery cause, and the traveler models the conversion experience of an uninformed northerner. As Listwell meditates on all the thoughts and feelings he has heard Washington express, "[t]he speech rung through the chambers of his soul, and vibrated through his entire frame," leading to Listwell's declaration: "From this hour I am an abolitionist. I have seen enough and heard enough, and I shall go to my home in Ohio resolved to atone for my past indifference to this ill-starred race, by making such exertions as I shall be able to do, for the speedy emancipation of every slave in the land" (135).

The conversion strains the reader's credulity, but such moments are a distinguishing feature of Douglass's autobiographies, including the change wrought by his fight with Covey, and they emerge from the same evangelical Christian tradition that informed Garrisonian immediatism. As David Brion Davis points out, "There are obvious links between immediate emancipation and a religious sense of immediate justification and presence of the divine spirit that can be traced through the early spiritual religions to the Quakers, Methodists, and evangelical revivals."[38] Listwell's response to Washington's patriotic strains are as religious as they are political. The forest becomes a "temple" for them, and Douglass calls Washington a "sable preacher" who "shuns the church, the altar,

FIGURE 4. Frederick Douglass.
Negative number 35765.
Collection of the New-York
Historical Society.

and the great congregation of christian worshippers" (the lowercase "c"
is Douglass's, who disdained the organized Christian denominations of
North and South alike).

Douglass further polishes Listwell's image in part 2 by having him
extend remarkable respect and kindness to Washington, who arrives by
chance at his cabin at night five years later as a fugitive making his way
north. The Listwells feed Washington, provide him with new clothes and
their best bedroom to sleep in, and help him on his journey to Canada.
Despite Douglass's use of the American Revolution as an analogue to
the revolt Madison Washington leads, he ironically lauds Great Britain in
the novella, primarily for its abolition of slavery throughout the empire,
including Canada (where Washington first travels as a fugitive) and then
Bermuda (where the *Creole* rebels seek and attain their freedom).[39] When
Washington with Listwell's help boards a British steamer in Cleveland,
Ohio, he meets the captain, and "[w]ith his usual generosity this true
subject of the emancipating queen welcomed Madison in and assured
him that he should be safely landed in Canada free of charge" (146).
After his arrival in Windsor, Canada, Washington writes Listwell, "I nestle
in the mane of the British lion, protected by the mighty paw from the

talons and the beak of the American eagle" (147). Douglass's own warm welcome as a fugitive in the British Isles in 1845–47 and his indebtedness to British abolitionist friends for purchasing him from Hugh Auld surely informed this favorable comparison of the two nations, despite his paradoxical use of revolutionary rhetoric once directed at British tyranny.

During his stay at the Listwell's home, the tired and hungry fugitive tells a tale of terror, adventure, and hardship. His accounts of whippings, torture, betrayal, separation from loved ones, living in a cave in the swamp, contending with wild animals, a forest fire, and bloodhounds are standard elements of the antebellum fugitive slave narratives Douglass knew well. These accounts serve to show the horror of slavery and provide a motive for the desperation that attends the fight for liberty on the *Creole* in part 4. Perhaps the most disturbing scene occurs when Washington tells of watching from hiding the whipping of a pious old slave caught buying supplies for him. "They tied him to a tree," Madison relates, "and began to whip him. My own flesh crept at every blow, and I seem to hear the old man's piteous cries even now" (144). Witnessing such wanton violence fuels the feelings of revenge Washington successfully represses when he later gains power on the *Creole*.

In part 3 we learn that Washington has had to deal with an even greater provocation, the killing of his wife. Listwell, traveling in Virginia near Richmond, has a third chance encounter with Washington, whom he comes upon enslaved in a chain gang about to be shipped to the deep South. He learns that Washington had returned to free his wife from slavery, but she was killed and he was captured during the escape. Douglass punctures Virginian pretensions to gentility by having Listwell enter a tavern where local whites reveal their ignorance, stupidity, and vulgarity. A loafer named Wilkes takes the abolitionist Listwell for a slave trader and says, "Well, 'pon my honor, sir, I never made any that way myself; but it stands to reason that it's a money making business; for almost all other business in Virginia is dropped to engage in this. One thing is sartain, I never see'd a nigger-buyer yet that hadn't a plenty of money, and he wasn't as free with it as water. I has known one on 'em to treat as high as twenty times in a night; and, generally speaking, they's men of edication, and knows all about the government" (149). After extricating himself from this lout, Listwell follows the gang of slaves to Richmond and slips Madison three files before he boards the *Creole*.

The setting for the final part of the novella is in the Marine Coffee-house at Richmond, where two white Virginia sailors, Jack Williams and Tom Grant, converse about the revolt with Grant, who was the first mate on the ship, telling what happened. Although the captain of the *Creole* and the owner of the slaves were killed during the revolt, Douglass elides the killing by having it occur while his narrator was unconscious on the deck. Douglass also uses Grant to argue for the bravery of Washington: "I confess, gentlemen, I felt myself in the presence of a superior man; one who, had he been a white man, I would have followed willingly and gladly in any honorable enterprise" (163). When Williams says, "I'll be hanged if you're not as good an abolitionist as Garrison himself," Grant becomes enraged, making Williams take back the insulting charge. Douglass thus frees Grant from the taint of abolitionist bias. He also makes it clear that the revolt succeeded not because of cowardice on the part of the whites but courage and cunning on the part of the blacks.

Douglass takes great pains to distinguish the violence on the *Creole* from murderous revenge. He emphasizes Washington's restraint, by having Grant report that the slave twice saved the mate's life. Washington also argues eloquently on his own behalf, as Grant quotes him saying, "You call me a *black murderer*. I am not a murderer. God is my witness that LIBERTY, not *malice*, is the motive for this night's work. . . . We have struck for freedom, and if a true man's heart be in you, you will honor us for the deed. We have done that which you applaud your fathers for doing, and if we are murderers, *so were they*" (161). Douglass assumes no one would believe the rebel colonists were murderers (although Hawthorne does suggest this interpretation in "Septimius Felton"), and he takes it as a given that national pride has elevated the American revolutionaries to the level of heroes. Richard Yarborough has traced the tensions within the work to Douglass's "sensitivity to and absorption of the values and expectations of his target audience." By trying to satisfy white northern readers, Douglass, according to Yarborough, "strips his fictional slave rebel of much of his radical, subversive force."[40] Yet, clearly, Douglass was trying to steer clear of black violence, which troubled him as well as his readers. He has his character Grant respond to Washington's restraint and declare, "The fellow loomed before me. I forgot his blackness in the dignity of his manner, and the eloquence of his speech. It seemed as if the souls of both the great dead (whose names he bore) had entered him" (161). Thus Douglass transforms, or at least attempts to transform, insurrection into patriotism. He makes sure no anger, no bloodlust, no spirit of revenge animates his protagonist. Love of liberty, not hatred of whites, motivates the killings on the fictional *Creole*. Washington is no Babo.

EBB AND FLOW OF RIGHTEOUS VIOLENCE

The Heroic Slave appeared at the midpoint of Douglass's transformation from a Christian pacifist to an advocate of violence. Within a year of its publication Douglass became an apologist for an apparent murder, the shooting of the Irish volunteer policeman Batchelder during the attempt to free Anthony Burns. The case provoked a strong emotion in Douglass, for unlike Burns's white would-be rescuers (Higginson and Alcott), Douglass, like Martin Stowell and Lewis Hayden, his black rescuers, identified with the fugitive and empathized with the desperation and terror he felt. As a result, Douglass was moved to justify the killing of Batchelder in a speech titled "Is It Right to Kill a Kidnapper?" In the speech, Douglass formulates the question somewhat disingenuously, declaring, "The occurrence naturally brings up the question of the reasonableness, and the rightfulness of killing a man who is in the act of forcibly reducing a brother man who is guilty of no crime, to the horrible condition of a slave" (*FDP* 2: 284).

He argues that to kill such a man "is in accordance with nature" because "society has the right to preserve itself even at the expense of the life of the aggressor." Placing Batchelder in the role of a "kidnapper," and a "bloodhound on the track of his crimeless brother Burns," Douglass asserts that this deputy "labeled himself the common enemy of mankind, and his slaughter was as innocent, in the sight of God, as would be the slaughter of a ravenous wolf in the act of throttling an infant" (*FDP* 2: 286–87). Douglass thus displays an unusual ferocity about the slain Batchelder, whom he dehumanizes as he had Covey in his *Narrative*, and he links his killing to a show of manhood, as he had also done in his *Narrative:* "Every slave-hunter who meets a bloody death in his infernal business, is an argument in favor of the manhood of our race. Resistance is, therefore, wise as well as just" (*FDP* 2: 289).

Douglass could not have been unaware that Batchelder's class and ethnicity made him a lowly and repellent figure, especially to African Americans, who regarded Irish immigrants with deep hostility, which was mutual. "The Irish people," Douglass declared in 1853, "warm-hearted, generous, and sympathizing with the oppressed everywhere when they stand on their own green island, are instantly taught on arriving in this Christian country to hate and despise the colored people. They are taught to believe that we eat the bread which of right belongs to them. The cruel lie is told the Irish that our adversity is essential to their prosperity" (*LW* 2: 249).[41] One wonders if Douglass would have justified the killing of someone other than Batchelder involved in Burns's return, such as Commissioner Edward Loring, who remanded Burns, Benjamin Hallett, the United States district attorney for Massachusetts who charged Burns, or President Franklin Pierce himself, who sent troops to Boston to make sure Burns was shipped back to his southern owner. By Douglass's logic, they, too, deserved to be killed. He does not venture this thought, but he does end by heaping contempt on the dead deputy: "The widow and orphans are far better off with such a wretch in the grave, than on the earth" (*FDP* 2: 288).

In the year following the turmoil caused by the Burns affair and the Kansas-Nebraska Act, Douglass became a founding member of the Radical Abolition Party and attended its inaugural convention in Syracuse, New York. As John Stauffer has pointed out, "The Radical Abolitionists embraced the immediate abolition of slavery; full suffrage for all Americans regardless of sex or skin color; the redistribution of land so that no one would be poor and no one rich; and violent intervention against the growing belligerence of proslavery advocates."[42] In 1856 a series of slave insurrections were discovered and brutally suppressed, and Douglass responded with a bitterly satirical poem, "The Tyrants' Jubilee!," which, as William Gleason has shown, "suggests that in the face of white recalcitrance, violent insurrection remains not only inevitable, but also natural: a volcanic eruption akin to the 'lightning, whirlwind, and earthquake' of God's millennial justice."[43] The last stanza features the metaphor of a slumbering volcano (which Douglass had previously used in his 1849 speech "Slavery, the Slumbering Volcano"):

> The pathway of tyrants lies over volcanoes;
> The very air they breathe is heavy with sorrows;
> Agonizing heart-throbs convulse them while sleeping,
> And the wind whispers Death as over them sweeping.[44]

At the time he wrote this poem, the warfare in "Bleeding Kansas" had raised the level of anger and hatred in the country and had also aroused slaves in the South, as Douglass's poem hauntingly suggests.

Despite the brutal reprisals that followed the slave rebellions of 1856, Douglass, characteristically, viewed them in a positive light. In his August 4, 1857, speech "West India Emancipation," he argued that the "insurrectionary movements of the slaves" could lead to emancipation in the South as they had in the British West Indies in 1834. The address has been called "one of Douglass' most radical orations,"[45] and perhaps its most shocking assertion is that "Virginia was never nearer emancipation that when General Turner kindled the fires of insurrection at Southampton" (*FDP* 2: 439). By redirecting attention from the violence of Turner's slave revolt to the discussions it prompted in the Virginia legislature about emancipation, Douglass makes his case for the effectiveness of violence as a political means.

At the beginning of 1858, when John Brown traveled to New England to raise more funds for his various plans, he found a receptive audience in Douglass, with whom he stayed for a month in Rochester. They apparently discussed Brown's plan to help slaves escape north through the Virginia and Maryland mountains. In *Life and Times*, Douglass says that Brown told him the freed slaves "were to be well armed, but were to avoid battle or violence, unless compelled by pursuit or in self-defense" (*A* 754). The plan was called off for a year, however, because of the betrayal of Hugh Forbes, one of Brown's men, but in the summer of 1859, as Brown was preparing to act, he met Douglass at night in a quarry near Chambersburg, Pennsylvania, and it was there that Douglass learned with dismay details of the Harpers Ferry raid.

Douglass approached the quarry carefully because he knew Brown was armed and dangerous. "He was then under the ban of the government," Douglass explained, "and heavy rewards were offered for his arrest, for offenses said to have been committed in Kansas. He was passing under the name of John Smith. As I came near, he regarded me rather suspiciously, but soon recognized me, and received me cordially. . . . His face wore an anxious expression, and he was much worn by thought and exposure" (*A* 758). During their conversation, Douglass was distressed to learn about Brown's new scheme, in particular his plan to kidnap leading citizens and hold them hostage. According to *Life and Times*, Douglass told Brown "he was going into a perfect steel-trap, and that once in he would never get out alive; that he would be surrounded at once and escape would be impossible." Brown responded by saying he would use the hostages to "dictate terms of egress from the town," which provoked Douglass to reply that "Virginia would blow him and his hostages sky-high, rather than that he should hold Harper's Ferry an hour" (*A* 759). Douglass seems to have known Virginians somewhat better than Brown, but his arguments were to no avail.

Although Douglass at the time was seeking social respectability and political influence, Brown cared nothing about either. He gloried in his outlaw status and had even refused to cooperate with the free-state settlers in Kansas, perceiving them as too passive and weak dealing with the Missourians. Leaders in Lawrence would later charge Brown with doing more harm than good in the region, but in 1856 they appreciated his help. When Douglass learned long after Brown's death about the Pottawatomie massacre, he justified it by saying, "To call out a murderer at midnight, and without note or warning, judge or jury, run him through with a sword, was a terrible remedy for a terrible malady. . . . In dealing with the ferocious enemies of the free-State cause in Kansas, [Brown] not only showed boundless courage but eminent military skill" (*A* 744).

After the Harpers Ferry raid, Douglass had to flee the United States for he became a wanted man. Virginia charged him with conspiring with Brown and "inciting servile insurrection." Although he had not joined Brown on the raid, he knew this would not prove his innocence in the prevailing hostile atmosphere of Richmond. As Foner has pointed out, "No evidence would have been required to sentence a Negro Abolitionist to death in Virginia during the weeks following the attack on Harpers

Ferry." If arrested, Douglass "would have followed Brown to the gallows" (*LW* 2: 92). In his speeches in Britain, Douglass openly praised Brown and linked him with Nat Turner and Madison Washington, calling him "a noble, heroic, and Christian martyr" (*FDP* 3: 315). In Edinburgh on June 30, 1860, Douglass claimed that Brown "emancipated some 300 slaves" (*FDP* 3: 315) (an exaggeration, perhaps provided by Brown) and asserted, "when a man had been reduced to slavery he had a right to get his freedom — (*applause*) — peaceably if he could, forcibly if he must (*prolonged applause*)." As for assisting people to get their freedom, as Brown attempted, which obviously differs from fighting for one's own freedom, Douglass suggests, "'Just make the case your own'" (*FDP* 3: 316). That is, would you want such help? Douglass offers a paragraph on Brown as a "peace man" and says Brown was not for peace to the wicked. "There could be no peace where there was oppression, injustice or outrage upon the right." He finally claims that John Brown did not invade a peaceable community. "Every slaveholder in America was an insurrectionist" (*FDP* 3: 317).

After Douglass returned to the United States in June 1860, he participated in the December 3, 1860, convention in Boston meant to mark the anniversary of the "Martyrdom of John Brown," amid a mob intent on silencing the speakers. As Blight has pointed out, "With the threat of disunion in the air and abolitionists railing against compromise, hostility to antislavery agitation rose to new levels of violence."[46] After struggling with a mob at Tremont Temple and relocating to the Martin's Joy Street Baptist Church, the gathered abolitionists heard one of Douglass's most bloodthirsty speeches. He welcomed the approaching civil war and defiantly asserted, "We must, as John Brown, Jr., has taught us this evening, reach the slaveholder's conscience through his fear of personal danger. We must make him feel that there is death in the air about him, that there is death in the pot before him, that there is death all around him" (*FDP* 3: 416). "The only way to make the Fugitive Slave Law a dead letter, is to make a few dead slave-catchers (*Laughter and applause*)" (*FDP* 3: 419).[47]

When the Civil War broke out four months later, Douglass was elated, and he kept pressure on Lincoln to make emancipation part of the war effort. He recruited more than one hundred men for the Massachusetts

54th, and in his "Men of Color to Arms! A Call by Frederick Douglass," he tells fellow blacks, "Remember Denmark Vesey of Charleston; remember Nathaniel Turner of Southampton; remember Shields Green and Copeland, who followed noble John Brown, and fell as glorious martyrs for the cause of the slave" (*LW* 3: 319). He holds before young blacks, in other words, the example of insurrectionists, whom they can now imitate but with the sanction of the state—in their case, the state of Massachusetts. He merges the causes of both as he tells his auditors to "fly to arms, and smite with death the power that would bury the government and your Liberty in the same hopeless grave" (*LW* 3: 318). As Yarborough has observed, the Civil War provided black men a "socially sanctioned opportunity to bear arms against their white American oppressors."[48]

When Lincoln issued his emancipation proclamation, Douglass, not surprisingly, was ecstatic, but as the war neared its end, he became impatient with Lincoln's gestures of reconciliation toward the southern states. After Lincoln's assassination, President Andrew Johnson further disheartened Douglass by his pardons of former Confederates, his veto of the 1866 Civil Rights Act, and his hostility to black suffrage. Ironically, in the years following the Civil War, Douglass returned to the pacifism that marked his early career. He also became more conservative in his politics, even as the failure of Reconstruction led to massive injustices being inflicted upon former slaves.

Douglass's "Self-Made Man" speech, given countless times, argued that freedmen needed to elevate themselves through their own efforts and to be patient about the federal government, which had been ignoring their oppression and abuse. His emphasis on self-reliance clearly echoed Emerson, who in his 1844 antislavery address, given with Douglass in the audience, declared: "If the black man is feeble, and not important to the existing races not on a parity with the best race, the black man must serve, and be exterminated. But if the black man carries in his bosom an indispensable element of a new and coming civilization, for the sake of that element, no wrong, nor strength, nor circumstance, can hurt him: he will survive and play his part" (*AW* 31). Similarly, Douglass would continually assert that "races, like individuals, must stand or fall by their own merits" (*A* 913).[49] He chose not to challenge the racist policies of his own government. In 1875 he even asserted, "Government is better than anarchy, and patient reform is better than violent revolution."[50]

The Heroic Slave, with its defense of violent revolution, stands as perhaps the best example of how Douglass tried before the Civil War to resolve his chosen role as representative of his fellow blacks suffering at the hands of whites with his comparable identification with white friends in the antislavery movement, and even with some southern whites. As a mulatto, Douglass saw himself as half-white and half-black, even though in the eyes of everyone he was simply a negro. As part of his response to the Dred Scott case, Douglass proudly identified himself as "an American, a citizen, a colored man of both Anglo-Saxon and African descent" (*FDP* 1: 178–79). Peter Walker has claimed that the basic fact of Douglass's life was that "he was half white, not simply a white man's offspring. Two cultures, and the claims of each, as well as two persons lived inside Douglass." More critically, Walker also argues that Douglass sought to escape not only slavery but also the blackness his mother, Harriet Bailey, had bequeathed him.[51] When Douglass took a white wife in 1884, to the dismay of prominent blacks, he joked that his first wife "was the color of my mother, and the second, the color of my father" (*LW* 4: 116). Black leaders, however, charged that he had shown "contempt for the women of his own race" (*LW* 116). More recently, the scholar Wilson J. Moses has argued that "black Americans have always rejected Douglass' vision of America," and that his "ideology was thoroughly inconsistent, usually opportunistic, and always self-serving."[52] Even McFeely, who presents Douglass's racial views in a positive light, has observed that Douglass's "stances between 1877 and 1881 were the least honorable and least helpful to his fellow former slaves of any in his long life" (291). Levine, Douglass's most brilliant interpreter, has called Douglass's attempt to elide issues of race "arguably a misguided strategy. For the elision of race went hand in hand with racism."[53]

Whether Douglass deserves criticism for his postwar politics remains a matter of debate. His admirers have ably defended him;[54] nevertheless, Douglass's perspective (and ambition) allowed the Republicans to exploit him for their own political ends, all the while ignoring the injustices suffered by the blacks he supposedly represented. Douglass's self-image as a man of two cultures goes far to explain his assimilationist thought and his reluctance before and after the Civil War to advocate the killing of white southerners. Some members of the white Auld family, with whom he had lived as a slave—such as his half-sister Lucretia, and his Baltimore mistress Sophia—he even regarded as beloved relatives. The role of holy avenger remained for him purely imaginary, arising out of sanguinary dreams, perhaps, yet more suited to desperate men he admired, such as Toussaint Louverture, Nat Turner, and Madison Washington. What Douglass sought for himself was not the martyrdom of a rebel leader but a place of honor within an integrated nation free of racial categories, where men and women, whatever the color of their skin, would treat one another with respect and civility. Near the end of his life, he declared, "I do now and always have attached more importance to manhood than to mere kinship or identity with one variety of the human family. Race, in the popular sense, is narrow; humanity is broad. The one is special, the other is universal. The one is transient, the other permanent."[55] Whereas Emerson's transcendental idealism grew weaker in the violent world of nineteenth-century America, Douglass's grew stronger. Unfortunately, in the unreconstructed nation, degraded by the lynching of hundreds of black men, this idealism exerted little practical power.

I found in myself, and still find, an instinct toward a higher, or, as it is named, spiritual life, as do most men, and another toward a primitive rank and savage one, and I reverence them both.

— THOREAU, "Higher Laws," *Walden*, 1854

CHAPTER FOUR

Contemplation versus Violence in Thoreau's World

In an essay titled "Emerson's Religion," published in 1885, Cyrus A. Bartol recalled asking Emerson if he approved of war, and the reply he received was, "Yes, in one born to fight."[1] This answer, with its unusual qualification, echoes a key point made in the Bhagavad Gita, a sacred Hindu poem that exerted a powerful influence on Emerson and his fellow transcendentalists. Emerson first learned about the Bhagavad Gita in 1831, when he read Victor Cousin's summary of it in his *Introduction to the History of Philosophy*. In Cousin's account, the god Krishna tells a young warrior, "You are, as a Schatrias, a man of the caste of warriors, doomed to the combat. Therefore, do battle; a fearful carnage will be the result. Be it so; tomorrow the sun will shine upon the world, and will illuminate new scenes, and the eternal principle will continue to subsist. Beyond this principle, every thing is illusion."[2] One sees in Cousin's summary much that anticipates Emerson's transcendentalism, including the notion that each individual, even a warrior, serves the interests of the divine principle impelling all creation. As Robert Richardson has observed, "From Emerson's excited reading of Cousin in 1831 came his first serious interest in and respect for Indic thought and expression."[3] When Emerson acquired Charles Wilkins's 1785 English translation of the Gita in 1845, he became even more engaged by it and excitedly shared it with many of his friends.

Thoreau was the one friend who became most deeply stirred by the Gita, and he regarded it as an incomparable source of inspiration. In *A Week on the Concord and Merrimack Rivers* (1849), he declares, "The reader is nowhere raised into and sustained in a higher, purer, or *rarer* region of thought than in the Bhagvat-Geeta. . . . It is unquestionably one of the noblest and most sacred scriptures that have come down to us."[4] Thoreau first read the Gita in 1846 during his second year at Walden Pond, and he studied it "off and on during the seven revisions of *Walden* that were generated over nine years."[5] The poem dramatizes a problem that Thoreau struggled with throughout his life: how to live in a world on the edge of violence and warfare. In Wilkins's translation, the Gita opens with the warrior hero Arjoon on the battlefield of Kooroo in the open space between two warring armies made up of his kinsmen. As he surveys the scene, he is filled with doubt and despair because he wishes to remain virtuous and nonviolent. He even declares himself more ready to be killed than to kill. Arjoon's charioteer is the supreme Hindu god, Kreeshna, who tells Arjoon to do his duty and fight: "Death is certain to all things which are subject to birth, and regeneration to all things which are mortal."[6] In the climactic eleventh section of the poem, Kreeshna reveals his overwhelming multiform divinity to Arjoon, providing him with even stronger arguments about why he must slay his kinsmen and thus become the agent of divine principle: "I am Time, the destroyer of mankind, matured, come hither to seize at once all these who stand before us. Except thyself not one of all these warriors, destined against us in these numerous ranks, shall live. Wherefore, arise! Seek honor and renown! Defeat the foe, and enjoy the full-grown kingdom! They are already, as it were, destroyed by me. Be thou alone the immediate agent" (93). Obviously, Kreeshna's words relieve Arjoon of responsibility for killing other men.

Much of the Gita's appeal for Thoreau came from its focus on the tension between contemplation and action, a tension that disquieted and inspired him. As he phrased it in a journal entry made while living at the pond, "The struggle in me is between a love of contemplation and a love of action — the life of a philosopher & of a hero."[7] Time and again he chose the former, but he remained sensitive to the call of the latter, which came from the Gita and other martial sites, including ancient Troy and contemporary Concord. In "The Bean-Field" chapter of *Walden*, Thoreau tells of music he hears coming from the village: "Sometimes it was a really noble and inspiring strain that reached these woods, and the trumpet that sings of fame, and I felt as if I could spit a Mexican with a good relish, — for why should we always stand for trifles?"[8] His statement is a satirical joke, of course, directed at supporters of the Mexican War, but the "distant drummer" (*W* 326) he stepped to indeed often played to a martial strain. In a journal entry of May 14, 1840, he declared, "Every man is a warrior when he aspires. He marches on his post. The soldier is the practical idealist — he has no sympathy with matter, he revels in the annihilation of it. So do we all at times."[9]

Despite these militant (and chilling) sentiments, in *A Week on the Concord and Merrimack Rivers*, where Thoreau discusses the Gita at length, he explicitly rejects Kreeshna's arguments on behalf of violent action, declaring that "no sufficient reason is given why Arjoon should fight. Arjoon may be convinced, but the reader is not. . . . The duty of which he speaks is an arbitrary one" (140). Similarly, in "Civil Disobedience" (1849), Thoreau seems to argue for nonviolent resistance as the best means to combat injustice. Wai Chee Dimock has traced the political philosophy of "Civil Disobedience" to the radical pacifism of Garrison and to the Gita as well, not Kreeshna's exhortation to fight, but "Arjuna's protest against it." Dimock explains that Thoreau came "to think of action, not as a feat of the body, proven on the battle field, but as a feat of the soul, proven by the will to disarm and to suffer the bodily consequences of disarming." Dimock acknowledges, however, that pacifism "only had a tenuous and rescindable sway on Thoreau. If anything, militancy was temperamentally more congenial to him."[10] As I will argue in this chapter, Thoreau's militancy accounts in large part for the attraction the Gita exerted on him, and he responded to Kreeshna's arguments just as strongly as he did to Arjoon's. They provided the religious rationale for the deep-seated violent impulses he periodically felt.

THE APPEAL OF VIOLENCE

Throughout his career, Thoreau revealed glimpses of his imaginary participation in warrior culture and his receptivity to the idea that to engage in violent warfare could bring honor to the warrior and justice to the land. In his early *Dial* essay "The Service," which he incorporated into *A Week,* he asserts, "Let not our Peace be proclaimed by the rust on our swords, or our inability to draw them from their scabbards, but let her at least have so much work on her hands, as to keep those swords bright and sharp."[11] In "Slavery in Massachusetts" and "The Last Days of John Brown," he likewise argues for the purifying benefits of righteous violence. "It is not an era of repose," Thoreau declares in "Slavery in Massachusetts." "We have used up all our inherited freedom. If we would save our lives, we must fight for them" (*RP* 108). In "A Plea," he argues on behalf of Brown's raid on the federal arsenal at Harpers Ferry, describing the United States government as a wounded yet dangerous "monster" that deserves to be slain, "a semi-human tiger or ox, stalking over the earth, with its heart taken out and the top of its brain shot away" (*RP* 129). Like all holy warriors, Thoreau felt compelled to dehumanize the enemy before calling for its annihilation.

Did Thoreau condone terrorism? He never committed a violent act, never tried to intimidate a population or government through violent means, yet his rhetorical support of political violence, even in *Walden,* responds positively to the contemporary violence surrounding the slavery issue. In the spring of 1854, Thoreau was preparing the final copy of *Walden* for the printer as President Franklin Pierce ("the Devil," Thoreau called him) sent federal troops to Boston to return Burns to his owner in an attempt, as he saw it, to defend the Constitution of the United States (and appease his southern base). Outraged, Thoreau declared in his journal, "Rather than thus consent to establish Hell upon earth — to be a party to this establishment — I would touch a match to blow up earth & hell together. I will not accept life in America or on this planet on such terms."[12] Thoreau engaged in no suicide bombing, of course, but he heaped contempt on the government and its representatives, especially the marines and militia who carried out orders from above. He heartily agreed with Higginson and Parker and Douglass that Batchelder deserved to be killed. He claimed that the police and marines "were not men of sense nor of principle—in a high moral sense they were not *men* at all."[13] In his most bloodthirsty entry, Thoreau asserts, "I am calculating how many miscreants each honest man can dispose of. I trust that all just men will conspire."[14] Though he did not conspire, his friends Parker, Higginson, and Sanborn did, joining five years later with Samuel Gridley Howe, Gerrit Smith, and George Luther Stearns to form a secret committee that provided John Brown with weapons and money for his activities in "Bleeding Kansas" and his raid on Harpers Ferry.

For Thoreau, Brown's violent behavior in Kansas, and later Virginia, was righteous work, comparable to Christ's driving the money changers from the temple: "The same indignation that is said to have cleared the temple once will clear it again," he asserted in "A Plea for John Brown." "The question is not about the weapon, but the spirit in which you use it" (*RP* 133). Given the Western belief in the reality of the body, one can question Thoreau's logic here and insist on the distinction between a hand and a bullet, yet it is Brown as agent of the divine, as enforcer of a "higher law," that inspires the rhetoric, or "transcendental slang," as Sophia Hawthorne called it.[15] In Thoreau's eyes, Brown was a Puritan warrior, an immortal avatar from the English Civil War, whose weapons and words were in service to his Lord. "It would be in vain to kill him," Thoreau declared. "He died lately in the time of Cromwell, but he reappeared here. Why should he not?" (*RP* 113).[16] Obviously identifying with Brown, Thoreau calls him "a transcendentalist above all, a man of ideas and principles" (*RP* 115), ignoring the bodily pain and death Brown inflicted upon others to achieve his ends, the instantiation of his principles. When speaking to William Dean Howells about his vision of John Brown, Thoreau recalled "a sort of John Brown type, a John Brown ideal, a John Brown principle,"[17] rather than John Brown himself.

Emerson, too, quoted with approval what Brown said to him privately about the Golden Rule and the Declaration of Independence: "Better that a whole generation of men, women and children should pass away by a violent death than that one word of either should be violated in this country" (*AW* 118). In other words, that which is spiritual and ideal renders mortal flesh and blood unimportant. In "The Last Days of John Brown," Thoreau thus asserts that before Brown died, "he had taken up the sword of the spirit—the sword with which he has really won his greatest and most memorable victories. Now he has not laid aside the sword of the spirit, for he is pure spirit himself, and his sword is pure spirit also" (*RP* 152). Brown's family, in gratitude for Thoreau's support, reportedly presented him with "a huge knife that had belonged to Brown,"[18] and one wonders what he felt when he held it in his hand.

For most readers, *Walden* seems unrelated to Thoreau's antislavery activities and violent impulses. After all, in "Economy," Thoreau ridicules reformers, argues for self-reform as opposed to social reform, including abolitionism, and makes only passing reference to the issue of slavery, as, for example, in "Visitors" when he mentions a runaway slave whom he helped "to forward toward the northstar" (152). A celebration of the simple pastoral life seems to be the main emphasis of the book. Yet despite *Walden*'s apparent quietude, beauty, and hopefulness, it reveals glimpses of violent forces at work beneath its calm surface. In his first chapter, he casually relates slaughtering a woodchuck and devouring him, "partly for experiment's sake" (*W* 59), and at the beginning of "Higher Laws," another woodchuck appears, evoking his confession, "I felt a strange thrill of savage delight, and was strongly tempted to seize and devour him raw; not that I was hungry then, except for that wildness which he represented" (*W* 210). In "Spring," Thoreau recalls the smell of a dead horse in the night air and asserts, "I love to see that Nature is so rife with life that myriads can be afforded to be sacrificed and suffered to prey on one another; that tender organizations can be so serenely squashed out of existence like pulp,—tadpoles which herons gobble up, and tortoises and toads run over in the road; and that sometimes it has rained flesh and blood!" (*W* 318). The expressed "love" of such violence, though jarring, suggests that while the explicit theme of *Walden* is the promise of rebirth and immortality, an additional undertone, implicit in the cycle of rebirth, is the appeal of death and destruction.

From the Gita, Thoreau acquired an understanding that the forces of destruction are inseparable from the forces of creation and that the divine encompasses them both. The supreme Hindu being, a form of elemental energy, is creator, preserver, and destroyer. In the introduction to his recent translation of the Gita, Stephen Mitchell explains why this concept is difficult for most westerners to grasp or accept: "There is little precedent for it in our own scriptures, which split the universe into good and evil and place God solely on the side of the good. The only exceptions are the Voice from the Whirlwind at the end of the Book of Job and a single, hair-raising verse from Second Isaiah: 'I form the light, and create darkness; I make peace, and create evil: I the Lord do all these things.'"[19] From the Gita and other Eastern texts such as the Laws of Menu, the Harivansa, the Vishnu Purana, the Sankhya Karika, the Vedanta, and the Upanishads,[20] Thoreau came to regard even the warfare within nations and between nations not as a matter of good or evil but rather a spectacle to rise above and regard with detachment. His poem "The Spirit of Lodin," which he entered in his journal on May 1, 1851, achieves this perspective:

> I look down from my height on nations,
> And they become ashes before me;
> Calm is my dwelling in the clouds;
> Pleasant are the great fields of my rest.[21]

Thoreau's apparent aloofness here (or Lodin's), like that displayed toward the Boston courthouse guard and John Brown's victims, is part of an Eastern spiritual process that transforms bloody actuality into heroic spiritual joy. Just as the intricate patterns of the flowing sand at the deep cut result from Nature "in full blast" within (*W* 308), so, too, *Walden* as a whole owes much to Thoreau's subtle and brilliant control of his inner fire, the violent aggression he attributes to some savage instinct within himself, like that of a "half-starved hound" (*W* 210), as he puts it, ranging the woods seeking prey to devour. At the beginning of "Higher Laws," he generalizes, "I found in myself, and still find, an instinct toward a higher, or, as it is named, spiritual life, as do most men, and another toward a primitive rank and savage one, and I reverence them both" (*W* 210). Thoreau's reverence for the savage grew out of his belief that violence can be a means of purification and enlightenment, contributing to an ongoing beneficent and deathless process. This process is addressed in the Gita, as Kreeshna explains, "These bodies, which envelope the souls which inhabit them, which are eternal, incorruptible, and surpassing all conception, are declared to be finite beings; wherefore, O Arjoon, resolve to fight. The man who believeth that it is the soul which killeth, and he who thinketh that the soul may be destroyed, are both alike deceived; for it neither killeth, nor is it killed" (36).

Emerson, who admired the Gita almost as much as Thoreau, expressed this idea in his poem "Brahma":

> If the red slayer think he slays,
> Or if the slain think he is slain,
> They know not well the subtle ways
> I keep, and pass, and turn again.[22]

Thoreau, likewise, responded to the idea that unity of the soul with the Supreme Being eliminated the fear of death, by revealing it as a temporal and temporary phenomenon.

THE APPEAL OF CONTEMPLATION

In *Walden*, the invisible counterpoints to the motifs of morning and rebirth are the darkness and death that necessarily precede them, and although John Thoreau's shocking 1842 death by lockjaw never rises to the book's surface, its absence looms as a powerful background to the book's hopefulness. Henry's sublimated reaction to the loss of his brother, I believe, informs not only his Eastern detachment but also his extravagance — "I do not propose to write an ode to dejection, but to brag as lustily as chanticleer in the morning" (84) — and his mocking treatment of violence and death. The personal and political merge in *Walden*, and its final drafts from the early 1850s were written as the country was experiencing growing violence over the slavery issue and as Thoreau was studying Eastern texts once more. (He had read the Gita in 1846 and returned to it in 1854.)[23] In *Walden*, one sees a split consciousness resulting from the contradictory demands of contemplation and action, of monk and warrior that grew in intensity within Thoreau as the slavery controversy struck home.

On the one hand, much of *Walden's* appeal flows from the Eastern contemplative life it celebrates, those moments when time stands still and the narrator grows "like corn in the night" (*W* 111). In "Sounds," "Spring," and "Conclusion," especially, spiritual enlightenment and rebirth seem the result of the narrator's ability to detach himself from the illusory world of getting and spending, drench himself in the reality of the natural world, and thereby achieve self-realization. On the other hand, for Thoreau, the peace, serenity, and emancipation one sought by contemplating nature involved a struggle, often one as ferocious as war; and in one of the most imaginative and striking passages of *Walden*, he uses a particular kind of weapon, the scimitar, a crescent-shaped Oriental saber, to suggest the overpowering effect of encountering ultimate Reality. "If you stand right fronting and face to face to a fact," he writes, "you will see the sun glimmer on both its surfaces, as if it were a cimeter, and feel its sweet edge dividing you through the heart and marrow, and so you will happily conclude your mortal career. Be it life or death, we crave only reality" (*W* 98). To a yogi, this would be the process by which the conscious self is annihilated and the essential self emerges. Thoreau's readings in the Gita may have inspired this vision, for it resembles the moment when Kreeshna reveals his true nature and becomes a "supreme and heavenly form; of many a mouth and eye; many a wondrous sight; many a heavenly ornament; many an up-raised weapon" (90), and the effect is that of the sun rising into the heavens with a thousand times more than usual brightness. The vision stuns and frightens Arjoon, but it represents, as does Thoreau's scimitar metaphor, the experience of enlightenment, which is the goal of the yogi.

As Arthur Christy long ago pointed out, Thoreau's life at Walden Pond, though in some sense a writer's retreat during which he finished *A Week* and wrote the first draft of *Walden*, can also be viewed as a yogi's search for self-realization through renunciation of desires and union with ultimate Reality.[24] In a letter to his admirer H. G. O. Blake on November 20, 1849, Thoreau declared, "Depend upon it that rude and careless as I am, I would fain practice the *yoga* faithfully. 'The yogin, absorbed in contemplation, contributes in his degree to creation: he breathes a divine perfume, he hears wonderful things.'"[25] Similarly, in one of the most serene and affecting passages in *Walden*, Thoreau shows his indebtedness to the yoga of meditation in "Sounds":

Sometimes, in a summer morning, having taken my accustomed bath, I sat in my sunny doorway from sunrise till noon, rapt in revery, amidst the pines and hickories and sumachs, in undisturbed solitude and stillness, while the birds sang around or flitted noiseless through the house, until by the sun falling in at my west window, or the noise of some traveller's wagon on the distant highway, I was reminded of the lapse of time. I grew in those seasons like corn in the night, and they were far better than any work of the hands would have been. They were not time subtracted from my life, but so much over and above my usual allowance. I realized what the Orientals mean by contemplation and the forsaking of works. (*W* 111–12)

Those who visited Thoreau at the pond sensed the success of his contemplative habits. In February 1847 Alcott recorded in his journal: "So vivid was my sense of escape from the senses while conversing with Henry today that the men, times, and occupations of coming years gave me a weary wish to be released from this scene and to pass into a state of noble companions and immortal labours."[26] A month later, Alcott reported: "His genius insinuates itself at every pore of us, and eliminates us into the old elements again. A wood-nymph, he abides on the earth and is a sylvan soul."[27] Hawthorne, when he visited, was also impressed, especially by the way Thoreau had tamed the wild birds who "ceased to be afraid of him, and would come and perch upon his shoulder, and sometimes upon his spade, when he was digging in the little croft that supplied him with potatoes and pumpkins."[28] In his prefaces to *Mosses from an Old Manse* and *The Scarlet Letter*, Hawthorne fondly recalls learning from Thoreau about pond lilies and Indian culture and of talking with him "about pine-trees and Indian relics, in his hermitage at Walden."[29]

In *Walden* itself, completed in the eventful spring of 1854, the undercurrent of violence is controlled by the recurrent argument that the contemplative life not only can alter one's consciousness but can indeed change the world. From a Western perspective, of course, the self resides within a Cartesian system of time and space, interacting within a world of objects, including other human beings. A yogic approach to life, however, seeks to dissolve this false conception as well as the false ego-self associated with it. Through silence, meditation, and detachment from desire, the true Self emerges and becomes one with Reality. At this moment, fact is penetrated by a new consciousness, and the world ceases to have an independent existence, becoming instead a fluid and receptive creation of the divine acting through the Self. In "The Pond in Winter," Thoreau dramatizes the dissolution of time and space such a moment involves:

> In the morning I bathe my intellect in the stupendous and cosmogonal philosophy of the Bhagvat Gita, since whose composition years of the gods have elapsed, and in comparison with which our modern world and its literature seem puny and trivial; and I doubt if that philosophy is not to be referred to a previous state of existence, so remote is its sublimity from our conceptions. I lay down the book and go to my well for water, and lo! There I meet the servant of the Brahmin, priest of Brahma and Vishnu and Indra, who still sits in his temple on the Ganges reading the Vedas, or dwells at the root of a tree with his crust and water jug. I meet his servant come to draw water for his master, and our buckets as it were grate together in the same well. The pure Walden water is mingled with the sacred of the "Ganges." (*W* 298)

The passage brilliantly captures the dissolution occasioned by the "cosmogonal philosophy" of the Gita. Thoreau's poem in the central "Ponds" chapter of *Walden* similarly puts into words the moment of spiritual enlightenment, when he and Walden Pond become one:

> I am its stony shore,
> And the breeze that passes o'er;
> In the hollow of my hand
> Are its water and its sand,
> And its deepest resort
> Lies high in my thought. (193)

As for the pain and suffering within nature and human society, viewed from an Eastern religious perspective, they become illusions best removed through self-realization, not by outward action. Because they derive from the false conception that the body and the senses are the basis of true identity, their elimination depends upon the liberation of the self from this misconception. In "Economy," Thoreau makes this point when he asserts, "I sometimes wonder that we can be so frivolous, I may almost say, as to attend to the gross but somewhat foreign form of servitude called Negro Slavery, there are so many keen and subtle masters that enslave both north and south. . . . What a man thinks of himself, that it is which determines, or rather indicates, his fate. Self-emancipation even in the West Indian provinces of the fancy and imagination,—what Wilberforce is there to bring that about?" (*W* 7–8). His idea here corresponds to one often ridiculed as Emerson expresses it in *Nature:* "As fast as you conform your life to the pure idea in your mind, . . . [s]o fast will disagreeable appearances, swine, spiders, snakes, pests, mad-houses, prisons, enemies, vanish."[30] Only when Thoreau's anger was aroused by injustice did his belief in the power of the awakened mind waver, to his regret. His antislavery activities, like Emerson's, were concessions to a materialist conception of reality.

In the conclusion to *Walden*, Thoreau uses the conceptual link between self-reform and social reform to argue disingenuously that the individual should not willfully oppose the laws of society: "It is not for a man to put himself in such an attitude to society, but to maintain himself in whatever attitude he find himself through obedience to the laws of his being, which will never be one of opposition to a just government, if he should chance to meet with such" (*W* 323). This "just" government emerges from the elevated thought of the individual, for "if one advances confidently in the direction of his dreams, and endeavors to live the life which he has imagined, he will meet with a success unexpected in common hours. He will put some things behind, will pass an invisible boundary; new, universal, and more liberal laws will begin to establish themselves around and within him; or the old laws be expanded, and interpreted in his favor in a more liberal sense, and he will live with the license of a higher order of beings" (*W* 323–24). Thoreau's well-known parable of the artist of Kouroo seems intended to illustrate the power of the liberated consciousness, as the artist, striving to create the perfect staff, arrests time and becomes endowed "with perennial youth." Centuries come and go and when he finishes his work, "it suddenly expanded before the eyes of the astonished artist into the fairest of all the creations of Brahma. He had made a new system in making a staff, a world with full and fair proportions" (*W* 327). This parable of Thoreau's own creation was likely inspired by the Gita. As Sherman Paul has pointed out, "Kouroo was clearly Kuru, Kooroo, or Curu, the nation that fought the Pandoos in the *Mahabharata*, the sacred land that

Arjuna was assigned to protect in the *Bhagavad-Gita.* . . . The lesson of the *Bhagavad-Gita*—not the lesson of passivity, but of disinterested work and contemplation—was already a part of his thought."[31]

THOREAU'S RECURRING CHALLENGE

Despite the power Thoreau attributes to the liberated mind, the repressed actual world periodically returns to haunt his thought and writings, evoking his hostility in the process. In *A Week*, one sees little evidence of Thoreau's combative instincts partly because, as Linck Johnson has argued, his main goal was "to depict the brothers' ideal society within a timeless pastoral world."[32] Despite this goal, there are nevertheless moments when an alternative world intrudes. In the "Monday" chapter, for example, after Thoreau's long paean to meditation, to the beauty and serenity of nature, he recalls that into the scene came a canal boat, "like some huge river beast, and changed the scene in an instant; and then another and another glided into sight, and we found ourselves in the current of commerce once more" (*WK* 144). Such moments are the recurring problem in Thoreau's life, the intrusion of the beastly and brutal into his serene consciousness, which challenges his sense of control. The slavery issue, more than any other circumstance in Thoreau's life, fell into this category. Yet it was not so much the suffering or oppression of the slaves themselves in the South that seemed to disturb him, though he certainly went out of his way to care for and assist runaway slaves; rather, it was what he perceived as *his* enslavement in Massachusetts caused by the state's compliance with "Webster's Fugitive-Slave Law" (*W* 232).[33]

In 1851 with the arrest of Thomas Sims, and again in 1854 with the arrest, trial, and remission of Anthony Burns, Thoreau's savage impulses overpowered his serenity, at least momentarily. Near the end of "Slavery in Massachusetts," he asks, "I walk toward one of our ponds, but what signifies the beauty of nature when men are base? . . . Who can be serene in a country where both the rulers and the ruled are without principle? The remembrance of my country spoils my walk. My thoughts are murder to the State, and involuntarily go plotting against her" (*RP* 108).[34] The anger Thoreau felt at injustice led him both to express it, in his journal and reform papers, and to subdue it, which was his preferred method. The latter represented voluntary, rather than involuntary, action.

In *Walden*, Thoreau for the most part represses his grievances against his government as well as his violent impulses. All but the beginning of "Higher Laws," in fact, argues on behalf of such repression and sublimation: "He is blessed who is assured that the animal is dying out in him day by day, and the divine being established" (*W* 219). Elsewhere he uses humor, the mock heroic, to mask his attraction to the values of warrior culture, so evident in the Gita and his other favorite books, Homer's *Iliad* and Carlyle's *Heroes and Hero-Worship*. In "The Bean-Field," the narrator becomes Achilles, the greatest of the Greek warriors and the slayer of Hector, while the Trojan enemy becomes the weeds he battles: "Daily the beans saw me come to their rescue armed with a hoe, and thin the ranks of their enemies, filling up the trenches with weedy dead. Many a lusty crest-waving Hector, that towered a whole foot above his crowding comrades, fell before my weapon and rolled in the dust" (*W* 161–62).

In similar humorous fashion, he describes in "Brute Neighbors" one of the ants "whose mother had charged him to return with his shield or upon it" (*W* 229). As he watches the ant battle, he assumes a detached Olympian perspective on the "red republicans" and "black imperialists," mocking their war and its human analogues: "For numbers and for carnage it was an Austerlitz or Dresden. Concord Fight! . . . I have no doubt that it was a principle they fought for, as much as our ancestors, and not to avoid a three-penny tax on their tea" (*W* 230). Yet after this mockery, he describes the fierce combat, as the ants gnaw off each other's legs and feelers, tear open chests, and sever heads from bodies. While Thoreau makes light of this violence, its connection to that which he and a growing number of abolitionists would later applaud gives it a grim resonance. He admits that "I felt for the rest of that day as if I had had my feelings excited and harrowed by witnessing the struggle, the ferocity and carnage, of a human battle before my door" (*W* 231), and he tells the reader the battle was fought "five years before the passage of Webster's Fugitive-Slave Bill," thus politicizing the event and allowing a glimpse of his own fierce political sentiments.

It was while living at Walden Pond during 1845–47 that the issue of slavery intruded upon his life in unavoidable ways. As Elise Lemire has shown, Walden Woods had long been the home of a community of former Concord slaves, and their experiences as outcasts "were one reason Thoreau was drawn to live in Walden Woods himself."[35] His mother and sisters had long been active members of the Concord Female Anti-Slavery Society, which successfully persuaded Emerson to deliver his famous August 1, 1844, "Address on the Emancipation of the Negroes in the British West Indies," and in September 1845 Thoreau helped the society get the address published as a pamphlet. A year later, on August 1, 1846, he co-hosted at his cabin the society's annual meeting to commemorate the freeing of the West Indian slaves, and the event marked the overt intersection of the political and the contemplative in his life. His own arrest by Sam Staples, in late July 1846, led to Thoreau's famous "Civil Disobedience" lecture and essay, published in Elizabeth Peabody's *Aesthetic Papers* (1849). Although "Civil Disobedience" argues for the active power of inaction (the refusal to pay one's poll tax to avoid contributing to the harm of others), the potential for more fierce action, for violence against the state, emerges at least once when he responds to the fear of bloodshed by declaring that "even suppose blood should flow. Is there not a sort of blood shed when the conscience is wounded? Through this wound a man's real manhood and immortality flow out, and he bleeds to an everlasting death" (*RP* 77). By accepting, while disregarding, literal bloodshed, Thoreau differentiates his antislavery ethic from those of William Lloyd Garrison and his followers, who religiously insisted on nonviolent resistance.

During the late 1840s and early 1850s, the antislavery movement turned sharply toward violence (as I pointed out in my introduction). The annexation of Texas, the war with Mexico, the European revolutions of 1848–49, and especially the hated Fugitive Slave Act spurred more and more New England abolitionists to accept the belief that the killing of oppressors was justified. Yet Thoreau tried his best to remain detached from the political scene. In *A Week*, he asserted that "to one who habitually endeavors to contemplate the true state of things, the political state can hardly be said to have any existence whatever. . . . It is unreal, incredible, and insignificant to him" (*WK* 129). He returned to this position in his journals, especially after becoming politically engaged, and in *Walden* he dismisses current events as "shams and delusions"

(*W*65), adding, "We inhabitants of New England live this mean life that we do because our vision does not penetrate the surface of things. We think that that *is* which *appears* to be" (*W* 65). In Hindu thought such illusion is *maya*, the mistaking of matter for reality, and it is through the practice of virtue—that is, knowing right as opposed to doing right—that the self achieves the understanding that spirit is the essential reality of the universe.[36]

When his friend Margaret Fuller died in a shipwreck off the coast of Fire Island on July 19, 1850, Thoreau tried to rise above the feelings evoked by the tragedy, which shocked all of New England. Emerson, deeply distressed, sent Thoreau to gather what remains he could from the wreck, especially the manuscript of Fuller's "History of the Italian Revolutions." On July 25 Thoreau, who had found little, reported to Emerson from Fire Island Beach, "At floodtide, about 3½ o'clock when the ship broke up entirely—they came out of the forecastle & Margaret sat with her back to the foremast with her hands over her knees—her husband & child already drowned—a great wave came & washed her off . . . Four bodies remain to be found—the two Ossoli's [Fuller and her husband]—Horace Sumner—& a sailor. I have visited the child's grave [Angelo's]. . . . I expect to go to Patchogue whence the pilferers much have chiefly come."[37] In a letter to his admirer H. G. O. Blake, he reported that he found a button torn from the coat of Ossoli: "Held up, it intercepts the light,—an actual button,—and yet all the life it is connected with is less substantial to me, and interests me less, than my faintest dream. Our thoughts are the epochs in our lives: all else is but as a journal of the winds that blew while we were here."[38] When he found bones that might have been Fuller's, he again asserted his detachment, though his repeated references to them in his journal make one question his assertion: he wrote Blake, "There was nothing at all remarkable about them they were simply some bones lying on the beach. They would not detain a walker there more than so much sea weed. I should think that the fates would not take the trouble to show me any bones again. I so slightly appreciate the favor."[39]

In his response to slavery, Thoreau evinced the same forced detachment. After joining the abolitionists at their famous July 4, 1854, meeting in Framingham Grove and publishing his "Slavery in Massachusetts"

speech, he wrote in a journal entry of August 1, 1854: "I feel the necessity of deepening the stream of my life—I must cultivate privacy. It is
dissipating to be with people too much."[40] A week later he wrote Blake,
"Methinks I have spent a rather unprofitable summer thus far. I have
been too much with the world, as the poet might say. . . . I find it, as ever,
very unprofitable to have much to do with men."[41] Thoreau's turn to the
white water lily at the end of "Slavery in Massachusetts" can be viewed as
escapist in Western terms. He calls the water lily "the emblem of purity
. . . extracted from the slime and muck of earth," and asserts, "What
a confirmation of our hopes is in the fragrance of this flower! I shall
not so soon despair of the world for it, notwithstanding slavery, and the
cowardice and want of principle of Northern men" (*RP* 109). Lawrence
Buell has called the image of the lily "disturbing" in "the insouciance
with which the persona turns away from social confrontation for the sake
of immersion in a simplified green world."[42] In Eastern terms, however,
the move is Thoreau's turn toward Reality. His persona has risen above
the illusory slime of the world.

Thoreau made a comparable move three years later, when, as Robert
Richardson has observed, "Thoreau's absorption in John Brown ceased almost as suddenly as it began."[43] Brown's hanging occurred on December 2,
1859, and by the summer of 1860, when Thoreau was asked about giving
a lecture, he declared that his subjects were "Transcendentalist & aesthetic. I devote myself to the absorption of nature generally,"[44] In April
1861, as the Civil War broke out, Thoreau wrote Parker Pillsbury, "As
for my prospective reader, I hope that he *ignores* Fort Sumpter, & Old
Abe, & all that, for that is just the most fatal and indeed the only fatal,
weapon you can direct against evil ever; for as long as you *know of* it, you
are *particeps criminis*. . . . I do not so much regret the present condition
of things in this country (provided I regret it at all) as I do that I ever
heard of it. . . . Blessed are they who never read a newspaper, for they
shall see Nature, and through her, God."[45] Whereas Fuller, Emerson, and
Douglass all became progressively more committed to political violence
as their careers developed, Thoreau's attention shifted like the tides between fierce engagement and serene detachment, with the latter holding
sway as his life and his nation approached dissolution. Thoreau died, at
peace by all accounts, on May 6, 1862.

HAWTHORNE ON THOREAU AND VIOLENCE

Perhaps the one contemporary of Thoreau's who best understood the struggle he waged within himself and the toll it took upon him was Hawthorne, who returned to Concord from abroad in 1860 and found himself marginalized due to his unwillingness to align himself with northern abolitionists. As Moncure Conway observed, "He had not the flexibility of principle displayed by so many in those days. He thus had no party,—then nearly equivalent to having no country."[46] Hawthorne and Thoreau had known each other for some twenty years when Thoreau died. During this period, Hawthorne had studied his friend closely, visiting him at Walden, reading his works, promoting his career, and using him as a model for a number of his characters, including the guide in "The Hall of Fantasy," Owen Warland in "The Artist of the Beautiful," Donatello in *The Marble Faun*, and finally, I believe, the title character of his unfinished romance, "Septimius Felton."[47] In fashioning these characters, Hawthorne captured the ambivalence of Thoreau's personality, the contradictory attractions of the wild and savage on the one hand and the detached and contemplative on the other.

In his notebooks and letters, Hawthorne invariably uses the term "Indian-like" to describe Thoreau, yet he also associates him with the classical world of Greece and Rome. In April 1843 Hawthorne identified Thoreau as "being one of the few persons, I think, with whom to hold intercourse is like hearing the wind among the boughs of a forest-tree; and with all this wild freedom, there is high and classic cultivation in him too."[48] Hawthorne was fascinated, if not obsessed, by the ways in which apparently noble individuals could fall under the sway of their passions and become burdened with sin, and he apparently saw Thoreau as capable of such a transformation. It is quite likely he read Thoreau's "Slavery in Massachusetts" while living in England and thus encountered clear evidence of Thoreau's violent impulses,[49] but even as early as "The Artist of the Beautiful" (1844), the protagonist Owen Warland, creator of ideal beauty, experiences a metaphorical war-land within himself when he lashes out at Annie, who represents the threat of the worldly to the spiritual.

In *The Marble Faun* (1860), published in England under the title

Transformation, the title character, Donatello, also shares traits Hawthorne attributed to Thoreau, and he is transformed from a simple, sylvan innocent, resembling the Faun of Praxiteles, into a guilt-ridden murderer. In a moment of rage he throws Miriam's persecutor, the model, over a cliff, and thus loses his innocence and his connection to the natural world.[50] Perhaps even closer to home — Concord, that is — Hawthorne creates in "Septimius Felton," one of the manuscripts he left unfinished at his death in 1864, a protagonist even more closely linked to Thoreau. Septimius is a hermitlike scholar, with Indian blood in his veins, who kills a foe during the war fever developing in Concord at the beginning of the American Revolution. Begun in 1862, the romance grew out of a story Thoreau told Hawthorne about a former inhabitant of the Wayside who resolved never to die.[51] As Hawthorne put it in his first memorandum to himself, this inhabitant "would sit there while oaks grew up and decayed; he would be always here. This was all that Thoreau communicated; and that was many years ago, when I first came to live at the old cottage. . . . I staid here but a little while; but often times, afar off, this singular idea occurred to me, in foreign lands, when my thoughts returned to this place which seemed to be the point by which I was attached to my native land."[52]

Like Thoreau, Septimius is a native of Concord who has studied at Harvard and returned home, there becoming "possibly a student of theology with the clergyman." His habits are meditative, and he studies nature closely: "Let him alone a moment or two, and then you would see him, with his head bent down, brooding, brooding, with his eyes fixed on some chip, some stone, some common plant, and commonest thing, as if it were the clue and index to some mystery; and when, by chance startled out of these meditations, he lifted his eyes, there would be a kind of perplexity, a dissatisfied, wild look in them, as if, of his speculations, he found no end" (6). Septimius, like Thoreau, prefers to remain detached from political events, yet finds himself drawn to them. Despite his isolation, Septimius ends up shooting and killing a British soldier in a face-to-face confrontation on the hillside behind his house, and Hawthorne attributes this act to Septimius's Indian blood, which represents a repressed savagery in his behavior. The sense of guilt Hawthorne projects upon Septimius, Thoreau himself never felt, of course, especially with regard to the "primitive rank and savage" instinct he confesses to in *Walden* and claims to reverence. To fight, and even to kill, the Gita had taught him, was not sinful during wartime, but rather one's duty to perform.

In gratitude to Thoreau for giving him the idea of "Septimius Felton," Hawthorne planned to include as his preface a short biography of Thoreau, "a little sketch," as he put it, because "it seems the duty of a live literary man to perpetuate the memory of a dead one, where there is such fair opportunity as in this case;—but how Thoreau would scorn me for thinking that *I* could perpetuate *him!*"[53] Hawthorne displays his habitual modesty here, of course, but indeed Thoreau's wild, contradictory, paradoxical personality is almost beyond capture. His combativeness, unlike that of Emerson and Fuller, was rooted in his character rather than his times, making his defense of violent action more difficult to track and grasp. For those who do not think that destruction is creation, death is life, inaction action, and detachment compassion, they cannot know well the subtle ways that Thoreau kept.

Great State Encampment here. Town full of
soldiers, with military fuss and feathers. I like a
camp, and long for a war, to see how it all seems.

— ALCOTT, *Journal*, September 1859

Sometimes I stopped to watch the passers in
the street, the moonlight shining on the spire
opposite, or the gleam of some vessel floating,
like a white-winged sea-gull, down the broad
Potomac, whose fullest flow can never wash
away the red stain of the land.

— ALCOTT, *Hospital Sketches*, 1863

CHAPTER FIVE

Violent Virtue and Alcott's *Moods*

Both Emerson and Thoreau were Louisa May Alcott's neighbors and
friends when she lived in Concord, and, as is well known, she came to
idolize them both. She paid visits to Emerson's study when she was a girl
and imagined the two of them replicating the relation between Goethe
and his young admirer Bettina von Arnim. She recalled Emerson as "my
beloved 'Master'" and counted it "the greatest honor and happiness of
my life to have known [him]."[1] Her feelings for Thoreau seem to have
been more romantic. As a child, she briefly attended the school he and
his brother John established in Concord, and his love of nature and
spirit of independence inspired her.[2] As Martha Saxton has observed,
"To Louisa, his disregard of conventions was an Indian love call."[3] In her
first novel, *Moods* (1865), which she wrote in her late twenties, Alcott
drew upon her knowledge of both men. Her portrayal of the gentle poet

Geoffrey Moor is based on Emerson, while that of the bold adventurer Adam Warwick is based in part on Thoreau. Both male characters become the competing suitors of Sylvia Yule, an eighteen-year-old heroine who possesses many of Alcott's own traits, including high spirits. The title and epigraph of the book, *Moods*, she took from Emerson's essay "Experience": "Life is a train of moods like a string of beads; and as we pass through them they prove to be many colored lenses, which paint the world their own hue, and each shows us only what lies in its own focus."[4] Although Emerson used the metaphor to address the issue of subjectivity, Alcott uses it to refer to the impulsiveness of her heroine.

Alcott began writing *Moods* in August 1860, revised it in February 1861, and again in the summers of 1863 and 1864, eventually seeing the novel into print at the end of 1864 (with a publication date of 1865). Although written in the wake of the Harpers Ferry raid and revised in the midst of the Civil War itself, Alcott makes no mention of Brown or the war. Nevertheless, the book resonates with these explosive political matters, especially through the character of Warwick, whose name suggests the incendiary features of his personality.[5] He becomes the novel's most heroic figure, demonstrating his courage by saving Sylvia's life during a forest fire, fighting alongside the republicans in Italy, and saving his best friend from drowning in a shipwreck. The young heroine from the outset cannot resist him: "To her imaginative and enthusiastic nature, there was something irresistibly attractive in the strong, solitary, self-reliant man" (38). The novel explores the nature of friendship and love, as well as marriage, but taking precedence over all these, and informing them as well, is what Alcott later identified as the "the mistakes of a moody nature, guided by impulse, not principle."[6] The mistakes are ostensively Sylvia's, yet Warwick's devotion to principle often makes him impulsive as well.

While Warwick stands as a masculine ideal in *Moods*, certain features of his personality make him clearly unsuitable as a mate. Heroic in the face of danger, he is also domineering and, at times, ruthless. He is just the man to fight to the death for a cause, but not one to treat a woman as his equal. When Sylvia asks her brother if Warwick is "good," Mark replies, "Violently virtuous. He is a masterful soul, bent on living out his beliefs and aspirations at any cost. Much given to denunciation of wrong-doing everywhere, and eager to execute justice upon all offend-ers high or low" (37). With regard to the struggle for women's rights, a struggle Alcott herself subscribed to, Warwick is more foe than friend. During his attempt to get Sylvia to marry him, ignorant of her marriage to their friend Moor, he declares, "Shy thing! I will tame you yet, and draw you to me as confidingly as I drew the bird to hop into my hand and eat. You must not fear me, Sylvia, else I shall grow tyrannical; for I hate fear, and like to trample on whatever dares not fill its place bravely" (127). His wooing obviously leaves much to be desired.

The question the book thus raises and that this chapter attempts to answer is, How does Alcott reconcile her favorable portrait of Warwick's domineering character with her commitment to women's rights? Given Alcott's sustained critique of male domination and oppression in a num-ber of her works, as a series of feminist scholars have pointed out, why did she portray this violently virtuous character so favorably?[7] She told her friend Caroline Dall, who objected to Warwick's character, "I have received a shock! You don't like Warwick, & he is my pride & delight & Moor is a pancake compared to him."[8] Several factors, I wish to argue, help explain her attitude. First, when she began the novel, her admira-tion for strong male abolitionists such as Thoreau, Parker, Higginson, and especially John Brown was at its peak. Second, her own warrior spirit had been aroused by the prospect of civil war. And finally, her height-ened interest in gender crossing, provoked by the war, gave Warwick's aggressive tendencies more appeal than they would otherwise have had. In fact, when Alcott revised *Moods* for publication in 1882, long after the war's end, she tamed Warwick's character considerably. He, like other strong men she depicted, including Brown and Thoreau, became more pacific and calm in her representation when the political violence they participated in lost its immediacy.

WARWICK, THOREAU, AND JOHN BROWN

When Alcott began writing *Moods*, most of Concord was deeply stirred by John Brown's character and fate. His willingness to fight on behalf of principle had not only altered the thinking of the transcendental-ists but affected Louisa as well. She imbibed their preference for action over thought as the slavery controversy became more and more violent, and the plot she constructed for *Moods* intentionally progresses from tranquility to warfare to death. The book opens with a series of pastoral chapters reflecting the youth and innocence of its heroine, then takes her deeper into the difficulties caused by misunderstandings and impulsiveness, and ends with her death from consumption and a prospective reunion with Warwick in heaven.

The opening scene of the novel (omitted in the 1882 edition) features Warwick and allegorizes national tensions, in particular the strained Union between the decadent South and the righteous North. In the scene, set in Cuba, the New Englander Warwick tries to extricate himself from an engagement to a dark seductress named Ottila, whose beauty and wiles have temporarily captivated him. When she asks where he intends to go, he replies, "Straight to the North. This luxurious life enervates me; the pestilence of slavery lurks in the air and infects me; I must build myself up anew and find again the man I was" (12). Like a good transcendentalist, he gives her a year to acquire "the moral sentiment" and promises that if "we find any basis for an abiding union, then, Ottila, I will marry you" (13). Clearly a disunionist, he plans to sever the relationship on moral grounds, and the next time we see him several chapters later, he, along with Moor and Sylvia's brother Mark, is setting out on a two-day camping trip on a beautiful New England river (inspired by Thoreau's *Week on the Concord and Merrimack Rivers*). Sylvia, an attractive tomboy, insists on joining her brother and his friends, and the trip provides the setting for Moor's and Warwick's falling in love with the wholesome young girl.

Moor, an idealized portrait of Emerson, is twelve years older than Sylvia and said to be of the "poetic" type. He "betrayed in every gesture the unconscious grace of the gentleman born. A most attractive face, with its broad brow, serene eyes, and the cordial smile about the mouth. A sweet, strong nature, one would say, which, having used life well had learned the secret of a true success. Inward tranquility seemed his, and it was plain to see that no wave of sound, no wandering breath, no glimpse of color, no hint of night or nature was without its charm and its significance for him" (36–37). While this sketch resembles the public Emerson of the 1840s, it does not capture the bellicose Emerson of the late 1850s. In order to establish a contrast between Moor and Warwick, Alcott obviously drew upon an earlier version of her "master," perhaps adding a portion of her father's mildness as well.

Warwick, in contrast, is a heightened version of Thoreau as he appeared in the wake of John Brown's raid, and Alcott fashions him into an Old Testament prophet in his prime. He stands "a head taller than his tall friend, broad-shouldered, strong-limbed, and bronzed by wind and weather. A massive head, covered with rings of ruddy brown hair; gray eyes, that seemed to pierce through all disguises, an eminent nose, and a beard like one of Mark's stout saints. Power, intellect, and courage were stamped on face and figure, making him the manliest man that Sylvia had ever seen" (36). While Sylvia responds to Moor as a platonic friend, she falls passionately in love with Warwick and he with her. After their river trip together, during which they float alone on the river, encounter a forest fire, and witness a country wedding, they exchange a meaningful look. His eyes "shed summer over her" and filled her "with a glad submission" (79). "In that moment," we are told, "each saw the other's heart, and each turned a new page in the romance of their lives" (80). Soon afterward, however, things go awry, because Warwick decides he must return to Cuba and break his engagement to Ottila before declaring his love for Sylvia. She unwittingly encourages him by answering a hypothetical question about what he should do, saying, "I think I should keep the promise as religiously as an Indian keeps a vow of vengeance" (77). Alcott thus foreshadows Warwick's "savagery," which is a latent feature of his character.

After he abruptly leaves New England and months pass, Sylvia, learning of his betrothal to Ottila at second hand, misunderstands and consents to marry Moor, now a dear friend who offers contentment and security. On their honeymoon in the mountains, however, Warwick returns and openly declares his love. Sylvia reluctantly sends him away, but Moor soon learns of his wife's feelings and leaves home, traveling abroad with Warwick. They become briefly separated in Italy, and in a village outside Rome, Moor finds Warwick lying wounded after single-handedly saving the village from invading Croats. Having received a message from Sylvia asking him to come home, Moor returns with Warwick, but there's a shipwreck as they approach the American coast, and Warwick drowns saving Moor's life.

The shipwreck, reminiscent of Margaret Fuller's tragic death, parallels Sylvia's struggles at home, for as she gains maturity and wisdom, she becomes fatally ill. In the closing scenes, she explains to Moor that she asked him to return because she needed him at her side. She tells him that she will soon join their friend in heaven, and describes an apocalyptic dream where "utter silence filled the world, and across the sky a vast curtain of the blackest cloud was falling, blotting out face after face and leaving the world a blank" (210). In "that universal gloom and stillness," she sees "the great word Amen . . . burning with a ruddy glory stronger than the sun," and through the "rift, between the dark earth and the darker sky, rolled in a softly flowing sea" (210–11). As floodwaters in the dream threaten to overcome Sylvia, she sees the dead Warwick's "beautiful, benignant face" regarding her (211), and she feels a joyful yearning to die. In the revised edition Alcott published in 1882, Sylvia does not die but comes to love Moor, and as they are reunited, she tells of seeing Warwick's "beautiful, benignant face, regarding us with something brighter than a smile."[9] In the revised version, he remains, in other words, a heroic ideal — "Death makes a saint of him," Moor says — yet not one Sylvia will soon join in heaven.[10]

As a number of scholars have pointed out, Warwick shares many traits with Thoreau, who would die in 1862. "Our Pan is dead," Alcott lamented in her moving poem "Thoreau's Flute," adding, "the Genius of the wood is lost."[11] Like Thoreau, Warwick disdains conventional society and evidences a deep love of nature that thrills the young heroine. In an early scene by the river, Alcott describes a little sparrow eating crumbs from his hand: "It was a pretty picture for the girl to see; the man, an image of power, in his hand the feathered atom, that, with unerring instinct, divined and trusted the superior nature which had not yet lost its passport to the world of innocent delights that Nature gives to those who love her best" (55).

Despite this similarity, Warwick differs from Thoreau in a number of ways. In addition to being much taller, he knows how to kill. Whereas Thoreau could be rhetorically violent, it was John Brown who actually fought and killed, as everyone in Concord knew. In fact, when Brown

FIGURE 5. Nahum Ball Onthank,
John Brown of Osawatomie. Oil on
canvas. Boston Athenæum.

visited Concord for the second time, in the spring of 1859, Bronson
Alcott described him in terms that anticipate those used by his daughter
to describe Warwick:

> He is of imposing appearance, personally tall, with square shoulders and
> standing, eyes of deep gray, and couchant as if ready to spring at the least
> rustling; dauntless yet kindly; his hair shooting backward from low down
> on his forehead; nose trenchant and Romanesque; set lips; his voice sup-
> pressed yet metallic, suggesting deep reserves; decided mouth; the coun-
> tenance and frame charged with power throughout. Since here last he has
> added a flowing beard, which gives him the soldierly air, and port of an
> apostle. . . . I think him about the manliest man I have ever seen.[12] (See
> figure 5.)

The attribution of manliness and sanctity to Brown, who traveled armed,
Bronson noted, clearly finds its echo in *Moods.*

Louisa, like her mother and father (and Emerson and Thoreau),
was captivated by the fifty-nine-year-old Brown and came to idolize him.
After the raid on Harpers Ferry in October 1859, she wrote to her friend
Alfred Whitman, "What are your ideas on the Harpers Ferry matter? If

you are *my* Dolphus you are full of admiration for old Brow[n]'s cour-age & pity his probable end. We are boiling over with excitement here for many of our people (Anti Slavery I mean) are concerned in it. We have a daily stampede for papers, & a nightly indignation meeting over the wickedness of our country, & the cowardice of the human race. I'm afraid mother will die of spontaneous combustion if things are not set right soon."[13] After Brown's arrest, Thoreau came often to the Alcott house to discuss how to respond to the trial and upcoming execution, and it was as if the personalities of Thoreau and Brown merged. On November 4, 1859, Bronson recorded in his journal:

> Thoreau calls and reports about the reading of his lecture on Brown at Boston and Worcester. Thoreau has good right to speak fully his mind con-cerning Brown, and has been the first to speak, and celebrate the hero's courage and magnanimity. It is these which he discusses and praises. The men have much in common: the sturdy manliness, straight-forwardness, and independence. It is well they met, and that Thoreau saw what he sets forth as none else can.[14]

The fact that Thoreau both identified with and resembled Brown, at least on a superficial level, helps explain Alcott's conflation of their traits in her characterization of Warwick.[15]

When Thoreau visited the Alcotts on November 19, he vented his frustration that few in the country, other than his friends, shared his admiration for Brown. Bronson reported in his journal that Thoreau "talks truly and enthusiastically about Brown, denouncing the Union, President, the States, and Virginia particularly. Wishes to publish his late speech, and has been to Boston publishers, but failed to find any to print it for him."[16] Louisa shared Thoreau's frustration and admiration. In her journal entry for November 1859 she wrote, "The Harper's Ferry tragedy makes this a memorable month. Glad I have lived to see the Antislavery movement and this last heroic act in it. Wish I could do my part in it."[17] A month later, she lamented in her journal, "The execution of Saint John the Just took place on the second. A meeting at the hall, and all Concord was there. Emerson, Thoreau, Father, and Sanborn spoke, and all were full of reverence and admiration for the martyr. I made some verses on it, and sent them to the 'Liberator.'"[18] Her poem subsequently appeared in Redpath's *Echoes of Harpers Ferry* (1860), along with the tributes of the other Concordians.

During the spring and summer of 1860, as *Moods* was taking shape in Alcott's imagination, Brown's influence permeated Concord, and the foiled attempt of federal agents to arrest Franklin Sanborn, one of Brown's co-conspirators, kept things stirred up in the village. Sanborn was at the Alcott house often, and Louisa was impressed with his successful resistance to his arrest through the help of his sister, his neighbor Anne Whiting, and Judge Hoar's writ of habeas corpus.[19] "Sanborn was nearly kidnapped for being a friend of John Brown; but his sister and A. W. rescued him when he was handcuffed, and the scamps drove off. Great ferment in town. A meeting and general flurry."[20] In February 1860 Brown's daughters Anne and Sarah came to Concord to live and to attend Sanborn's school. In July, Brown's widow, Mary, and her daughter-in-law Belle also arrived and briefly visited with the Alcotts. During four weeks in the following month, Louisa wrote furiously on *Moods:* "Genius burned so fiercely that for four weeks I wrote all day and planned nearly all night, being quite possessed by my work. I was perfectly happy, and seemed to have no wants. Finished the book, or a rough draught of it, and put it away to settle. Mr. Emerson offered to read it when Mother told him it was *Moods* and had one of his sayings for motto."[21] In March 1861 Alcott wrote a poem at Emerson's request to be read at the Concord school festival. Because it mentioned Wendell Philips and John Brown favorably, "some of the old fogies objected," but, according to Louisa, "Emerson said, 'Give it up? No, no, *I* will read it.' Which he did, to my great contentment."[22] At least during the first composition of *Moods*, Alcott's thoughts were never far from the political turmoil in her town and her country. In the periods during which she revised, the turmoil became war, and the times seemed to demand additional heroic acts.

After *Moods* was published in 1865, some readers objected to Warwick, including a young Henry James, whose review of the book speculated that "Miss Alcott has probably mused upon Warwick so long and so lovingly that she has lost all sense of his proportions. . . . [A]pparently as a natural result of being thoroughly conscientious, he is essentially disagreeable."[23] Alcott stoutly defended her hero much as she and others in

Concord had defended Brown, praising his masculinity and devotion to a "higher law." In a letter dated March 19, 1865, to a reader she did not know, Mr. Ayer, she declared: "Warwick has been pronounced an impossible character, but as he was drawn from life he must stand for what he is worth. . . . He too makes his mistakes, endeavors to amend them, & is true to his belief of what is right in defiance of the world's opinion."[24] On one level, Alcott recognized that Warwick's high-mindedness made him less than desirable as a husband for Sylvia. "Adam touch[ed] both heart & mind, kindled both intellect & soul, & she was his in spirit," Alcott wrote Dall, "though not strong or old enough to mate with him. One may love any great & noble thing, but it is not always best to try to gain it or be wretched because it is denied."[25] In *Moods,* Sylvia's older friend Faith Dane cautions her against Warwick for many of the same reasons: "He clings to *principles;* persons are but animated facts or ideas; he seizes, searches, uses them, and when they have no more for him; drops them like the husk whose kernel he has secured. . . . With him you would exhaust yourself in passionate endeavour to follow where he led. . . . It is like a woodbird mating with an eagle" (180–81). Elizabeth Keyser has called this Alcott's "inner wisdom," and it complicates the reader's sense that Warwick is Sylvia's true love.[26]

When Warwick establishes himself as a military hero by joining in the struggle for liberty in Italy, his behavior, though apparently admired by Alcott, suggests an unsettling thirst for violence. As he tells Moor of his exploits, which involve driving off the Croats by manning a cannon, he becomes larger than life and his weapon embarrassingly phallic: "I came to watch, but found work ready for me. It is not clear to me even now what I did, nor how I did it. One of my Berserker rages possessed me I fancy; my nerves and muscles seemed made of steel and gutta percha, the smell of powder intoxicated, and the sense of power was grand. The fire, the smoke, the din were all delicious, and I felt like a giant, as I wielded that great weapon, dealing many deaths with a single pair of hands" (199–200). Moor responds, "The savage in you got the mastery just then; I've seen it, and have often wondered how you managed to control it so well. Now it has had a holiday and made a hero of you." To which Warwick declares, "The savage is better out than in, and any man may be a hero if he will" (200). Although Warwick's assertion can be read as a form of modesty, it also reveals an attitude that gained adherents during the 1850s, as the United States prepared for war.

Radical abolitionists, especially, came to regard the savage as a fitting symbol of masculinity. As John Stauffer has pointed out, John Brown and his admirers "justified and accepted savagery as a means for furthering civilization by vanquishing slavery. They found in the symbol of the savage Indian grounds for striking violently against a corrupted civilization." Brown "emerged from the guerrilla warfare in Kansas referring to himself by the Indian name Osawatomie Brown and became widely known as a brave warrior."[27] Not surprisingly, Thoreau, who studied and admired Indian culture, found Brown a kindred spirit. As previously mentioned, in an 1845 journal entry Thoreau recorded, "I find an instinct in me conducting to a mystic spiritual life—and also another—to a primitive savage life."[28] When Higginson suggested in a January 1860 lecture titled "Barbarism and Civilization" that the positive traits of the savage should be adopted by men of his class, his friends Thoreau and Bronson Alcott agreed but thought he had not gone far enough. Alcott wrote in his journal that Higginson "defends civilization against Thoreau's prejudices for Adamhood, and celebrates its advantages—of health chiefly, among the rest. After the lecture Thoreau and I go to Emerson's and talk further on it. . . . Thoreau defends the Indian from the doctrine of being lost or exterminated, and thinks he holds a place between civilized man and nature, and must hold it."[29] As the Civil War began, even Emerson, as I have shown, seemed ready to indulge his savage impulses, declaring that "Passions, resistance, danger, are educators. We acquire the strength we have overcome."[30] Thus Louisa's positive treatment of Warwick's savagery accords with the attitudes of her family and friends at the time. As she later asserted, "'Earth's fanatics often make heaven's saints,' you, know, and it is as well to try for that sort of promotion in time."[31]

ALCOTT'S WARRIOR SPIRIT

Clearly, Warwick's endorsement of "savage" behavior bodes ill for those unable to withstand it. Moreover, it runs counter to the emergent struggle of women to attain social and political equality. His assertive masculinity threatens to overpower Sylvia especially, yet Alcott presents this trait in a favorable light because she, like Thoreau and Brown, possessed a warrior spirit of her own. Given her ambiguous sexuality and strong theatrical bent, Alcott found switching gender roles appealing and easily assumed male personae who were fierce as well as brave. In a letter of March 1860 she explained, "I was born with a boy's nature & always had more sympathy for & interest in them than in girls, & have fought my fight for nearly fifteen [years] with a boys spirit under my 'bib & tucker' & a boys wrath when I got 'floored.'"[32] In an interview Alcott gave in 1883, she became even more explicit about herself: "Now I am more than half-persuaded that I am a man's soul, put by some freak of nature into a woman's body . . . because I have fallen in love in my life with so many pretty girls, and never once the least little bit with any man."[33] As is well known, Alcott often crossed gender in home theatricals, but she also took these performances beyond the stage. Julian Hawthorne related the humorous story about a young English gentleman who outraged him by speaking condescendingly and presuming to put an arm around Louisa's sister Abby May, upon whom Julian had a crush. When Julian reacted menacingly to the gentleman's insults, the stranger "snatched off his soft black hat and with the same movement pushed a hand up through his hair, which broke from its fastenings and cascaded down his back in joyous tumult," leaving Julian "with a new respect of Louisa's histrionic ability."[34]

In *Little Women*, Jo plays the villainous Hugo and the dashing Roderigo in bedroom dramas, but she also expresses her affinity for masculine character traits. She often gets "into a fury" and at one point tells Marmee, "It seems as if I could do any thing when I'm in a passion; I get so savage, I could hurt any one, and enjoy it."[35] It is difficult to know how much Alcott drew upon her own personality in her portrait of Jo, but we do know that when she was a child her father recorded her "ferocity, ungovernable energy, [and] passionate obstinacy."[36] Edna Cheney was one of the first to point out that Alcott's sensational stories provided an outlet for the passion and anger Alcott suppressed in her children's and sentimental writings. Cheney observed, "She had a passion for wild, adventurous life, and even for lurid passion and melodramatic action, which she could indulge to the utmost in these stories. Louisa was always a creature of moods; and it was a great relief to work off certain feelings by the safe vent of imaginary persons and scenes in a story."[37] These "certain feelings" most often involved resentment, anger, and thirst for revenge. Her short story "Pauline's Passion and Punishment" (1863), for example, opens with the following description of the revengeful protagonist: "To and fro, like a wild creature in its cage, paced that handsome woman, with bent head, locked hands, and restless steps. Some mental storm, swift and sudden as a tempest of the tropics, had swept over her and left its marks behind."[38] Similarly, in "Behind a Mask: *or, A Woman's Power*" (1866), the protagonist, Jean Muir, a governess intent on coming between the privileged Gerald Coventry and his fiancée, tells a friend: "I hated them both, of course, and in return for their insolence shall torment her with jealousy, and teach him how to woo a woman by making his heart ache. They are an intensely proud family, but I can humble them all, I think," which she does, to the reader's delight.[39]

Alcott's passionate interest in violence and revenge fed into her political activities as well as her thrillers.[40] When she paid tribute to her heroes, this was particularly the case. Following Preston Brooks's caning of Senator Charles Sumner, New England's most eminent abolitionist, in the U.S. Senate, Alcott thus described her response when after his long recovery Sumner returned to Boston and a grand reception in his honor: "I could not hear the speeches at the State House so I tore down Hancock St & got a place opposite his house. . . . I was so excited I pitched about like a mad woman, shouted, waved, hung onto fences, rushed thrọ crowds, & swarmed about in a state [of] rapturous insanity till it was all over & then I went home hoarse & worn out."[41] The reason for her mad tumult was admiration for Sumner's heroic efforts on behalf of the antislavery cause and the suffering he endured because of it. Like Brown, who empathized deeply with Sumner, the senator had become a saintlike martyr in the eyes of many New Englanders. While Alcott was working as a nurse in Washington, D.C., she visited the Senate chamber, "sat in Sumner's chair, and cudgeled an imaginary Brooks within an inch of his life."[42] In October 1862, a month before she went to Washington, she wrote in her journal, "I like the stir in the air, and long for battle like a war horse when he smells powder. The blood of the Mays is up!"[43]

Alcott's most recent biographer, John Matteson, has suggested that Alcott may have suffered from a form of manic-depressive illness, which would explain her "evident interest in mood disorders, her own mercurial character, and her seemingly obsessive work habits." He adds, "Louisa's struggles with emotional control were a frequent source of profound distress to herself and her family during her years of growing up. Bronson's response to all emotional discontents was to urge self-mastery and self-denial. . . . There was no obvious place in Bronson's theory of the mind for mental states that the individual could *not* control—no room for the idea that the roots of an unbalanced temperament might be medical instead of moral."[44] Matteson provides a useful update to nineteenth-century male claims about hysterical women, but I would suggest that a complementary way to explain Warwick's "savagery" and Alcott's own aggression is to consider the influence of romantic warrior figures whom Alcott admired, including Joan of Arc and Britomart, Spenser's powerful female knight in *The Faerie Queene.*

A number of Alcott's characters display the chivalric virtues she had read about and admired. In her story "M.L.," written in 1860, she endows her heroine, Claudia, with the noble courage to defeat racial prejudice. Claudia leaves "the world of wealth, and fashion, and pretense" behind to marry her lover, Paul, a quadroon former slave. As a result, she finds within herself "a truer chivalry than she had known before, for heroic deeds shone on her in the humblest guise, and she discovered knights of a nobler court than Arthur founded, or than Spenser sang." Her models all "fight for love of God and universal right."[45] Alcott, like her own role model Margaret Fuller, overflowed with militant energy when aroused by a righteous cause, and as a number of feminists have pointed out, Alcott's anger was a source of her creative power and a useful response to male oppression. Madeleine Stern was one of the first to observe that in Alcott's thrillers of the 1860s, "her own anger at an unjust world she transformed into the anger of her heroines, who made of it a powerful weapon with which to challenge fate."[46]

Alcott's passion and warrior spirit seem to have informed her depiction of Warwick's hypermasculine behavior as well, and it seems probable that she identified with him, especially during his fighting in Italy. In the novel, the tribute paid to him by Garibaldi (who places his famous gray robe on him) was surely evoked by current events and by previous struggles in Italy during 1848–50. In 1860 the newspapers and magazines were filled with accounts of the second Italian war of independence and Garibaldi's successful invasion of southern Italy, when, along with his "One Thousand," he gave essential support to the popular revolt against the King of Naples. Garibaldi's invasion was viewed as an Italian version of John Brown's Harpers Ferry raid and was used to justify Brown's violence (even though Brown sought to start an insurrection, not join one). As Paola Gemme has pointed out, "Given the enormous popularity enjoyed by Garibaldi in the United States at that time, the equation of John Brown and the Italian patriot functioned to domesticate, even glorify, the use of violence rather than Garrisonian 'moral suasion.'"[47]

Bronson Alcott cut out a number of newspaper articles about the struggle, which he pasted in his journal. He also put there a contemporaneous four-column tribute to Margaret Fuller that Horace Greeley wrote for his *New-York Daily Tribune*. Greeley recalled Fuller's own efforts on behalf of Italian liberty ten years earlier, and Louisa, like her father, must have found the account stirring, despite its tragic features. Greeley concludes,

> . . . the hour of overwhelming reaction, of deadly perils, of priestly maledictions and popular consternation, of mustering legions and gleaming bayonets converging from France, from Austria, from Naples, to quench the beacon-fires of Liberty still burning brightly if not cheerily on the ramparts of the seven-hilled city, found [Fuller] calm, resolute, tearless, leaving her young babe in its rural nest to stand through the night-watches beside her husband in the batteries on the ramparts of the beleaguered city, and give her days to sympathizing labors in the hospitals where the wounded soldiers of the Republic, torn with cannon-shot and parched with fever, were breathing their last in the bitter consciousness that they had poured out their life-blood in behalf of a hopeless, ruined cause.[48]

Fuller was one of Alcott's heroines, and they shared an admiration for women warriors. In *Woman in the Nineteenth Century*, Fuller pays tribute to Emily Plater, the Polish freedom fighter who dressed as a man and led troops into battle against the Russians. Fuller calls her "the figure I want for my frontispiece," compares her to Joan of Arc, and observes that some officers "talked of the delicacy of her sex, advised her to withdraw from perils and dangers, and had no comprehension of the feelings within her breast that made this impossible."[49]

As Sarah Elbert points out, Alcott shared Fuller's support of both anti-slavery and women's rights: "The identification of the white woman with Afro-American bondage is crucial to understanding *Moods*, although neither the peculiar institution nor the Civil War appear in the novel."[50] Fuller makes such a connection in *Woman in the Nineteenth Century* when she explains that "champions of the enslaved African" make "the warmest appeal in behalf of woman."[51] In Concord especially, women were at the forefront of the antislavery and the women's rights movements, despite the higher visibility of the town's leading male citizens. In a letter to Thomas Niles, February 19, 1881, Alcott recalled, "I can remember when Anti slavery was in just the same state that Suffrage is now, and take more pride in the very small help we Alcotts could give than in all the books I ever wrote or ever shall write."[52] Abolitionism and suffrage both gave content and focus to Louisa's romantic, tempestuous side, and informed her exalted bursts of rhetoric, often focused on fighting.

As the Civil War approached, Alcott longed to give vent to her anger about slavery, and she viewed the war rather naively as an opportunity to display a heroism she had long admired. She chafed at the limitations that prevented women from participating in battle. Young men were allowed to fight, she complained, but women were not. Her conception of war, however, made it seem a romantic enterprise, and a number of young men in New England in 1861 shared her outlook. They saw the war as an opportunity to attain glory and return as heroes. Few, in the North or the South, thought the war would last longer than a few months. In her journal, Alcott wrote, "1859 September. — Great State Encampment here. Town full of soldiers, with military fuss and feathers. I like a camp, and long for a war, to see how it all seems."[53] In a letter to Alfred Whitman, May 19, 1861, the young woman asked, "Are you going to have a dab at the saucy Southerners? I long to fly at some body & free my mind on several points, but there is no opening for me at present so I study Dr Home on 'Gun shot wounds,' & get my highly connected self ready to go as a nurse."[54] (She would begin her nursing duties at the Union Hotel Hospital in Georgetown some eighteen months later.)

Like everyone else in Concord, Alcott was impressed by the departure of the young recruits on April 19, 1861, and again expressed her desire to join them: "At the station the scene was very dramatic, as the brave boys went away perhaps never to come back again. I've often longed to see a war, and now I have my wish. I long to be a man, but as I can't fight, I will content myself with working for those who can." A month later, she got closer to the impending fighting on a walk to Cambridge and back: "Took a sail to the forts, and saw our men on guard there. Felt very martial and Joan-of-Arc-y as I stood on the walls with the flag flying over me and cannon all about."[55] Given Alcott's enthusiasm for war before she had witnessed its effects, one can certainly charge her with naïveté. Cheney has called her "an unformed girl" who "had not studied herself or life very deeply,"[56] and yet the Harvard-educated men who were her idols were no more circumspect or restrained in their attitudes. What is perhaps different about Alcott is her theatrical bent. She often struck poses, and one of her favorites was that of a knight riding to the rescue of a damsel in distress. Thoreau never fancied himself in such a role, but Emerson claimed that "the oath of gentle blood and knighthood" was what led him and other gentlemen to admire John Brown's efforts on behalf of "the weak and lowly" (*AW* 123).

FEMINIZED WARRIORS

Even though Alcott professed to want to charge into battle and fight like a man, she often in her works made men more feminine as she made women more masculine. While she glorified moments of fury in her writings and depicted both men and women as heroic, she also softened her warrior figures after battle, making them more sensitive and peaceable. Elizabeth Young in her analysis of *Hospital Sketches* has shown how Alcott "valorizes the injured soldier for his feminine characteristics" and "relocates traits of masculinity within the figure of the female nurse."[57] *Hospital Sketches* (1863), which originated with Alcott's letters home during her two months' service as a nurse, were adapted for publication in the abolitionist newspaper *The Commonwealth* and then as a book.

In the published letters, Alcott used the Dickensian name Tribulation Periwinkle for her first-person narrator, and as Periwinkle prepares to leave on her nursing assignment, she declares, "I turned military at once, called my dinner rations, saluted all comers, and ordered a dress parade that very afternoon" (55). At work in the hospital, she continues to use military metaphors half-facetiously to describe her activities, including her debilitating illness, which forces her to proclaim "a defeat before I was fairly routed" (107).

The soldiers, on the other hand, whom Periwinkle attends, acquire feminine traits in her descriptions, especially the Virginia blacksmith John, who in the chapter titled "A Night" dies on her watch: "A most attractive face he had, framed in brown hair and beard, comely featured and full of vigor, as yet unsubdued by pain; thoughtful and often beautifully mild while watching the afflictions of others, as if entirely forgetful of his own. His mouth was grave and firm, with plenty of will and courage in its lines, but a smile could make it as sweet as any woman's; and his eyes were child's eyes, looking one fairly in the face, with a clear, straightforward glance, which promised well for such as placed their faith in him" (86–87). When John tells his best friend goodbye, before he dies, "They kissed each other, tenderly as women." After his death, John's face takes on a "lovely expression" and his body appears to Periwinkle "stately and still as the statue of some young knight asleep upon his tomb" (93). Alcott thus drains the bellicosity from John and those other "young knights" who have gone to war and replaces it with mildness and calm.

Alcott engaged in a similar process after the deaths of John Brown and Thoreau, and she would do the same when she revised *Moods*. Her male warriors would become tamed at her hand. In "With a Rose, That Bloomed on the Day of John Brown's Martyrdom," Alcott converts Brown the killer into a figure of serenity and love, and if one looks closely at her poem, it is Brown as a man of peace that she emphasizes:

> Each cheerful word, each valiant act,
> So simple, so sublime,
> Spoke to us through the reverent hush
> Which sanctified that time.

> That moment when the brave old man
> > Went so serenely forth
> With footsteps whose unfaltering tread
> > Re-echoed through the North.
>
> The sword he wielded for the right
> > Turns to a victor's palm;
> His memory sounds forever more,
> > A spirit-stirring psalm.
> No breath of shame can touch his shield,
> > Nor ages dim its shine;
> Living, he made life beautiful,—
> > Dying, made death divine.[58]

Her use of such words as "sublime," "reverent," and "divine" almost make Brown seem a pacifist. The poem obviously contrasts with Thoreau's "A Plea for John Brown," which celebrates the man's use of weapons.

Similarly, in her poem "Thoreau's Flute," written after Thoreau's death, she recalls him not as the savage abolitionist whose thoughts were "murder to the state" but, rather, as her gentle and serene childhood teacher. Through the flute come the words,

> Above man's aims his nature rose.
> > The wisdom of a just content
> Made one small spot a continent,
> > And turned to poetry life's prose.

Calling him a "large-hearted child," Alcott ends the poem with the following stanza:

> O lonely friend! he still will be
> > A potent presence, though unseen,—
> Steadfast, sagacious, and serene;
> > Seek not for him—he is with thee.[59]

As Matteson points out, "Once a voice on behalf of nature, Thoreau's voice is now one with nature; the breath that no longer fills his consumptive lungs still carries its message of peace to those sensitive enough to hear."[60] Alcott wrote "Thoreau's Flute" one night in the hospital as she watched over a wounded soldier, which may explain the pacific tone of the poem.

One of the antislavery pieces that Alcott published while *Moods* was still in its formative stages also argues for peace over righteous violence. The story, called "An Hour," stages the contest between love and peace on the one hand and hate and insurrection on the other. "An Hour" takes place between 11:00 p.m. and midnight on a plantation where a slave insurrection is about to occur, which will result in the killing of the family of slaveowners—a cruel mother, her daughters, and her stepson, Gabriel, a liberal-minded person from the South now living in the North. He has come home after his father's death and plans to free the slaves, a fact unknown to them. Milly, a beautiful house slave in love with Gabriel, and he with her, faces the decision of whether to betray the insurrection by informing Gabriel or going through with the plan and letting justice take its course. He looks into her eyes, which "filled slowly till two great tears rolled down her cheeks, wetting the hands that touched them; and when Gabriel said, softly, 'For my sake you will save us?' she straightway answered, 'Yes.'"[61] Thus, love wins out over righteous violence in this plot, for after she informs Gabriel, he bravely confronts the rebellious slaves and persuades them to lay down their arms: "Out from the darkness Gabriel came among them. To their startled, superstitious eyes he seemed no mortal man, but a beautiful, benignant angel, bringing tidings of great joy, as he stood there, armed with no weapon but a righteous purpose, gifted with no eloquence but the truth."[62] He proclaims them free. They drop their arms. And hoofbeats are heard in the distance, signaling approaching troops, who will have no insurrection to put down. The story thus suggests that white philanthropy can arrest black insurgency and bloodshed, at least in Alcott's imagined world.

Another story contemporaneous with *Moods*, "My Contraband," published in the *Atlantic Monthly* (November 1863), more explicitly argues against a freed slave's righteous violence directed at his former master. In this story, nurse Faith Dane (from *Moods*) acts as an ethical agent once more while working in a wartime hospital. There she persuades one negro patient, Robert, not to kill another patient, a Confederate captain named Ned—Robert's white half-brother and former master.

Faith relates, "Robert's deep eyes filled, the clenched hands were spread before his face, and all I heard were the broken words, — 'My wife, — he took her — .'"[63] Faith knows that the wife, Lucy, after being raped and whipped, committed suicide by cutting her own throat, yet Faith tells Robert, "There is a better way of righting wrong than by violence; — let me help you find it."[64] Robert relents and departs. Ned, too, recovers and leaves in a prisoner exchange, and both meet again during the Massachusetts 54th's famous attack on Fort Wagner. In battle, Ned fatally wounds Robert, before being killed himself by a "dark freeman." Nurse Dane, at a nearby hospital, witnesses Robert's last breath and reports, "As he turned his face from the shadow of the life that was, the sunshine of the life to be touched it with a beautiful content, and in the drawing of a breath my contraband found wife and home, eternal liberty and God."[65] As Matthew R. Davis has pointed out, "My Contraband" "promotes an egalitarian and interracial brotherhood that shifts responsibility for violence to those who would deny brotherhood's promise."[66] Ned, rather than Robert, becomes the killer in this story, making Robert into both martyr and victim. By pacifying Robert through appeals to his love of Lucy, Faith Dane conquers his rage and apparently saves his soul. As for the "dark freeman," he operates impersonally as the hand of fate.

SICK AT HEART: POSTWAR RE-VISIONS

Although Alcott longed for war and seemed imbued with a romantic ideology gained from her readings in Spenser and Scott, her attitude toward political violence obviously underwent a change, especially after she served as a nurse during the Civil War. The typhoid fever she contracted and the doses of mercurous chloride she received left her frequently weary and in pain the rest of her life. She also experienced an emotional alteration, as Matteson has pointed out. At times, "it seemed that her illness and the haunting memories of the hospital had marked her with an indelible air of gravity and melancholy."[67] One has to probe beneath the surface of Alcott's multiple personae to glimpse her suffering and change of heart, for in her fiction and letters, she uses humor and lightheartedness to mask her true feelings. In September 1863, for example, after she had recovered from the typhoid fever that prostrated her, she wrote Alfred Whitman: "Our Concord company is to return tonight & the town is in as wild a state of excitement as it is possible for such a dozy old place to be without dying of brain fever. [She always speaks of Concord as a conservative collective.] Flags are flapping every where, wreaths 'Welcome home' are stuck on every stickable place & our drum corps, consisting of eight small boys with eight large drums, keep a continual rub-a-dubbing."[68] When the company arrived in town, Alcott participated gleefully along with others, yet as Julian Hawthorne later reported, "her smiles had the pathos of remembered pain. . . . After the column had vanished she didn't stir for several moments. . . . At last her old mother went up to her and put an arm gently round her waist. Then the tall girl faltered and drooped, and rested her forehead on her mother's shoulder; but she recovered herself quickly and passed hurriedly up the pathway to the porch of the old house and disappeared within. We saw no more of her that day."[69] After the war, Alcott labored heroically to support her impoverished family, while struggling with physical and emotional ills that would have prostrated most other souls, yet she consistently displayed a sense of humor that masked her pains.

In her postwar writings, Alcott's bellicosity diminishes, apparently due to the distress she has witnessed and suffered. In *Little Women* (1868), of course, Jo becomes less angry and defiant at the end of the novel, under the influence of Professor Bhaer. And when Mr. March returns from the war, his weariness undermines any sense of jubilation the family might otherwise exhibit. Although some critics have registered regret at Jo's loss of anger and her new conventionality, Keren Fite points out that "Jo's willingness to experiment within a principled framework, to let go of a passion in favor of a sober exploration of her circumstance, suggests a union of creation and relation, the sweetness of self-control that is more socially productive than savage passion."[70]

In the revised edition of *Moods*, published in 1882, Warwick is also tamed considerably by the novel's end. One can argue that Alcott wishes to satisfy her readers through such plot constructions. Yet I would argue that the romance of revolution and warfare faded for Alcott as years passed and she reflected on what the country had experienced. In her revisions to *Moods*, she makes Warwick into a supporter of women's rights. He's given a "sermon" in which he decries "the base legislation which decrees liberty to the white and slavery to the black, the false public opinion that grants all suffrages to man and none to woman yet judges both alike."[71] She also omits the passage where Mark speaks of Warwick as "virtuously violent." Although she makes Warwick's wildness and boldness more pronounced at the beginning, by adding scenes featuring a thunderstorm, this addition seems designed to dramatize the change he undergoes in the last half of the novel. After Sylvia demonstrates her acting talent before Moor and Warwick, the latter comments, "It is a perilous gift, but has its uses, for the pent-up emotions can find a safer vent in this way than in melancholy dreams *or daring action*" (emphasis added).[72] Whether he means his remarks to apply only to Sylvia and not to himself and other men remains unclear, although in the new chapter "Sermons," we learn that his ideal woman is "an heroic creature, strong and sweet, aspiring as a flame, and true as steel. Not an impossible woman, but a rare one; and the charm Sylvia had for him was a suggestion of this possibility when time had taught and discipline tamed the wildness that was akin to his own."[73]

In the same chapter, Alcott lets Warwick express his belief system, which accords with that of Thoreau, yet she does not wholly support it. She uses the New Testament to criticize his Old Testament outlook: "Those who listened, while they owned the sincerity, felt the power, admired the enthusiasm, saw that this valiant St. George rode without a Una, and in executing justice forgot mercy, like many another young crusader who, in his ardor to set up the New Jerusalem, breaks the commandments of the Divine Reformer, who immortalized the old."[74]

Though motivated by high principle, Warwick's words and deeds are made to seem excessive at times, and thus he, like Sylvia, is subject to "moods" that color his outlook. Moor says as much in the revised edition, when he tells Sylvia, "You must not let Adam's thunder and lightning disturb you. We have seen the world through his glass, which, though a powerful one, is not always well regulated, so we get a magnified view of things. He is a self-reliant genius, intent on his own aims, which, fortunately, are high ones, for he would go vigorously wrong if it were not for the native integrity which keeps him vigorously right." He adds that Warwick is going through a "storm and stress period," and the observation gives the steady and serene Moor a newly elevated stature.

When Sylvia replies, "I like it because I think I am in a little period of my own. If I dared, I should like to ask you how best to get out of it."[75] Her turn to Moor, as someone to help her rise above the impulsiveness she shares with Warwick, substantially undermines the stature accorded to Warwick in the first version of the romance.

In the first edition, Warwick experiences "a peaceful mood" after his fighting in Italy yet admits it "may not last perhaps" (203). In the revised edition, Alcott softens Warwick's character even more in the last half of the book, just as she makes it more bold in the first half, and he, as well as Sylvia, overcomes his storminess and fury. In the chapter "Sylvia's Honeymoon," in the first edition, the speech he makes to her, in ignorance of her marriage, contains off-putting aggressiveness: "I hate fear, and like to trample on whatever dares not fill its place bravely." (127). In comparison, the 1882 version reads: "I hate fear, and love to see people freely and bravely accept what belongs to them, as I do now to you."[76] He no longer seeks to "trample," but to "love" instead.

Apparently, Alcott came to believe that perhaps the "savage" should be kept within rather than let out, which would put her in agreement with Hawthorne, who explained that revolutionary times allow for the display of individual virtue but are destructive of social relations. Ultimately, Alcott was not the idealist her father and Emerson and Thoreau and John Brown were. In fact, she once claimed not to have understood transcendentalism. Principles mattered to her but human beings did more, as her "Transcendental Wild Oats" (1873) reveals. In this important way, she resembled Margaret Fuller, who, while serving as a nurse in Rome during the revolution there, confessed to a friend: "You say, you are glad I have had this great opportunity for carrying out my principles. Would it were so! I found myself inferior in courage and fortitude to the occasion. I knew not how to bear the havoc and anguish incident to the struggle for these principles. . . . I forget the great ideas, to sympathize with the poor mothers, who had nursed their precious forms, only to see them all lopped and gashed."[77] Louisa May Alcott, it seems, came to regard the romance of revolution in the same way.

> This war, in which the country was so earnestly
> and enthusiastically engaged, had perhaps an
> influence on Septimius's state of mind; for it
> put everybody into an unnatural and exaggerated
> state, raised enthusiasms of all sorts, heightened
> everybody either into its own heroism, or into
> the peculiar madness to which each person
> was inclined.
>
> — HAWTHORNE, "Septimius Felton"

CHAPTER SIX

Pacifism, Savagery, and Hawthorne's Last Romances

When Nathaniel Hawthorne returned to the United States after seven years abroad in the summer of 1860, the hero worship of John Brown was radiating throughout the land from its center in Concord. In the months that followed, the Alcotts found Hawthorne, who lived next door, aloof and shy. According to Louisa, "Mr. H. is as queer as ever and we catch glimpses of a dark mysterious looking man in a big hat and red slippers darting over the hills or skimming by as if he expected the house of Alcott were about to rush out and clutch him."[1] Similarly, Bronson Alcott wrote in his journal: "I get glimpses of Hawthorne as I walk up the sledpaths, he dodging about amongst the trees on his hill-top as if he feared his neighbor's eyes would catch him as he walked."[2] Louisa counted it a great triumph when she finally finagled an invitation to visit Hawthorne's towered study. John Brown's daughter Annie recalled, "One day Miss Louisa came bounding in, whirled around and

clapped her hands above her head, exclaiming 'I came, I saw, I've conquered.' . . . She had for a long time been trying to get Hawthorne to
ask her up into his tower, which he used as a study . . . and on that day
he told her he was too busy to look in a certain volume in his library and
invited her to come up and look it out herself."[3] Louisa enjoyed one of
the rare occasions when Hawthorne allowed someone to share his personal space during his final years.

Hawthorne's furtiveness and his struggles to finish his late romances
have been commonly attributed to his deteriorating health, anxiety
about his reputation and finances, and the distractions of the Civil War.
In this chapter, I argue that Hawthorne's peace principles, which he
knew were at odds with the bellicosity of his Concord neighbors, left him
conflicted about the narratives he was attempting to construct. Although
one part of him wished to join in the "enthusiasm of all sorts" animating New Englanders, especially John Brown's supporters, his pacifism
caused him to question both the validity of their support of political
violence and the morality of his own. Hawthorne had long considered
warfare barbaric and senseless, and thus in Concord in the early 1860s,
he became uncertain about his politics and those of his fictional characters. Consequently, he was accused of treason, even by himself at times.

Bronson Alcott would later claim, "Of all our literary men, he openly
espoused the side of the South, and was tremendously disturbed at the
Northern victories."[4] This false and hurtful notion, shared by many of
Hawthorne's New England contemporaries, arose from Hawthorne's
reserve, his public friendship with Franklin Pierce, and his opposition
to all forms of political violence. Hawthorne's essay "Chiefly about War-
Matters. By a Peaceable Man," published in the *Atlantic Monthly* in July
1862, contributed to his questionable reputation because it brought
multiple perspectives to bear upon its topic and disappointed those
readers who expected ardent partisan commentary. Moreover, in the
piece, Hawthorne created a fictional "editor," who questions the author's
patriotism. A number of readers followed suit. After the essay's appearance, Hawthorne wrote to an English friend, "The war-party here do not
look upon me as a reliably loyal man, and, in fact, I have been publicly
accused of treasonable sympathies;—whereas, I sympathize with nobody
and approve of nothing; and if I have any wishes on the subject, it is

that New England might be a nation by itself."[5] Hawthorne's detached and critical perspective on the contemporary scene, including the "war party," isolated him on high ground, and as he labored in his towered study or paced the hilltop path behind his house, he seems to have felt like his character Septimius, "strangely ajar with the human race," and "would have given much, either to be in full accord with it, or to be separated from it forever."[6] Hawthorne would die on May 19, 1864, before the war ended.

PACIFISM, DRAGON'S TEETH, AND FRATRICIDE

Hawthorne's position on the Civil War was complex, for he disapproved of slavery and the South as a whole, yet he also disapproved of the activities of the abolitionists, or at least "the fiercest, the least scrupulous, and the most consistent of those, who battle against slavery."[7] He called himself "more of an abolitionist in feeling than in principle,"[8] and he blamed the radical abolitionists in part for precipitating the Civil War, which, he told his sister-in-law Elizabeth Peabody, "will only effect by a horrible convulsion the self-same end that might and would have been brought about by a gradual and peaceful change."[9] Hawthorne had long considered war a childish activity that seldom produced beneficial results. Despite this outlook, on November 14, 1861, he wrote his English friend Henry A. Bright, "Emerson is breathing slaughter, like the rest of us; and it is really wonderful how all sorts of theoretical nonsense, to which we New Englanders are addicted in peaceful times, vanish in the strong atmosphere which we now inhale." In the same letter, he added, "I never imagined what a happy state of mind a civil war produces, and how it invigorates every man's whole being. . . . I truly regret that my youth was not cast in these days, instead of in a quiet time."[10] He soon lost his enthusiasm, however, and a year and a half later, he confessed to Bright, "The play (be it tragedy or comedy) is too long drawn out, and my chief feeling about it now is a sense of infinite weariness. I want the end to come, and the curtain to drop, and then to go to sleep. I never did really approve of the war, though you may have supposed so from the violence and animosity with which I controverted your notions about it, when I wrote last."[11]

Whereas Thoreau's attention to the divine led to his eventual disinterest in warfare, Hawthorne's attention to moral behavior led to his eventual conflicted attitude toward the Civil War. In Hawthorne's earlier books, especially his children's stories where he foregoes his characteristic irony, he provides his young readers with a strong antiwar, antimilitary perspective. In *Grandfather's Chair* (1841), for example, he has Grandfather point out that "the great game of war is easily shown to be ridiculous. . . . And would not [snow-ball fighting] be as reasonable a mode of settling national disputes, as if swords, bayonets, tomahawks, bullets, and cannon-balls, were the instruments of warfare?"[12] Grandfather insists that the children should admire men of peace over warriors and magistrates. When the boy Charley asks about King Phillip's War, Grandfather impatiently replies, "I have no time to spare in talking about battles," and when Charley persists by asking who the captain of the English was, he is told, "Their most noted captain was Benjamin Church — a very famous warrior. . . . But I assure you, Charley, that neither Captain Church, nor any of the officers and soldiers who fought in King Philip's war, did any thing a thousandth part so glorious, as Mr. Eliot did, when he translated the Bible for the Indians."[13]

Some nine years later, in *The Scarlet Letter* (1850), Hawthorne responded to the turmoil in Europe by referring to the myth of the dragon's teeth, which his friend Margaret Fuller had also referred to in her European dispatches. (In Greek myth, Cadmus and Jason must confront a race of fierce earth-born warriors who spring fully grown from the sown teeth of a dragon sacred to the war-god Ares.) Writing from Europe in 1850, Fuller prophesied the continued fighting of the revolutionaries against "the old tyrannies" and asserted: "Their imprisonments and executions of the most generous men, only sow more Hydra teeth; the crop shoots up daily more and more plenteous" (*SG* 278). In *The Scarlet Letter*, inspired in part by Fuller, Hawthorne dramatizes Pearl's combative nature by writing, "She never created a friend, but seemed always to be sowing broadcast the dragon's teeth, whence sprung a harvest of armed enemies, against whom she rushed to battle."[14] Pearl's combative "curse," as Hawthorne calls it, is lifted only in the final scene, when her tears pledged "that she would grow up amid human joy and sorrow, nor for ever do battle with the world, but be a woman in it."[15] Pearl's salvation from a life of conflict and turmoil stands as the major positive outcome of the novel.

In his *Life of Franklin Pierce* (1852), Hawthorne lauded Pierce's peace principles and defended Pierce's support of the Compromise of 1850 (along with the Fugitive Slave Act, which Hawthorne hated as much as others in the North). In the *Life,* Hawthorne includes an account of Pierce's service in the Mexican War ("a gallant soldier in the hour of your country's need") yet works to present him essentially "as a man of peaceful pursuits. 'Cedant arma togae.' ['Let wars yield to peace.']"[16] Like others who voted for the compromise, Pierce hoped thereby to avoid a civil war, a prospect that horrified him. He agreed with Webster, who in his infamous March 7, 1850, speech on behalf of the compromise, asserted, "There can be no such thing as peaceable secession. Peaceable secession is an utter impossibility. . . . I will not state what might produce the disruption of the Union; but, Sir, I see as plainly as I see the sun in heaven what that disruption itself must produce; I see that it must produce war, and such a war as I will not describe."[17] The massive death toll of the Civil War confirmed at least one part of Webster's vision. Whereas Emerson and other antislavery proponents vilified Webster, Clay, and Pierce as morally bankrupt, Hawthorne, who also found the compromise repellent, justified his friend Pierce's support of it by emphasizing the candidate's desire for peace and his love of country. For him, Pierce was no mere political opportunist.

In the group of children's stories entitled *Tanglewood Tales* (1853), which Hawthorne wrote in the months after he completed *Life of Franklin Pierce*, he satirizes those men and monsters who rely on aggression and force rather than intelligence and kindness. In his tale "The Pygmies," he ridicules the militarism of the little men who mindlessly and constantly engage in warfare. He also offers a moral about reason over violence. After describing how Hercules defeated the enraged giant Antaeus (protector of the pygmies) by lifting him off the ground, Hawthorne calls this a "secret . . . it may be well for us all to remember, . . . in case we should ever have to fight a battle with a fellow like Antaeus. For these earthborn creatures are only difficult to conquer on their own ground, but may easily be managed, if we can contrive to lift them into a loftier and purer region."[18] Apparently, Hawthorne felt southerners should be dealt with through civilized means, as Emerson once suggested. The triumph of moral suasion over brute force links "The Pygmies" to the stories that follow. In "The Dragon's Teeth," Hawthorne returns to the myth that had long fascinated him, and he describes the conversion of "earthborn creatures," sprung from dragon's teeth, into wise and peaceable men who help the protagonist, Cadmus, found a city and rule over it with Harmonia, a daughter of the sky. Hawthorne writes that the savage dragon-men are taught by Cadmus "to feel that there was more true enjoyment in living at peace, and doing good to one's neighbor, than in striking at him with a two-edged sword" (1380).

The final Tanglewood tale, "The Golden Fleece," again uses the story of the dragon's teeth to show the mindlessness of civil war (which the radical abolitionists were attempting to ignite). After taming the brazen bulls (who become happy cows), Jason confronts the army of warriors who have sprouted from the ground, "boiling over with the red-hot thirst for battle." When he throws a stone in their midst, to agitate them, they engage in fratricide: "Instead of running any farther towards Jason, they began a fight among themselves. The confusion spread through the host; so that it seemed scarcely a moment before they were all hacking, hewing, and stabbing at one another, lopping off arms, heads, and legs" (1463). Hawthorne thus gives his readers a sense of what a civil war might be like, and to make sure they do not miss his antiwar sentiments, he has Princess Medea tell Jason, "The world will always have simpletons enough, just like them, fighting and dying for they know not what, and fancying that Posterity will take the trouble to put laurel wreaths on their rusty and battered helmets!" (1464). The chivalric ideal that motivated so many of Hawthorne's contemporaries, and that even he drew upon in his treatment of the Mexican War in his *Life of Franklin Pierce,* he here critiques for his young readers.

When the Civil War began, Hawthorne saw the same kind of confusion animating the warring participants. He informed his English friend Francis Bennoch that we "have gone to war, and we seem to have little, or, at least, a very misty idea of what we are fighting for. It depends upon the speaker, and that, again, depends upon the section of the country in which his sympathies are enlisted. The Southern man will say, We fight for state rights, liberty, and independence. The middle and Western states-man will avow that he fights for the Union; whilst our Northern and Eastern man will swear that, from the beginning, his only idea was liberty to the Blacks, and the annihilation of slavery. All are thoroughly in earnest, and all pray for the blessing of Heaven to rest upon the enterprise."[19] The annihilation of slavery was the only cause that Hawthorne thought worth fighting for, and after Lincoln issued the Emancipation Proclamation in September 1862, Hawthorne became more supportive of the war effort. In fact, he opposed any peace agreement that did not result in the elimination of slavery. With some irritation, he wrote his sister-in-law Elizabeth Peabody in July 1863, "You do not in the least shake me by telling me that I shall be supposed to disapprove of the war; for I always thought that it should have been avoided, although, since it has broken out, I have longed for military success as much as any man or woman of the North."[20]

BROWN, CROMWELL, AND THE AMERICAN CLAIMANT

Like many of his fellow countrymen, Hawthorne in the 1850s saw civil war looming on the horizon, especially after passage of the Kansas-Nebraska Act and the remission of Anthony Burns. In a letter to Horatio Bridge of December 14, 1854, he told his friend that the United States had become "so convulsed with party-spirit as it is, so crochetty, so restless, so ill-tempered. From this distance, it looks to me as if there were an actual fissure between the North and the South, which may widen and deepen into a gulf, anon."[21] He also realized that the residual Puritanism of New England animated those most vigorously castigating the South. As the Civil War approached, admiration for the Puritan spirit grew in New England, and more and more writers referenced the Old Testament rather than the New in support of their views. While the southern secessionists made a conscious effort to link their rebellion to the American Revolution of 1776, John Brown reminded New Englanders of their Puritan heritage and the English Revolution of 1642–49, when Oliver Cromwell and his roundheads defeated the cavaliers of King Charles I and beheaded the king. As Moncure Conway later observed, "It appears to me now that there had remained in nearly every Northern breast, however liberal, some unconscious chord which Brown had touched, inherited from the old Puritan spirit and faith in the God of War. I had been brought up in no such faith, but in the belief that evil could be conquered only by regeneration of the evil-doer."[22]

The American Civil War made many New Englanders appreciate even more the virtues represented by Cromwell and Brown—that is, the energy, bravery, and piety both displayed. James Russell Lowell's "Sunthin' in the Pastoral Line," one of the most fierce and funny of his antislavery pieces, appeared in the *Atlantic Monthly* in June 1862, one month before "Chiefly about War-Matters," and in it Hosea Biglow dreams of being visited by his great-great-great grandfather, a Puritan father and former colonel in Cromwell's army, who tells him how to deal with the Southerners:

> 'Smite 'em hip an' thigh!'
> Sez gran'ther, 'an' let every man-child die!
> Oh for three weeks o' Crommie an' the Lord!
> O Israel, to your tents an' grind the sword!'

Hosea argues for the complexity of the war, much as Hawthorne would, by saying,

> The moral question's ollus plain enough,—
> It's jes' the human-natur' side thet's tough;
> Wut's best to think may n't puzzle me nor you,—
> The pinch comes in decidin' wut to *du;*

As a committed abolitionist, Lowell gives the last word to the Puritan warrior, who tells Hosea that the rebellion is merely the rattlesnake's tail, while slavery is "the fangs an' thinkin' head" that must be crushed:

> 'Strike soon,' sez he, 'or you'll be deadly ailin',—
> Folks thet's afeared to fail are sure o' failin';
> God hates your sneakin' creturs thet believe
> He'll settle things they run away an' leave!'
> He brought his foot down fercely, ez he spoke,
> An' give me sech a startle thet I woke.

One of the most insightful of the abolitionist poets, Lowell understood and appreciated the perspective of pacifists and gradualists such as Hawthorne, yet he rejected it. After Hawthorne's death, George W. Curtis, in an 1864 review, pointed out: "The Puritan spirit was neither gracious nor lovely, but nothing softer than its iron hand could have done its necessary work. . . . The moral and physical tenacity which is wrestling with the Rebellion was toughened among these flinty and forbidding rocks."[23]

The transcendentalists saw Brown as an avatar of Cromwell, as I have already pointed out, and according to David Reynolds, they "were *prepared* to support him by their initiation into the Cromwell cult."[24] Sanborn, in his recollection of Brown, observed, "He had, like Cromwell and Spartacus, a certain predestined relation to the political crisis of his time, for which his character fitted him and which, had he striven against it, he could not avoid. Like Cromwell and all the great Calvinists, he was an unquestioning believer in God's fore-ordination and the divine guidance of human affairs; but he was free from the taint of guile that disfigured Cromwell's greatness."[25] Although Cromwell had been "reviled as a murderer and a harsh dictator," Thomas Carlyle had made him "a figure worthy of emulation." According to Reynolds, Brown even kept a copy of Joel Tyler Headley's 1848 biography of Cromwell "on his bookshelf next to the Bible. Headley portrayed Cromwell as a God-directed Calvinist whose murderous tactics were justifiable because they fostered the democratic spirit behind the American Revolution."[26]

Brown's self-fashioning as Cromwell became remarkably effective. Not only did Sanborn, Emerson, and Thoreau identify him as an avatar from "the time of Cromwell" (*RP* 113), but Wendell Phillips did as well in his discourse titled "The Puritan Principle": "Puritanism went up and down England and fulfilled its mission. It revealed despotism. Charles the First and James, in order to rule, were obliged to persecute. Under the guise of what seemed government, they had hidden tyranny. Patriotism tore off the mask, and said to the enlightened conscience and sleeping intellect of England, 'Behold! That is despotism!' It was the first lesson; it was the text of the English Revolution. . . . John Brown has done the same for us to-day."[27]

As is well known, Hawthorne disdained John Brown, calling him a "blood-stained fanatic" who was "justly hanged,"[28] yet there are indications in his later romances that he, too, associated Brown with Cromwell and regarded both with mixed feelings. Perhaps no writer in the country was more steeped in knowledge of Puritan history than Hawthorne, and while he abhorred Puritan cruelty and intolerance, he admired Puritan piety and fortitude. Early in his career, Hawthorne hints at the complex features of Cromwell's democratic righteousness, which could transform into unholy self-righteousness. In "The Gentle Boy" (1831), he indicates this shift most clearly as the good Puritan Tobias Pearson separates himself first from Cromwell and then New England Puritans, eventually becoming a Quaker. We learn that Tobias "had remained in England during the first years of the civil war, in which he had borne some share as a cornet of dragoons, under Cromwell. But when the ambitious designs of his leader began to develop themselves, he quitted the army of the parliament, and sought a refuge from the strife, which was no longer holy, among the people of his persuasion, in the colony of Massachusetts."[29] He soon comes to question the holiness of these intolerant "people" as well.

Some ten years later, in a sketch entitled "Cromwell," in *Biographical Stories for Children* (1842), Hawthorne lauds Cromwell for his battle against the tyranny of the king. He explains, "King Charles had fallen, because, in his manhood the same as when a child, he disdained to feel that every human creature was his brother. He deemed himself a superior being, and fancied that his subjects were created only for a King to rule over. And Cromwell rose, because, in spite of his many faults, he mainly fought for the rights and freedom of his fellow-men; and therefore the poor and the oppressed all lent their strength to him."[30] Cromwell as democratic rebel fighting for oppressed people evoked Hawthorne's approval; Cromwell the ruthless king killer did not.

When Hawthorne set out to write *The Scarlet Letter*, he chose as his historical period 1642–49, the years of the English Civil War, which he used to enhance the treatment of revolutionary themes in the novel and critique the excesses of political radicalism.[31] The decapitated surveyor of the Custom House, victim of "blood-thirsty Whigs," identifies with whoever becomes a martyr upon the scaffold, including Charles I. In *Peter Parley's Universal History on the Basis of Geography*, Hawthorne showed sympathy (perhaps borrowed from his sources) for Charles, as he described his beheading:

The steel-clad soldiers of Cromwell surrounded the scaffold. But the king walked to his death with as firm a step as when he went to his coronation. . . . When King Charles had knelt down and prayed, he cast a pitying glance upon the people round the scaffold; for he feared that direful judgments would come upon the land which was now to be stained with its monarch's blood. He then calmly laid his head upon the block; the executioner raised his axe, and smote off the king's head at a single blow; then lifting it in his hand, he cried aloud, "This is the head of a traitor!" But the people shuddered; for they doubted whether it was the head of a traitor, but they did know that it was the head of a king.[32]

Charles's concern for his people and their respect for him contribute to the sympathetic tone of Hawthorne's account.

In the months before he wrote *The Scarlet Letter*, Hawthorne refreshed his knowledge of this event by reading François Guizot's *History of the English Revolution of 1640, Commonly Called the Great Rebellion* (1846), which emphasizes Cromwell's coarse behavior while signing the king's death warrant: "Gay, noisy, daring as ever, [he] gave way to his usual coarse buffoonery; after having signed himself—he was the third to do so—he smeared with ink Henry Martyn's face who sat beside him and who immediately did the same to him."[33] In contrast, Guizot shows King Charles, on the scaffold, behaving courageously. Andrew Marvell's famous "An Horatian Ode," similarly does as well:

> While round the armèd bands
> Did clap their bloody hands.
> *He* nothing common did nor mean . . .
> But bowed his comely head,
> Down, as upon a bed.[34]

In Hawthorne's novel, at this moment, Arthur Dimmesdale bows "his head forward on the cushions of the pulpit, at the close of his Election Sermon. Meanwhile Hester Prynne [stands] beside the scaffold of the pillory, with the scarlet letter still burning on her breast!"[35] When Arthur joins her on the scaffold and meets his death, as Charles I meets his across the sea, Arthur mirrors the courage and dignity Hester showed in the opening chapters, surrounded by brutish Puritans.

Hawthorne's imagination often returned to that climactic moment in English history when Charles I was beheaded by Puritans acting on behalf of an oppressed people. The moment, which was becoming so relevant in his own country, fascinated and perplexed him. In *True Stories*, written in the spring of 1851, a year after publication of *The Scarlet Letter*, he speculated that Cromwell may have said to himself when Charles was beheaded: "It is a righteous deed. . . . Now Englishmen may enjoy their rights!"[36] The moment gained additional drama for Hawthorne in England when he held in his hands the prayer-book King Charles used on the scaffold. "It opens most readily at the commencement of the Communion Service," Hawthorne observed, "and there, on the left hand page, there is a discoloration about as large as a sixpence, of a yellowish or brownish hue, which, two hundred years ago, and a little more, was doubtless red. For, on that page, had fallen a drop of King Charles's blood."[37]

Bennoch, who was with Hawthorne at the time he held this book, reported that Hawthorne experienced "an intensity of satisfaction,—not pleasure, not delight, but—a sort of thrilling excitement. . . . Of this scene and circumstance Hawthorne frequently spoke, dwelling upon it as one of the facts far exceeding any he had ever imagined."[38] For Hawthorne, it was as if the history he had studied so thoroughly had come to life before his eyes. As for the behavior of Cromwell and his soldiers, Hawthorne also witnessed the results of their iconoclasm and lamented it. At the Lincoln Cathedral, he reported that they "stabled their steeds in the nave, and hacked and hewed the monkish sculptures at their wicked pleasure."[39] As Frederick Newberry has observed, "In England, [Hawthorne] sees more fully than he had imagined to what extremes his forebears had gone to rid themselves of Anglo-Catholic art. They may not have felt deprived, but he certainly does."[40]

The evidence of Cromwell's extremism, the resurgence of a Puritan spirit in New England, representations of Brown as a heroic Cromwellian figure, and the American Civil War itself all encouraged Hawthorne during his final years to revisit in his fiction the scene of the English Civil War, and he focused on the question of whether the killing of an oppressor was righteous or not.[41] In the first version of his claimant story, titled "The Ancestral Footstep," he did not address this issue but instead focused on comparing English and American values. The draft he wrote in Italy in 1858 features a young American who has returned to England to search after his ancestry and perhaps claim an estate and a title. Hawthorne had seen a brown stain in the shape of a human foot at the bottom of a great staircase during a visit to Smithell's Hall in England in 1855 and learned the legend about its being made by the blood of the nonconformist clergyman George Marsh, martyred in 1555. This inspired him to attribute a bloody footstep in his romance to the first emigrant to America who left two hundred years before the returning American claimant arrives.

The image of a bloody footstep lay deep in Hawthorne's imagination, where it symbolized the strife between Puritan righteousness and Quaker martyrdom. In "The Gentle Boy" (1831), he had created an old Quaker who tells of being banished and beaten by Puritans "from village to village, towards the wilderness. A strong and cruel hand was wielding the knotted cords; they sunk deep into the flesh, and thou mightst have tracked every reel and totter of my footsteps by the blood that followed. As we went on — ."[42] In a notebook entry in 1842, Hawthorne made the notation: "The print in blood of a naked foot to be traced through the street of a town."[43] This recurrent bloody image, though gothic in nature, perhaps held personal associations for Hawthorne because, as he explains in "The Custom-House," his own Puritan ancestor had been "a bitter persecutor; as witness the Quakers, who have remembered him in their histories, and relate an incident of his hard severity towards a woman of their sect, which will last longer, it is to be feared, than any record of his better deeds, although these were many."[44] The woman was Ann Coleman who, by order of William Hathorne, was whipped through Salem, Boston, and Dedham, bleeding profusely.[45] In the claimant manuscript, whether the footprint was a sign of aggression or martyrdom Hawthorne could not quite decide.

From July 1860 to July 1861, as Hawthorne worked on the second and third versions of this claimant romance, talk of the American civil war surrounded him, and the contemporary political implications of his materials started to become clear. As Rita Gollin points out, "the footstep signifies 'brotherly hatred and attempted murder.' All are glosses on America's ties to and severance from England, the archetypal fratricide of Cain, and the inherent fratricide of all civil wars."[46] In the two later drafts, called "Etherege" and "Grimshawe," he sets the beginning of the action not in England (as in "The Ancestral Footstep") but in Salem, where the young boy and a girl live in a gloomy old house in Charter Street as wards of a quirky old doctor.

In "Etherege," Hawthorne devotes page after page to ruminations on the nature of the first emigrant and the old pensioner in England, who will befriend the boy when he arrives there as a young man twenty years later. Thoughts of John Brown and of Alcott seem to have floated to the surface of Hawthorne's mind as he struggled to define his characters and their motives. In a long meditation midway through "Etherege," written in the nationally tense winter months of 1860–61, the figure of "a fierce and bloody rebel" enters, and "all harsh roundhead traits shall seem to have been collected in his character."[47] Hawthorne speculates that he is "involved in some guilt of murder or high-treason, or the suspicion of it, which precludes him from returning to England" (12: 114). After asking himself, "What did the emigrant do?," Hawthorne answers himself, "he was the man in the masque who beheaded Charles I" (12: 202). Yet Hawthorne quickly rejects this idea, and transforms him from a bloody Puritan regicide to Quaker pacifist. He writes, "The emigrant must be made out to have been, in that chaos of strange opinions, a man of peace, and a follower and friend of George Fox" (12: 203). The track of blood will thus not signify some secret guilt but instead persecution. "The original emigrant," Hawthorne tells himself, "must have been the model of a Christian, and therefore misunderstood by everybody—therefore maligned—therefore bitterly hated always. . . . He was on the scaffold to support and comfort the dying monarch, to die for him if possible; everywhere, he was sacrificing himself" (12: 204).

Hawthorne had long been fascinated by George Fox, the founder of the Quaker movement. He apparently read Fox's *Journal* at some time in the 1820s, and in "The Virtuoso's Collection" (1842), he refers to him as "perhaps the truest apostle that has appeared on earth for these eighteen hundred years."[48] The notion that a Quaker advocate of peace and compassion could be mistaken for a fierce Puritan rebel was an idea that in Hawthorne's contemporary world attached to the figure of John Brown. The Quaker poet John Greenleaf Whittier captured this duality in his controversial poem "Brown of Osawatomie," where he describes Brown's walk to the gallows past a slave mother:

> Then the bold, blue eye grew tender,
> And the old, harsh face grew mild,
> As he stooped between the jeering ranks
> And kissed the negro's child!

> The shadows of his stormy life
> That moment fell apart:
> Without, the rash and bloody hand,
> Within, the loving heart.
> That kiss, from all its guilty means,
> Redeemed the good intent,
> And round the grisly fighter's hair
> The Martyr's aureole bent![49]

In "Chiefly about War-Matters," Hawthorne acknowledged: "I shall not pretend to be an admirer of old John Brown, any further than sympathy with Whittier's excellent ballad about him may go."[50] His "sympathy" for the poem seems consonant with the conflicted notions about the original emigrant in his claimant romance.

As Hawthorne struggled to decide whether this figure was a violent Puritan or loving Quaker, he also became distressed about the development of this character's descendant, the old pensioner living in a hospital in England. "This wretched old pensioner keeps recurring to me, insisting that I have not sufficiently provided for him, nor given him no time enough—or, any indeed." Hawthorne's character apparently had a personality of his own that the author could not quite understand. "There must be something in this old man," Hawthorne wrote to himself, "that shall put to shame hereditary distinction, and make the reader feel that he must have stooped from a position of higher dignity, had he taken up the rank he had inherited" (12: 219). With the issue of the "higher law" in mind, Hawthorne writes, "The Pensioner inherits the religious spirit of his ancestor; a mild, gentle, sweet, unyieldingness of character, which has always distinguished this branch of the family. . . . He has made no impression on the world, being of too mild and meek a spirit, though he has the possibility of a martyr in him, as his forefather had. Perhaps his forefather was hanged by the Puritans—I think so" (12: 334). In a concluding note to himself, Hawthorne adds, "He might be a Fifth Monarchy Man; that is to say, obedient to the higher law within himself, and rejecting human law when it interfered. In figure, Mr. Alcott" (12: 335).

Despite his avoidance of the Alcotts, Hawthorne was apparently fascinated by Bronson, whose personality he liked but whose politics he questioned. The fact that Thoreau admired Alcott inordinately probably contributed to Hawthorne's uncertainty about him. In the "Hall of Fantasy" (1843), he describes him as "this great mystic innovator. So calm and gentle was he, so holy in aspect, so quiet in the utterance of what his soul brooded upon, that one might readily conceive his Orphic Sayings to well upward from a fountain in his breast, which communicated with the infinite abyss of Thought."[51] In a facetious poem he wrote in the fall of 1861, Hawthorne was less kind:

> There dwelt a Sage at Apple Slump
> Whose dinner never made him plump;
> Give him carrots, potatoes, squash, parsnips and peas,
> And some boiled macaroni without any cheese,
> And a plate of raw apples to hold on his knees,
> And a glass of sweet cider to wash down all these;
> And he'd prate of the Spirit as long as you'd please—
> This airy Sage of Apple Slump![52]

While obviously amused by Alcott, Hawthorne came to believe that his devotion to "the higher law" could prove dangerous, as his support of John Brown and eagerness to go to war had shown. When Rebecca Harding Davis visited Concord in the spring of 1862, after Hawthorne's tour of the front lines, she recorded a scene that reveals Hawthorne's bemused attitude toward his neighbors' combined mildness and bloodlust. During a conversation that took place in the parlor at the Wayside involving Alcott, Emerson, and Hawthorne, Davis registered shock at what she heard. Alcott apparently held forth about the beneficial results of the war, which he characterized as "an armed angel . . . wakening the nation to a lofty life unknown before," while Emerson bowed his head in approval, and Hawthorne looked on with "laughing, sagacious eyes" that were "full of mockery."[53] Davis identified with Hawthorne, whom she calls "an alien among these men, not of their kind," and in her memoirs she asserts, "I had just come up from the border where I had seen the actual war, the filthy spewing of it; the political jobbery in Union and Confederate camps, the malignant personal hatreds wearing patriotic masks, and glutted by burning homes and outraged women. . . . This would-be seer [Alcott] who was talking of [the war], and the real seer [Emerson] who listened, knew no more of war as it was, than I had done in my cherry-tree when I dreamed of bannered legions of crusaders debouching in the misty fields."[54]

In Hawthorne's claimant manuscripts, he tried to capture how he felt about such a well-meaning yet dangerous person as Alcott. In an aside to himself about the pensioner, Hawthorne writes, "He is partially crazed; yet in a benevolent way, and so as to craze all that associates with him, having a great spiritual fever queerly done up with his weakness and folly. I can't get hold of it. I will" (12: 220). Several sentences later, he writes, "A certain property shall attend him wherever he goes; a bloody footstep. Pshaw! He shall have the fatality of causing death, bloodshed, wherever he goes; and this shall symbolize the strife which benevolence inevitably provokes, because it disturbs everything around it. Make this out" (12: 220). As a background, Hawthorne tells himself that the pensioner must have been a peddler, a pauper, an American rambling in quest of his country, yet there must also be "Secret mischief—bloody consequences connected with his mild and beautiful nature" (12: 220–21). These consequences remain unspecified in "Etherege."

In "Grimshawe," the third and final draft of his claimant romance, Hawthorne tried to solve the problems of characterization he was facing by letting both legends about the first emigrant stand through the introduction of a new character named, significantly, Seymour, also modeled on Alcott. Dr. Grimshawe, now a more cruel figure, relates the negative legend of the first emigrant; Seymour the more favorable legend. Seymour, a Yankee schoolteacher, turns out to be the old pensioner twenty years before he is encountered in England. As Edward Davidson has pointed out, Seymour, also known as Colcord (Concord), is "a remarkable portrait of Bronson Alcott" (see figure 6).[55]

FIGURE 6. Amos Bronson Alcott. Bettmann/ CORBIS.

Hawthorne describes Seymour as "a person of singularly impressive presence; a thin, mild looking man, with a peculiar look of delicacy and natural refinement about him, . . . plain in dress, and simple in manner; not giving the idea of remarkable intellectual gifts, but with a kind of spiritual aspect, fair, clear complexion, gentle eyes. . . . He looked middle-aged, and yet there was a kind of childlike, simple expression, which . . . would make you suppose him much younger" (12: 386–87). Seymour appears on the scene as Doctor Grimshawe is being attacked by a violent mob in the streets of Salem. He stands in front of Grimshawe, calls out "Christian men, what would you do! Peace! Peace!," and is knocked down unconscious. Taken to the doctor's home, he tells his story about his bloodied ancestor.

In Seymour's version, the emigrant is the mild second son of a fierce Catholic father. After becoming one of the earliest Quakers converted by George Fox and marrying a young lady loved by his eldest brother, he is kidnapped, imprisoned, and tortured by a Jesuit priest, who crushes his foot. After escaping, he flees to America and is joined there by his son, whom his wife sends to him before she dies (12: 395). "There are two ways of telling that legend" (12: 421), remarked the doctor, and Hawthorne realized that his inability to resolve the differences between the two versions arrests the progression of his narrative, not to mention the weaknesses contributed by all the gothic machinery he finds himself shoveling into the plot, especially as the draft nears its end in England. As James Mellow has pointed out, Hawthorne became "lost in a thicket of possibilities, unable to find his way out."[56] His inability to get a fix on the motives and morality of the first emigrant and his puzzlement about the Christ-like pensioner Colcord especially frustrated him. Grimshawe, after observing Colcord's gentleness and weakness, is said to know "scarcely, whether to despise the man in whom he saw them, or yield to a strange sense of reverence" (12: 390), and the remark surely reveals much about Hawthorne's conflicted attitude toward the advocates of righteous violence living in Concord.

ELIXIR OF LIFE MANUSCRIPTS

Soon after Fort Sumter was fired upon in April 1861 and the Civil War began, Hawthorne abandoned his claimant romance and turned to another, set in Concord at the beginning of the American Revolution and focused on the search for the elixir of life. When the protagonist thinks he has concocted this elixir, of course, it proves poisonous rather than salvific. Not coincidentally, in a July 20, 1863, letter to Elizabeth Peabody, Hawthorne lamented "the potent elixir of political opinions" she had imbibed from the abolitionist newspapers,[57] for they too, in his eyes, brought death and destruction to the country and hardship to the freed slaves. To seek the secret to earthly immortality in the midst of political upheaval was the task he gave his young protagonist named Septimius. Yet whether this was an admirable task or a foolish and unpatriotic one was a question he could never decide. He again became stymied as he sought to determine whether his protagonist should show a commitment to war or to peace—that is, to violent engagement or pacific detachment.

He begins the narrative on April 18, 1775, the day before the British marched into Concord and confronted the militia at the Old North Bridge. At first, Septimius, studying for the ministry, remains an observer of the frenetic activities of his neighbors as they prepare for battle, and Hawthorne claims that his romance will focus on internal rather than external events. "Our story," he writes, "is an internal one, dealing as little as possible with outward events, and taking hold of these only when it cannot be helped, in order by means of them to delineate the history of a mind bewildered in certain errors."[58] Yet the war constantly intrudes upon the minds of all, including Septimius. Hawthorne relates that "Horsemen galloped past the line of farm-houses shouting alarm! There were stories of marching troops coming like dreams through the midnights" (13: 15). He then emphasizes the intoxication such a scene can generate and compares it to his own historical moment: "It was a good time, everybody felt, to be alive, a nearer kindred, a closer sympathy between man and man; a sense of the goodness of the world, of the sacredness of country, of the excellence of life; . . . The ennobling of brute force; the feeling that it had its godlike side; the drawing of heroic breath amid the scenes of ordinary life, so that it seemed as if they had all been transfigured since yesterday. Oh, high, heroic, tremulous juncture, when man felt himself almost an angel; on the verge of doing deeds that outwardly look so fiendish! Oh, strange rapture of the coming battle! We know something of that time now . . ." (13: 15). While capturing the tension between thought and feeling caused by the rebellion, Hawthorne also hints at the loss of free will also involved. He almost suggests that it is a god of war sweeping up the people in a mock religious conversion: "[We have] felt how a great impulse lifts up a people, and every cold, passionless, indifferent spectator, —lifts him into religion, and makes him join in what becomes an act of devotion, a prayer, when perhaps he but half approves" (13: 16–17). The final clause of the statement puts all that precedes it under a cloud of doubt.

Doubt about the morality of the war fever in Concord grows in the narrative as the British soldiers enter the town. Septimius and a young neighbor girl, Rose, his love interest, stand their ground and humanize the British through their dialogue: "'O heavens, Mr. Felton!' whispered Rose, 'why should we shoot these men, or they us? They look kind, if homely. Each of them has a mother and sister, I suppose, just like our men.'" Septimius agrees that "It is the strangest thing in the world that we can think of killing them. Human life is so precious" (13: 19). Their mutual friend and neighbor, Robert Hagburn, however, spoils for a fight and becomes caught up in the contagion of the moment, going off to join the revolution. He becomes susceptible to the "news of the battle that had gone rolling onward along the hitherto peaceful country road, converting everywhere (this demon of war, we mean), with one blast of its red sulphurous breath, the peaceful husbandman to a soldier thirsting for blood" (13: 31).

Septimius, too, succumbs to the "demon of war" when he kills a British soldier in a face-to-face confrontation on the hillside behind his house. After burying this young gentleman (who, out of a sense of kinship, has given him papers with clues to making the elixir), "Septimius wondered at the easiness with which he acquiesced in this deed; in fact, he felt in a slight degree the effects of that taste of blood, which makes the slaying of men, like any other abuse, sometimes become a passion. Perhaps it was his Indian trait stirring in him again; at any rate, it is not delightful to observe how readily man becomes a blood-shedding animal" (13: 35). Hawthorne thus presents war as an unfortunate event that even a scholar training for the ministry cannot escape. "War," he writes, "had filled the whole brain of the people, and enveloped the whole thought of man in a mist of gunpowder" (13: 43).

Once the revolution has begun, Hawthorne stages a key debate between Septimius and the local minister, who sounds much like Krishna in the Bhagavad Gita. He tells Septimius, "Go to the wars, and do a valiant part for your country and come back to your peaceful mission when the enemy has vanished" (13: 44). When Septimius demurs, the minister insists, "Pray for success before a battle, help win it with sword or gun, and gives thanks to God, kneeling on the bloody field; at its close" (13: 44). Septimius, however, is "inclined to think that women and clergymen are, in matters of war, the most uncompromising and bloodthirsty of the community" (13: 44), and he replies to the minister that "he was of opinion that war was a business in which a man could not engage with safety to his conscience, unless his conscience actually drove him into it; and that this made all the difference between heroic battle and murderous strife" (13: 45). Hawthorne thus denies righteousness to killing for political, as opposed to moral, reasons.

In Hawthorne's narrative, Septimius acquires a burden of guilt for killing the young British officer in an unnecessary duel. Hawthorne then constructs a scene that puts Septimius's character at a turning point, as he looks down upon the houses of Rose and Hagburn and wonders if those two, rather than he and Rose, should be together. At this point, Hawthorne has yet to decide how to proportion the reader's regard for the three, and his indecision grows out of the politically violent context in which he has placed them and in which, in 1862, he found himself.

As he rewrites in the draft titled "Septimius Norton," he decides to make Rose Septimius's sister, rather than his fiancée, and he adds depth and maturity to Robert Hagburn's character as he subtracts these qualities from Septimius's. In fact, his young scholar becomes fanatical in his quest to discover the formula of the elixir. In a key scene, Hawthorne allows Robert, now home from the battlefront, to criticize Septimius's behavior, and the author's as well. Robert enters a decorated officer, "and certainly there was a kind of authority in his look and manner, indicating that heavy responsibilities, critical moments, had educated him, and turned the ploughboy into a man" (13: 114). This new man then observes the change in Septimius and declares, "I never saw such a discontented, unhappy-looking fellow as you are. You have had a harder time in peace than I in war. You have not found what you seek, whatever that may be. . . . If war is holy work, a priest may lawfully do it, as well as pray for it. Come with us, my old friend Septimius, be my comrade" (13: 115). When Septimius resists this suggestion, Robert directs a telling criticism at Hawthorne, his creator, as well as at Septimius: "This is not a generation for study, and the making of books; that may come by and by. This great fight has need of all men to carry it on, in one way or another; and no man will do well, even for himself, who tries to avoid his share in it" (13: 116).

Hawthorne's inveterate skepticism and pacifism surely made it repugnant to write such a self-critical scene. Yet he knew that not to become passionately involved in a "great fight," whether the American Revolution or the Civil War, left one open to the charge of treason, the thought of which tormented him. As Brenda Wineapple observes, "Though Hawthorne wanted somehow to participate in the war, he also wanted to shut it out. So he watched."[59] And the more he watched, the more frustrated and guilty he felt. Before he abandoned the manuscript, he described Septimius's home in Concord, which was also his home, as "a more forlorn and wretched place than he could endure; a dismal dungeon, and his hillside, a growth of gloomy pines, among which he would gaze around seeking one on which to hang himself" (13: 447). A page later, the manuscript abruptly stops, as the protagonist contemplates "the readiest passage out of [his] existence" (13: 448). Hawthorne's pacifism had taken its toll.

TREASON AND WAR MATTERS

When Hawthorne put the manuscript of Septimius aside in the spring of 1862, the issue of treason was much on his mind, and he knew what a sensitive issue it was. In his essay "Chiefly about War-Matters," he begins by speaking about himself the way Hagburn speaks about Septimius. The war, he writes, compelled him to suspend "such unsubstantial business" as "the contemplation of certain fantasies," and he "magnanimously considered that there is a kind of treason in insulating one's self from the universal fear and sorrow, and thinking one's idle thoughts in the dread time of civil war." He had spent a month touring the area around Washington, D.C., at the invitation of his friend Horatio Bridge, a commodore working in the city. He visited Alexandria, Fort Ellsworth, Harpers Ferry, Fortress Monroe, and Manassas. He saw General McClellan reviewing the troops and encountered refugee slaves making their way north. The essay he wrote on his return, "Chiefly about War-Matters," appeared in the *Atlantic Monthly,* under the byline "By a Peaceable Man," and the word "treason" sounds like a drumbeat throughout. In the account of his visit to Alexandria, he addresses the so-called "treason" of the rebel soldiers and points out that it arose "not from any real zeal for the cause, but because, between two conflicting loyalties, they chose that which necessarily lay nearest the heart. There never existed any other government, against which treason was so easy, and could defend itself by such plausible arguments, as against that of the United States."[60] Hawthorne also defends General McClellan, the cautious commander of the Union army, from the charges of "treasonable purposes" by describing his bearing and the troops' support of him: "If he is a coward, or a traitor, or a humbug, or anything less than a brave, true, and able man, that mass of intelligent soldiers, whose lives and honor he had in charge, were utterly deceived, and so was this present writer; for they believed in him, and so did I" (23: 424).

When he returned from his various excursions to Washington, D.C., Hawthorne observed in the hall and parlors of Willard's Hotel "a miscellany of people," including governors, generals, statesmen, orators, "office-seekers, wire-pullers, inventors, artists, poets, prosers," and so on (23: 438), and he recalls that "The question often occurred to me,—and, to say the truth, it added an indefinable piquancy to the scene—what proportion of all these people, whether soldiers or civilians, were true at heart to the Union, and what part were tainted, more or less, with treasonable sympathies and wishes, even if such had never blossomed into purpose" (23: 441). He denounces actual traitors but explains the perspective of southern sympathizers: "They have a conscientious, though mistaken belief, that the South was driven out of the Union by intolerable wrong on our part, and that we are responsible for having compelled true patriots to love only half their country, instead of the whole, and brave soldiers to draw their swords against the Constitution which they would once have died for" (23: 441). He ends the essay by saying if a "truer union" cannot be won, then let the South go, like Lucifer and his rebel angels, making heaven "perhaps all the more heavenly," but his fictional "editor" has the last word, attacking the author's "kindness": "We should be sorry to cast a doubt on the Peaceable Man's loyalty, but he will allow us to say that we consider him premature in his kindly feelings towards traitors and sympathizers with treason" (23: 442). In a letter to the editor, James T. Fields, about the essay, Hawthorne half-facetiously declared, "I found it quite difficult not to lapse into treason continually; but I made manful resistance to the temptation."[61] A number of readers, including his neighbors, thought he failed.

Although Hawthorne assumed the controversial persona of "A Peaceable Man," he should not have been categorized as a Peace Democrat, that is, a southern sympathizer who wished to end the war and return to the status quo. Rather, he should be aligned with the Quakers, who opposed the war based on principle, not politics. There were two advocates for peace before and during the Civil War, and the Quakers made it clear in articles they wrote for public consumption that their stance did not put them in sympathy with the Peace Democrats, also known as Copperheads. In an article titled "Misconceptions of Peace," one Quaker wrote: "The friends of our cause have come of late to be confounded in some minds with a set of demagogues and their partisans, misnamed 'peace men.' Peace men! Yet in sympathy and collusion, if not in active alliance, with a rebellion, second in magnitude and atrocity only to that of Satan against the throne of God!"[62]

Like the Quakers, Hawthorne detested slavery and had no desire to make peace with the South if it were not abolished. In this sense, he was not unlike Emerson, who foresaw the dangers of the Peace Democrats in the North. Without emancipation, the thousands of men killed in the war would have died in vain. In a July 20, 1863, letter to Elizabeth Peabody, Hawthorne points out to her that unless the South is totally defeated, slavery will persist. Recent northern successes, he explains,

> will suggest to the rebels that their best hope lies in the succor of the Peace Democrats of the North, whom they have heretofore scorned, and by amalgamation with whom I really think that the old Union might be restored, and slavery prolonged for another hundred years, with new bulwarks; while the people of the North would fancy that they had got the victory, and never know that they had shed their blood in vain, and so would become peace Democrats to a man. . . . You cannot possibly conceive (looking through spectacles of the tint which yours have acquired) how little the North really cares for the negro-question, and how eagerly it would grasp at peace if recommended by a delusive show of victory. Free soil was never in so great danger as now.[63]

Although Hawthorne throughout his career considered slavery but one of a multitude of evils afflicting mankind, he came to believe during the Civil War that it had to be destroyed, despite the cost of the war in lives and suffering. Like Emerson and Douglass, he abandoned his peace principles while still clinging to his self-image as a peaceable man. In the last written work he was able to complete, *Our Old Home*, he attempted to reenvision the war and war fever by raising them to a moral plane he admired. Comparing the American public with the English one, he writes, "Our excitements are not impulsive, like theirs, but, right or wrong, are moral and intellectual. For example, the grand rising of the North, at the commencement of this war, bore the aspect of impulse and passion only because it was so universal, and necessarily done in a moment. . . . We were cool then, and have been cool ever since, and shall remain cool to the end, which we shall take coolly, whatever it may be."[64] Hawthorne thus transforms the unwieldy "demon of war" of "Septimius Felton" into a "grand rising," coolly done. One wonders if he believed what he wrote. In any case, he clearly tried to make peace with his neighbors and himself before he died.

When a patched-together version of *Septimius Felton*, edited by Hawthorne's daughter Una, was published in 1872, Higginson, in an otherwise favorable review, critiqued Hawthorne's treatment of political violence in the book. He faulted Hawthorne's lack of emphasis on self-sacrifice, "which might have kept the book within the pale of warm human sympathies."[65] He apparently wanted Hawthorne to endow Septimius with the ferocity and even fanaticism he admired in Brown: "Why should not the love of his fellow-men have entered largely into the original dreams of Septimius? Might there not have been an element of sentimental fanaticism, if you please, introduced as the motive power, and subtly intertwined with egotism, as we often see it in life?" (102). Citing their mutual friend Margaret Fuller, Higginson asserts that Hawthorne should have explained and condemned Septimius's antiwar attitudes: "I waive the moral question; but it seems to me irresistibly clear that this is a defect of art. It was one of the profound critical sayings of Margaret Fuller Ossoli, that we need in fiction to 'hear the excuses men make to themselves for their worthlessness'" (103).

Even in his favorable comments on the book, Higginson seems to impugn Hawthorne's pacifism: he quotes a passage and writes, "In the whole literature of our civil strife there is no more vivid description than this of the way the sounds of a skirmish pass away into the distance; and yet it is the work of a peaceful novelist, who sits down at the wayside to describe a scene in the Revolutionary War" (102). Higginson's subtext here is that while he (Higginson) had been on the battlefield experiencing warfare, Hawthorne had been merely sitting in his study imagining it. The compliment anticipates the criticism leveled at Hawthorne for years after his death.[66] Whereas Emerson, Fuller, Douglass, Thoreau, and even Alcott were praised for their militant ardor, Hawthorne was accused of escapism, cowardice, and proslavery sympathies.

It seems an inconsistency to assert unconditional democracy in all things, and yet confess a dislike to all mankind—in the mass. But not so.

—MELVILLE, letter to Hawthorne, June 1851

CHAPTER SEVEN

The Revolutionary Times of Melville's *Billy Budd*

In many ways, Herman Melville's attitude toward political violence coincided with Nathaniel Hawthorne's. Like Hawthorne, he possessed a constitutional aversion to social and political upheaval. Yet it was the French Revolution of 1789, as opposed to the English Rebellion of 1642, that especially fascinated him and informed his belief that violence and warfare resulted from the primeval savageness of mankind.[1] In *White-Jacket*, he observed that "the whole matter of war is a thing that smites common sense and Christianity in the face; so every thing connected with it is utterly foolish, unchristian, barbarous, brutal, and savoring of the Feejee Islands, cannibalism, saltpeter, and the devil."[2] Melville's *Battle-Pieces and Aspects of the War* (1866), his collection of poems about the Civil War, makes many of the same points as Hawthorne's "Chiefly about War-Matters," especially in Melville's prose supplement. There he argues for compassion toward one's enemy, and with the radical Republicans in mind, he rejects self-righteousness and revenge: "Zeal is not of necessity religion, neither is it always of the same essence with poetry or patriotism."[3]

In his notes to *Battle Pieces*, he compares misgivings about the war to "the eclipse which came over the promise of the French Revolution" (150); yet despite these misgivings, he supports the Union cause and exults in the downfall of slavery. In the war's aftermath, he, like Hawthorne, warns his readers of unintended consequences, especially regarding emancipation: "Benevolent desires, after passing a certain point, cannot undertake their own fulfillment without incurring the risk of evils beyond those sought to be remedied" (163). He gives as an example a race war: "In our natural solicitude to confirm the benefit of liberty to the blacks, let us forbear from measures of dubious constitutional rightfulness toward our white countrymen — measures of a nature to provoke, among other of the last evils, exterminating hatred of race toward race." For him, avoiding the outbreak of additional fighting was a primary concern at the time.[4]

Like Hawthorne, he was criticized for his pacifism by radical Republicans. "Gentlemen of Mr. Melville's class," a reviewer for the *New York Independent* declared, "are mischievous men in these troubled times. Only absolute justice is safe. Peaceable, by all means peaceable, in God's name; but *first pure*, in God's name, also."[5] The search for "absolute justice," Melville knew, and *Moby-Dick* illustrates, was fraught with physical and psychological danger. Nothing in his late career caused him to relinquish his pacifism or his aversion to political violence. In the turbulent 1880s, when he returned to prose fiction with *Billy Budd*, he revisited for the last time the issues of peace and warfare, revolution and established authority, which had long concerned him, and dramatized the value and cost of a conservative stance toward them.

LABOR UNREST

Despite the nostalgia that permeates Melville's last collection of poems, *John Marr and Other Sailors* (1888), the contemporary strikes and riots that unsettled America surely caught his attention. Current events had always interested him, and in the last decades of his life, he had ample opportunity to follow them. He lived in the country's largest city; he read its papers; he walked its streets. From 1866 to 1885 he was a district inspector of customs in New York City, working first along the North River Waterfront at 207 West Street, then at 62 Harrison Street (which was nearer his home at 104 East 26th Street), and finally at 76th Street and the East River. As he began *Billy Budd* early in 1886 by writing the prose headnote to the ballad "Billy in the Darbies," labor unrest broke out near at hand.

In March 1886 the city was disrupted by a series of violent streetcar strikes, which led to massive police action against the strikers (see figure 7). During the first week of March, New York horse-car drivers and conductors tied up every major road in the city, from the Battery to East 34th Street. After attempts to run a car through Grand Street failed when strikers blocked the tracks with lumber, bricks, barrels, and cobblestones, city officials called out the police, and 750 of them escorted the same car along its route, encountering opposition from workers and their sympathizers. At Eldrige Street, when a baggage truck was overturned to block the way, the police charged the crowd, and according to one report, "With wild cries of alarm the crowd scattered in all directions, a few badly clubbed, some injured by being trampled upon, while show windows were smashed, and hats and bonnets were strewn on the street as the result of the fray."[6] The striking drivers and the railroad company reached an agreement the following day, yet the "labor agitation" persisted in the months that followed.

The sensational bombing in Haymarket Square in Chicago—and the trial and hanging of four anarchists found guilty of provoking the violence—riveted the attention of Americans at the time and found its way into Melville's fiction. "The similarities of historical moment—of mass unrest and challenges to authority, of issues brought to law and settled by authorized force—resound too insistently to be ignored," as Alan Trachtenberg has pointed out.[7] Moreover, distinctive features of the Haymarket affair—the harsh justice, the scapegoating, the death by hanging—have persuaded several critics that this event served as a particular source for Melville's narrative.[8] Like the Haymarket defendants, Billy is an innocent man hanged to preserve order during a time of revolutionary strife. Whether, like them, he is also the victim of a biased judge and unfair trial, however, remains an open question. Critical con-

FIGURE 7. T. De Thulstrup, *The Street Railroad Strike in New York — The Police Opening the Way for a Horsecar.* From *Harper's Weekly* 30 (March 13, 1886): 168–69.

troversy has long surrounded Melville's authority figure, Captain Vere, a learned man, like Melville, with that "bias toward those books to which every serious mind of superior order occupying any active post of authority in the world naturally inclines."[9]

On the one hand, one can argue that Vere prejudges the case against Billy, uses irregular proceedings to convict him, and then executes him in a gross miscarriage of justice. On the other, one can argue that Vere, though filled with compassion for Billy, acts with a heroic presence of mind during a crisis, preserving the social order by an act of stern yet necessary justice. Milton Stern has been the most prominent advocate for this second view, and he has persuasively argued that "in *Billy Budd*, with many modifications and exceptions, with anger and depression, Melville is making a tortured choice for conservatism."[10] Vere's conservative rationale for hanging Billy, of course, is that it will silence and tame the sailors, who otherwise will take the captain's inaction as a sign of weakness and an excuse to rebel. "You know what sailors are," Vere says, in response to the Sailing Master's suggestion of clemency. "Will they not revert to the recent outbreak at the Nore? Ay. They know the well-founded alarm — the panic it struck throughout England. Your clement sentence they would account pusillanimous. They would think that we flinch, that we are afraid of them — afraid of practising a lawful rigor singularly demanded at this juncture, lest it should provoke new troubles" (112–13). Although a number of critics have perceived irony at work here, Melville's earlier treatments of revolutionary action suggest that he linked it with anarchy and bloodshed. In other words, he shared Vere's conviction that "with mankind, forms, measured forms are everything" (128), and he applied this to disruptions at home and abroad throughout his life.

MELVILLE'S POLITICS

Melville's political views were complex and at times self-contradictory, for they involved an "unconditional democracy" based on faith in man in the ideal and a conservative elitism based on distrust for the mass of mankind.[11] Melville's democracy obviously figures prominently in *Billy Budd*, especially in the portrayal of Billy as an ideal common sailor, "an angel of God" (101), at times transfigured like Christ. Nevertheless, his conservatism also informs the novel, especially in the positive portrayal of Vere as a humane and rational captain struggling to do what is right in a world that is wrong. In many respects the novel dramatizes the dilemma posed in the famous "The Journey and the Pamphlet" chapter of *Pierre* (1852), where Melville elaborates upon the difficulties of reconciling celestial (chronometrical) time with terrestrial (horological) time — Heaven and Earth, the Ideal and the Actual. As the pamphlet states, "he who finding in himself a chronometrical soul, seeks practically to force that heavenly time upon the earth; in such an attempt he can never succeed, with an absolute and essential success."[12] Absolutists such as Ahab and Pierre exemplify the truth of this assertion, of course. And although Melville himself could identify with such characters, he also appreciated the reserve and moderation some men displayed in a crisis. Vere must confront the momentous question of whether to execute a morally innocent man in order to secure the welfare of his ship, his nation, and civilized society. Because he inhabits a fallen world, his decision must accord with earthly realities or be doomed to failure.

Melville had served as a common sailor himself aboard five different ships during 1839–44, and in his early writings, *White-Jacket* (1850) especially, he vigorously affirms the inherent dignity and equality of the common sailors and castigates naval officers who abuse their authority and deny sailors their basic human rights. Flogging, in particular, he represents as a bloody and reprehensible practice. His character White-Jacket contemplates suicide and murder when confronted with the possibility that he might be flogged. Nevertheless, Melville also describes the depravity and ignorance of the "people" and shows disdain toward them. He reserves his highest regard for grand and glowing individuals, such as Jack Chase, who possess superior social, moral, and intellectual gifts. "[W]e have seen that a man-of-war is but this old-fashioned world of ours afloat," White-Jacket observes, "full of all manner of characters—full of strange contradictions; and though boasting some fine fellows here and there, yet, upon the whole, charged to the combings of her hatchways with the spirit of Belial and all unrighteousness" (390).

In *Moby-Dick* (1851), the two sides of Melville's political thought come to the fore when Ishmael declares, "take high abstracted man alone; and he seems a wonder, a grandeur, and a woe. But . . . take mankind in mass, and for the most part, they seem a mob of unnecessary duplicates."[13] For Melville, the dark side of mankind surfaced most noticeably and frighteningly during riots, mutinies, rebellions, and revolutions. Although it can be argued that Starbuck should have saved the crew of the *Pequod* by murdering Ahab in his sleep or leading a mutiny against him, the role of deadly rebel was Ahab's alone, and it apparently cost him his soul. Hell, at least, seems his destination.

Since the beginning of Melville's career as a writer, political violence had fascinated him (see the murderous end of *Typee*), but like most of his countrymen, he regarded it warily, even when oppression and injustice were clearly its cause. In *White-Jacket*, he concludes, "Oh, shipmates and world-mates, all round! We the people suffer many abuses. . . . Yet the worst of our evils we blindly inflict upon ourselves; our officers can not remove them, even if they would. . . . Whatever befall us, let us never train our murderous guns inboard; let us not mutiny with bloody pikes in our hands" (399–400). *Moby-Dick* can be read as his most emotional treatment of self-destructive rebellion (the red flag of revolt signals Ahab's violent radicalism), while *Billy Budd* is his most sustained analysis of the difficulties inherent in suppressing such action.

During his early career, scenes from the French Revolution of 1789 were fresh in his mind, thanks to stories heard in his youth, from his Uncle Thomas especially, who was a banker in Paris during 1795–1811. The revolution possessed for Melville an immediacy and reality that have been lost to us due to the passage of time. The French revolutions of 1848 and 1871 reawakened memories of the "Reign of Terror" and provided their own dramas of violence and bloodshed that Melville and other Americans found appalling. The political allegory he added to *Mardi* (1849) in response to the European revolutions of 1848 contains an explicit anticipation of the treatment of French and English radicalism in *Billy Budd*. When the Mardian travelers approach Franko (France) in the earlier work, they see a violent eruption accompanied by the din of warfare, showers of embers, and whirling blasts. "The fiery storm from Franko, kindled new flames in the distant valleys of Porpheero [Europe]," Melville writes, "while driven over from Verdanna came frantic shouts, and direful jubilees. Upon Dominora [England] a baleful glare was resting." Media, the king, cries, "See! how the flames blow over upon Dominora!" while the philosopher Babbalanja answers, "Yet the fires they kindle there are soon extinguished. No, no; Dominora ne'er can burn with Franko's fires; only those of her own kindling may consume her."[14] In *Billy Budd*, Melville reuses this fire imagery as he describes the Nore mutiny: "Reasonable discontent growing out of practical grievances in the fleet had been ignited into irrational combustion as by live cinders blown across the Channel from France in flames" (54).

The distinction between "reasonable discontent" and "irrational combustion" made in both cases points to a key aspect of Melville's political thought. For him, practical grievances and reasonable discontent needed to be addressed through reform; when they burst into "irrational combustion" or revolution, his sympathy turned to antipathy. His support for reform never developed into support for insurrectionary violence; rather, he urged readers to value existential reality over abstract principles when it came to the revolutionary trinity of *liberté, égalité,* and *fraternité.* In *Mardi,* Melville comments upon the Paris workers' revolt of June 1848 by introducing a mysterious scroll that expresses a number of Burkean reflections on recent events. This scroll asserts, "Better, on all hands that peace should rule with a scepter, than the tribunes of the people should brandish their broadswords. Better be the subject of a king, upright and just; than a freeman in Franko, with the executioner's ax at every corner" (527). Violence brings only harm, the scroll maintains: although "great reforms, of a verity, be needed; nowhere are bloody revolutions required. Though it be the most certain of remedies, no prudent invalid opens his veins, to let out his disease with his life" (529). The travelers in *Mardi* accuse one another of being the scroll's author, but Melville terms it "a Voice from the Gods" (523).

Melville's response to the Astor Place Riots in May 1849 was consistent with his response to revolutions abroad. Along with forty-seven prominent citizens of New York City, he signed a letter of support for the British actor William Charles Macready, whose appearance at the Astor Place Opera House was protested by members of New York's laboring classes, supporters of Macready's archrival, the American actor Edwin Forrest. On the evening of May 10, a mob of ten to twenty thousand gathered to disrupt Macready's performance in *Macbeth;* when they threw rocks and invaded the theater, the militia opened fire, and some 31 persons were killed and 150 wounded. The letter Melville signed assured Macready "that the good sense and respect for order prevailing in this community will sustain you on the subsequent nights of your performance."[15] As Dennis Berthold has persuasively argued, "The Astor Place riot was an explosion of class conflict in which Melville found himself on the side of cosmopolitanism and vested authority against the forces of nationalism and Jacksonian democracy."[16] Melville's family lived dangerously close to the site where the second night of rioting occurred, which probably added to his support of those authorities trying to suppress the violence.[17]

A decade later, when civil war broke out, it seemed a bloody rebellion to many in the North, and Melville, who joined a local militia in Pittsfield, Massachusetts, offered conservative reflections upon it in his

Battle-Pieces.[18] Several of his poems express a Vere-like commitment to law and order as he indicts the forces of rebellion. "Dupont's Round Fight," for example, which treats the battle fought at Port Royal Sound, South Carolina, on November 7, 1861, ends with the declaration:

> The rebel at Port Royal felt
> The Unity overawe,
> And rued the spell. A type was here,
> And victory of LAW.[19]

A comparable poem, "The House-Top, a Night Piece," treats the New York draft riots of 1863, when hundreds of (mostly Irish) laborers set fires, attacked, beat, mutilated, and killed blacks and their supporters throughout the city. After five days, federal troops, using artillery, were able to quell the rioting. In his poem, Melville (who was not in the city at the time) assumes an elevated view of the masses who give voice to "the Atheist roar of riot," and illuminate themselves by "red Arson," until the militia, "wise Draco," arrives and restores order. The thrust of the poem is that the author's countrymen are unaware of the challenge to democratic ideals implied in their approval of armed force to quell the riots:

> . . . the Town, redeemed,
> Give thanks devout; nor, being thankful, heeds
> The grimy slur on the Republic's faith implied,
> Which holds that Man is naturally good,
> And—more—is Nature's Roman, never to be scourged.[20]

As Milton Stern has pointed out, "In 'The House-Top' what is clear is a dominant distrust of men, a sense of the limitations of fallen man, and a consequent need for formal imposition of law and order."[21]

Some thirteen years later in his long poem *Clarel* (1876), Melville responded in a similar vein to the recent French revolution of 1871, when the communists took over Paris for two months (establishing the Paris Commune) and thousands of people were killed before and after government troops retook the city. In the poem, he portrays the "Reds" as even more reprehensible than the French revolutionaries of 1789:

> The Revolution, whose first mode,
> Ere yet the maniacs overrode,
> Despite the passion of the dream
> Evinced no disrespect for God; . . .
> But yesterday—how did they then,
> In new uprising of the Red,
> The offspring of those Tuileries men?
> They made a clothes-stand of the Cross
> Before the church; . . .
> Transcended rebel angels.[22]

In other words, the revolutionaries become like Lucifer's minions, angels who revolt against God and are cast into hell. This demonization of French revolutionaries is attributed to Ungar, the disillusioned Confederate soldier in *Clarel*, but it forms part of the overall political conservatism of the poem. As Walter E. Bezanson has pointed out, "A major political theme of *Clarel* [is] intense distrust of French revolutionary politics in the nineteenth century, and of radicalism generally."[23] Throughout *Clarel*, a number of Melville's characters, including Rolfe, the Dominican, Mortmain, and Ungar, heap contempt upon the "Vitriolists," "Red Caps," "Communists," and "Atheists."

As he worked on *Billy Budd*, until shortly before his death in 1891, Melville returned to the 1789 revolution in France, surely because of contemporary social unrest.[24] He addressed this unrest obliquely, reasserting his sense of the cyclical nature of human events and making his indictment of radicalism transhistorical and sweeping. The "Great Mutiny," we are told, was precipitated by revolution in France, yet it resembled "what a strike in the fire-brigade would be to London threatened by general arson" (54). Melville thus links mutiny, revolution, strikes, and arson through their common destructiveness. The special urgency of the situation on the *Bellipotent* arises because Billy's killing of Claggart occurs during wartime, at a time when the future of the Western world depends on Vere's ability to maintain control of his ship. As the narrator explains, "The year 1797, the year of this narrative, belongs to a period which, as every thinker now feels, involved a crisis for Christendom not exceeded in its undetermined momentousness at the time by any other era whereof there is record."[25] The "crisis" provides the justification for, and clarifies the stakes involved in, Vere's stern justice.

In the early drafts of *Billy Budd*, one can see Melville's strong antipathy toward the French Revolution of 1789, as he stresses its violence and bloodshed. In subsequent drafts, perhaps in an effort to emphasize Vere's solidity and reason, he tones down the narrative's extremism and adds weight to its conservative thrust. For example, in the first account of Vere's opposition to French thought, Melville writes that the "newfangled" ideas from abroad so far partook "of the unsound as to border on the insane." He later revised this to read "at war with the peace of the world and the true welfare of mankind."[26] French radicalism thus becomes a momentous social danger rather than a temporary psychotic state. The red flag, associated with anarchy in contemporary America as well as revolution in France, received attention in the contemporary press and became another image Melville altered as he worked on his text. When *Harper's Weekly* applauded Chicago election results in the spring of 1887, it used a cartoon by W. A. Rogers showing an anarchist being tossed in a ragged red flag (see figure 8). Melville's first description of the transformation of the British flag by the mutineers at the Spithead and the Nore likewise treats the red flag contemptuously, as it details how the sailors wiped out the union and the cross and thereby transmuted their flag into the enemy's "red rag of revolt and universal revolution." Melville later changed this to "red meteor of unbridled and unbounded revolt,"[27] thereby granting the red flag more consequence and power.

The British colors at the time had no cross to be wiped out,[28] yet the historical inaccuracy allows Melville to suggest symbolically the anti-Christian and atheistic dimensions of revolution, as he had done previously in *Moby-Dick* and *Clarel*, where he alluded to the French revolutions of 1848 and 1871, respectively. In *Moby-Dick*, the red flag of revolt flying on the masthead of the *Pequod* is linked symbolically not only to Ahab's mad rebellion against God but also to the recent "Bloody June Days" in Paris, when workers, shouting communist slogans, clashed with government troops. The tableau at the end of the novel, with its vivid conjunction of the red flag, the red arm, the hammer, the sinking ship,

FIGURE 8. W. A. Rogers, *The Latest Chicago Idea: Tossing the Anarchist in His Own Blanket—The Red Flag.* From *Harper's Weekly* 31 (April 16, 1887): 280.

and the imminent descent to Hell, reflects both Melville's conservatism and contemporary attitudes toward European "Red Republicanism," which frightened Americans at midcentury.[29] Viewed in the context of Melville's earlier treatments, Captain Vere's death in *Billy Budd*, the result of a musket ball fired from a French man-of-war, the *Athée* (the "Atheist"), can be seen as Melville's last and most dramatic example of the murderous nature of French radicalism.

BILLY BUDD AND BIOGRAPHY

Melville's antipathy toward revolutionary action, his appreciation for law and order, flowed from a number of sources, many of them biographical. The French Revolution of 1789 was linked in his memory with the reversals of fortune of his father, his uncle Thomas, and especially himself, and it formed the basis for his latent antipathy; the French Revolution of 1848 inspired him to express this antipathy in his works, *Mardi* and

Moby-Dick, especially; and the revolution of 1871 intensified what he already felt and believed. Violence and warfare appalled him, and he had little faith that political uprisings, even when they led to new forms of government, brought lasting benefits. One of his deepest convictions was that "All is Vanity. ALL," a quotation from Ecclesiastes, which he called the "fine hammered steel of woe."[30] To his mind, revolutions merely resulted in one oppressor replacing another in an endless chain of oppositions. In *Mardi,* the mysterious scroll declares that "though crimson republics may rise in constellations, like fiery Aldebarans, speeding to their culminations; yet, down must they sink at last, and leave the old sultan-sun in the sky; in time, again to be deposed" (527).

In "Benito Cereno," Melville uses masked images on the stern-piece—"a dark satyr in a mask, holding his foot on the prostrate neck of a writing figure, likewise masked"[31]—to suggest that revolt, such as that on the *San Dominick,* makes victim and victimizer indistinguishable and interchangeable. Although a prolonged debate has focused on where Melville's sympathies lie with regard to the main characters in this work, this knot resists untying. While "Benito Cereno" is based on an actual slave revolt described in Amasa Delano's narrative, Melville's changes, as other scholars have observed, reflect the fears and delusions of antebellum Americans. On the *San Dominick,* Babo shows Toussaint's intelligence and shrewdness, and perhaps even Madison Washington's restraint (by preserving the lives of some of the crew); however, his sadistic treatment of Cereno places him among those slaves of San Domingo known for their cruelty toward whites during their revolt. It thus becomes difficult to place Babo on a higher moral plane than his dead master, Don Alexandro Aranda. As Jason Richards has astutely observed, the ironic reversals suggest "that black and white identities are mutually constitutive, mutually destructive, and constantly in flux."[32] To expect right to replace wrong in Melville's fallen world is to be guilty, like Delano, of less than "ordinary quickness and accuracy of intellectual perception." In most of Melville's works, "Shadows present" foreshadow not a new day, but only "deeper shadows to come" (164).

In *Clarel,* Rolfe reflects on the European revolutions of 1848, declaring:

> The flood weaves out—the ebb
> Weaves back; the incessant shuttle shifts
> And flies, and wears and tears the web.
> Turn, turn thee to the proof that sifts:
>
> What if the kings in Forty-Eight
> Fled like the gods? even as the gods
> Shall do, return they made; and sate
> And fortified their strong abodes.[33]

The poem alludes to the failures of the revolutions of 1848 and the re-institution of new absolutist governments in almost all the countries in which revolutions occurred. In *Billy Budd*, Melville as narrator reasserts this fatalistic view of revolution, as he historicizes his narrative: "The opening proposition made by the Spirit of that Age," he writes, "involved the rectification of the Old World's hereditary wrongs. In France, to some extent, this was bloodily effected. But what then? Straightway the Revolution regency as righter of wrongs itself became a wrongdoer, one more oppressive than the Kings. Under Napoleon it enthroned upstart kings, and initiated that prolonged agony of Continental war whose final throe was at Waterloo."[34] It is as if some fateful tautology dominated all attempts to effect political progress, especially using violence.

Despite this fatalistic attitude, tied to his pessimistic view of mankind, Melville in his later life evidenced a Vere-like sense of duty that sustained him. As Stanton Garner has shown, the New York Custom House, where Melville worked for nineteen years until 1885, was "a genuinely malign instrument of corruption." "Out of its continual round of politics and ruthless manipulation, as well as its demand for obsequious compliance, he was forced to salvage as best he could the self-respect and dignity which were the defenses of his old age."[35] When Melville began his service, he wore a badge on the outside of his coat, and beginning early in 1878, he and the other inspectors wore Navy-like uniforms modeled on those of the Revenue Cutter Service.[36] When Vere tells his drum-head court that the buttons on their uniforms attest that their allegiance is to the king, not to nature, he expresses a sense of duty that Melville evidenced in his own service to the state. In 1873 his brother-in-law, John C. Hoadley, described Melville's conduct: "Surrounded by low venality, he puts it all quietly aside,—quietly declining offers of money for special services,—quietly returning money which has been thrust into his pockets behind his back, avoiding offence alike to the corrupting merchants and their clerks and runners, who think that all men can be bought, and to the corrupt swarms who shamelessly seek their price."[37]

On points of honor, Melville was obstinate, and despite his explorations of cultural relativism and epistemological uncertainty, much of his thought rested upon a foundation of ethical certainty. At the heart of Melville's great work, *Moby-Dick*, lies an obsession with justice, and Ahab's quarrel with the god or gods who allow the faithful and innocent to suffer can be read as an insistence that life should resemble a boxing match where strict rules apply. *Billy Budd* marks Melville's final exploration of this topic and offers the insight that justice itself can cause the faithful and innocent to suffer. It should be added, though, that Billy's violent streak and his failure to report a mutiny in the making call into question his putative innocence.

In his interactions with members of his family, especially his sons, Melville displayed a firmness much like Vere's, which set him apart. Vere, we are told, "though a conscientious disciplinarian, . . . was no lover of authority for mere authority's sake" (104), and one suspects Melville thought of himself in the same way. As Merton Sealts has pointed out, Melville "was a strict disciplinarian, given to moodiness and irascibility that some of his relatives by marriage came to interpret as outright insanity."[38] In his dealings with his own children, he seems to have been inflexible, and circumstantial evidence suggests that the suicide of his son Malcolm in 1867 may have been precipitated by Melville's harsh discipline. Hennig Cohen and Donald Yannella have posited that "For Malcolm, caught between a kindly though inept mother and a domineering father and trapped within an atmosphere of matrimonial tension, there was no substitute for pistol and ball."[39] Though one hesitates to accept this assertion, knowledge of Melville's troubled relations with Malcolm accentuates the poignancy of the last embrace between Billy and Vere, which remains veiled from our eyes. Melville writes of the scene, "Two of great Nature's nobler order embrace. There is privacy at the time, inviolable to the survivor; and holy oblivion, the sequel to each diviner magnanimity, providentially covers all at last" (115). If Melville's treatment of Vere draws on the author's own experiences, then Billy's forgiveness of Vere should perhaps be read as a father's wishful fantasy about hearing his dead son speak.[40]

The fact that Vere and Billy are portrayed as exceptional men gives us additional reason to view them in the context of Melville's life and career. Vere's rigidity as well as Billy's goodness are Christ-like within Melville's sociopolitical system of values. Sometime after receiving a copy of *New Testament and Psalms* as a gift in 1846, Melville copied and underscored the following description of Christ into the book:

> In Life he appears as a true Philosopher—as a wise man in the highest sense. He stands *firm to his point;* he *goes on his way inflexibly;* and while he exalts the lower to himself, while he makes the ignorant, the poor, the sick, partakers of his wisdom, of his riches, of his strength, he, on the other hand, in no wise conceals his divine origin; he dares to equal himself with God; nay to declare that he himself is God.
>
> In this manner is he wont from youth upwards to *astonish his familiar friends;* of these he gains a part to his own cause; irritates the rest against him; and shows to all men, who are aiming at a certain elevation in doctrine and life, *what they have to look for from the world.*[41]

This interpretation of the character and life of Christ not only captures Melville's sense of his own "inflexibility" but also illuminates his admiration for Vere's firmness. Near the end of his life, as he was revising *Billy Budd*, Melville marked several book passages that reveal his continued fascination with the superior individual. In Balzac's *Fame and Sorrow*, he scored a passage describing "the horrible strife, the incessant warfare which mediocrity wages against superior men," and in Schopenhauer's *Studies in Pessimism*, he underlined, "If he is a man of genius, he will occasionally feel like some noble prisoner of state, condemned to work in the galleys with common criminals; and he will follow his example and try to isolate himself."[42] These passages help us understand Melville's conception of himself, of Vere, and perhaps even of Billy.

Of all the qualities linking Vere and Billy to each other, the noble blood flowing in their veins is the most telling, and it sets them apart from the turbulent masses. Despite his democracy, Melville believed that "blood will tell," and we should see no irony in his insistence that "noble descent was as evident in [Billy] as in a blood horse" (52). Melville had made the same point about King Mehevi in *Typee* (1846), Jack Chase in *White-Jacket*, and Queequeg in *Moby-Dick*. Like his own father and mother, Melville prided himself on his ancestry, and he named his son Malcolm after Scottish nobility. In 1850 Melville told Sophia Hawthorne, and she reported to her sister, that he was "of Scotch descent — of noble lineage — of the Lords of Melville & Leven, & Malcolm is a family name."[43] Like Jack Chase, to whom *Billy Budd* is dedicated, Billy is a "by-blow," a noble foundling, whose "small and shapely" ear, "the arch of the foot, the curve in mouth and nostril," expression, attitude, and movement all "strangely indicated a lineage in direct contradiction to his lot" (51). As many readers have noticed, he could be Vere's actual, as well as surrogate, son.

While Melville privileged blood and respected the elevation it conferred, he had no blind faith in authority. *Billy Budd* argues on behalf of law, order, social stability, and family solidarity, but our reading is complicated by indications that here, as in *White-Jacket*, Melville views with contempt those who represent established order yet act to subvert it. The villain, Claggart, after all, is master-at-arms, the chief policeman on the ship; it is he who seeks to engage Billy in mutiny. This feature of the book returns us to the 1880s and the labor unrest surrounding Melville as he wrote. Although the police were applauded in the press for protecting citizens and preserving order during turbulent times, the public had gradually become aware that some law enforcement officers actively engaged in infiltrating labor organizations and inciting the riots that brought the law to bear upon striking workers. Having gained its reputation in the suppression of the Molly Maguires during the 1870s, the Pinkerton Agency advertised its espionage services by claiming that "corporations and individuals desirous of ascertaining the feeling of their employees and whether they are likely to engage in strikes or are joining any secret labor organization with a view of compelling terms from corporations or employers, can obtain . . . a detective suitable to associate with their employees."[44] Pinkerton agents, however, often acted, like Claggart, as *agents provocateurs*, who created trouble rather than prevented it. As John McBride, president of the United Mine Workers, pointed out, the Pinkertons "had an interest in keeping up and creating troubles which gave employers opportunity to demand protection from the state militia at the expense of the state."[45] In some cities, the police operated in a similar fashion. In an interview given in May 1889, Chicago chief of police Frederick Ebersold admitted that in the wake of the Haymarket bombing, the police had organized anarchist societies, planted bombs and weapons at their headquarters, and then raided these. One anarchist and *agent provocateur* may even have thrown the Haymarket bomb.[46]

Though Claggart and Vere both represent the forces of law and order on the *Bellipotent*, the former forsakes his duties while the latter does not, and Melville suggests that the foreign element in Claggart's blood is tied to his despicable behavior. Unlike Billy and Vere, he is not English by birth. He speaks with "a bit of an accent" (65) and seems vaguely French. Rumor has it that he was a "*chevalier*" previously involved in "some mysterious swindle" (65). Melville's lifelong association of France with revolutionary violence may thus inform his characterization of Claggart, as may American prejudice against foreigners as a whole. As Susan Mizruchi has pointed out, "Claggart's story resembles a type of fantasy about immigration that captivated Americans in the 1880s, especially those of Vere's class: . . . the arrival of the alien serpent introduces social chaos."[47] Like Satan, Claggart reveals his demonic "otherness" through his subversive activities.

As for the "people" on the *Bellipotent*, Melville portrays them, as he does the common sailors in his other works, as easily manipulated by both the Veres and Claggarts of the world. More ignorant than depraved, they lack the acuity to do more than respond to the material facts of their existence. "Yes, as a class, sailors are in character a juvenile race," the narrator declares. "Even their deviations are marked by juvenility" (87). What then is the appropriate response to these undeveloped men when they become lawless and violent? Superior force seems to be one answer couched in the story of Billy's encounter with Red Whiskers on *The Rights of Man*. After the fellow "insultingly gave him a dig under the ribs," Billy "gave the burly fool a terrible drubbing" (47). As a result, this fiery fellow ends up loving Billy. Vere, too, evokes Billy's love, or at least his blessing, when he uses force against him. "Baby" Budd's crime is that he strikes—instinctually, irrationally, murderously. Vere, after "the father in him . . . was replaced by the military disciplinarian" (100), strikes back—thoughtfully, rationally, lawfully. In Melville's eyes, at this time in his life, Vere appears to demonstrate a right response to popular violence, when the times are revolutionary.

Doubts of all things earthly, and intuitions of some
things heavenly; this combination makes neither
believer nor infidel, but makes a man who regards
them both with equal eye.

— MELVILLE, *Moby-Dick,* 1851

EPILOGUE

The struggle with righteous violence, as this book has tried to show, was
central to the writers of the American Renaissance, for it persistently engaged their imaginations and deeply informed their writings. They lived
in violent times. The United States experienced unprecedented bloodshed on its own soil during the years 1830–1890, caused not only by the
state terror of slavery, conflict with Native Americans, and the waging of
civil war, but also by the unlawful revolts, insurrections, riots, and strikes
that surrounded those more spectacular tragedies. Oppression, exploita-
tion, and denial of human rights were the primary causes of the killings
that challenged these authors' ethical and moral values, often forcing
them to choose the lesser of two evils.

During the American Renaissance, appeals to "higher law" doctrine
often served to justify criminal acts on behalf of oppressed peoples. The
English Revolution of 1642–49, the American Revolution of 1775–83,
the French Revolutions of 1789 and 1848, the Haitian Revolution of
1791–1804, and the Italian Revolutions of 1848–49 also served as major
analogues for contemporary unlawful violence, and these prior revolutions were widely represented as struggles for liberty against the be-
nighted forces of tyranny. Liberty (or the rights of man) and peace (or
law and order) stood as the two magnetic poles that attracted arguments

for and against the use of violent force, by those with power and those without it. The incomplete *Billy Budd* wavers between the two poles, as do many other writings of the age.

Fuller, Emerson, Douglass, Thoreau, Alcott, Hawthorne, and Melville all detested slavery, yet all evidenced strong misgivings about political violence and warfare. For the most part, they rejected the idea that one group could prove its moral superiority by inflicting suffering and death on another. Nevertheless, all of them shifted their attitudes under the influence of different contingencies, such as Joseph Mazzini and John Brown, and even became bloodthirsty at times. Their passions were aroused by threats to themselves, to their imagined communities, or to others with whom they sympathized. When the threat seemed urgent, immediate, and severe, their pacifism, no matter how much an intrinsic part of their personal moralities, disappeared.

Fuller, in the midst of the Roman revolution, applauds the assassination of the pope's prime minister, vilifies the Catholic powers of Europe, and calls on Heaven to "waft a fire that will burn down all, root and branch, and prepare the earth for an entirely new culture."[1] Emerson recruits young men in the colleges and tells them it's a good time to die (though not for his son). Douglass urges his fellow free blacks to take up arms and "smite with death the power that would bury the government and your liberty."[2] Thoreau threatens to "touch a match to blow up earth & hell together."[3] Alcott writes a friend, "I like the stir in the air and long for battle like a war horse when he smells powder."[4] Hawthorne tells a correspondent, "I never imagined what a happy state of mind a civil war produces."[5] And even Melville, at age forty-two, joins the Pittsfield militia, ready to fight.

External stimuli often contributed to the mind-altering process these authors and their contemporaries experienced. The heightened rhetoric of newspapers, broadsides, and political speeches, the flare of bombs, the beating of drums, martial music, the sight of muskets, bayonets, pistols, and uniforms, the clank of chains, the sound of gunfire, the smell of gunpowder—all served as catalysts for what Freud would later identify as Thanatos, the irresistible destructive impulses that can overpower one's individual inhibitions. In *Moods*, Alcott dramatizes the process when she has Warwick in Italy relate, "One of my Berserker rages possessed me I fancy; . . . the smell of powder intoxicated, and the sense of power was grand. The fire, the smoke, the din were all delicious, and I felt like a giant, as I wielded that great weapon, dealing many deaths with a single pair of hands."[6] Hawthorne puts it more critically when he describes the Concord of 1775 (and 1861): "War had filled the whole brain of the people and enveloped the whole thought of man in a mist of gunpowder."[7]

As a student of witchcraft in Salem, Hawthorne understood, perhaps better than his contemporaries, the effects the sensational could have on individuals and groups in the grip of religio-political frenzy. He had studied how his Puritan ancestors had become fanatical in their killing of Quakers, Indians, witches, and other enemies of the Lord. In a climate of ignorance and fear, systems of values and beliefs — call them ideologies — offer members of an aroused and threatened group a sense of unity, justice, and righteousness. This is especially the case when these ideologies advocate the use of violence against others, which heightens their intensity and value. At times the lure of group zeal proves almost irresistible. For example, Hawthorne argued against violence his entire career, yet said about the young recruits in Concord, in 1861, "When I hear their drums beating, and see their banners flying, and witness their steady marching, I declare . . . I feel as if I could catch the infection, shoulder a musket, and be off to the war myself!"[8] And yet, he did not. Like Douglass, Melville, and most of his Concord neighbors, he was a pacifist at heart.

Perhaps the most valuable aspect of the thought and writings discussed in this study is not the authors' ardent participation in the struggle for liberty (as others have argued), or even their conservative commitment to peace and civil order, but, rather, the glimpses they reveal of the complexities, ambivalences, and uncertainties of their views. Fuller, for example, wondered if the Roman Republic was worth the suffering of the young men she tended in the hospitals; Emerson disdained war as barbaric but also argued it could exalt the age; Douglass called himself a peace man yet advocated slave revolt; Thoreau cautioned a correspondent to ignore the newspapers, as he had not been able to do, and focus on Nature and God; Alcott critiqued the savagery of her favorite character, Warwick; and Hawthorne equated his pacifism with treason in notes he wrote as "editor" of his own essay. Such intellectual self-criticism and capaciousness allowed these writers to resist the totalizing ideologies (both religious and political) always ready to overdetermine one's thought.

Today we remain in need of imaginative artists, writers, and intellectuals able to illuminate the multiple sides of controversial issues, especially when technologically advanced media are spreading ignorance, fear, and anger throughout the world. Righteous violence has a history that extends thousands of years into the past (think Jael and Sisera; Judith and Holofernes), yet it now seems more prevalent, especially when religious and state-sanctioned killing of civilians is termed "righteous." As John W. Dower has observed, referring to the terror bombings of World War II and the attacks of 9/11, modern targeting of noncombatants reflects "the cycle of now almost naturalized crimes against humanity perpetuated by implacable antagonists who share rage and righteousness in common, and have no doubt that reason, morality, destiny, and divine Providence itself all stand on their side."[9] The writers discussed in this study, in addition to creating some of the most stirring works in American literature, provide examples of how imaginative men and women can struggle, sometimes successfully, sometimes not, to overcome the groupthink that declares certain killings righteous, others murder. Their example, if followed, puts one at risk of losing the satisfaction and safety of group unity, but it also holds out the promise of intellectual growth that difference can provide. Such growth is the first step toward a deeper and more informed understanding of righteous violence, past and present.

NOTES

PREFACE

1. Emerson, *Collected Poems*, 125.

2. Hawthorne, *The Elixir of Life*, 13: 24.

3. The dates, authors, and texts of this study differ from those of F. O. Matthiessen's classic study, *American Renaissance: Art and Expression in the Age of Emerson and Whitman* (1941). They do so because I wish to show how centrally important political violence was to the cultural history of the period. As will become clear, a number of my chapters support Betsy Erkkila's persuasive argument that "[w]e need to revise and more fully historicize Matthiessen's story and chronology by relocating the Revolution not *outside* but *inside* the American Renaissance, as its underlying logic and specter, and in relation to its post-history in the Civil War, Reconstruction, and the ongoing global crisis of capitalism and democracy in the present" ("Revolution in the Renaissance" 20).

4. Sundquist, *To Wake the Nations*, 34. The present study has been heavily influenced by Sundquist's work.

5. Emerson, "Man of Letters," 257.

INTRODUCTION. *Righteous Violence*

1. Fuller, "'The Impulses of Human Nature,'" 107.

2. *Woman in the Nineteenth Century*, 15.

3. "The Jubilee," 127.

4. Petrulionis, *To Set This World Right*, 11.

5. "The Jubilee," 127.

6. Sundquist, *Empire and Slavery*, 143.

7. Sanborn, *Life and Letters of John Brown*, 629.

8. See Murdock, *The Nineteenth of April*, 72.

9. Hawthorne, *Mosses from an Old Manse*, 10: 10–11.

10. Hallahan, *The Day the American Revolution Began*, 40.

11. Gross, *The Minutemen*. My summary of the events of April 19, 1775, is indebted to Gross's excellent study.

12. Hancock, "Monthly Intelligence," 333.

13. McWilliams, "Hinge of the Future," 5.

14. McWilliams, "Hinge," 2.

15. Emerson, "Dedication of the Soldiers' Monument," 349, 351–52.

16. "Declaration of Sentiments," 7–8.

17. Fuller, *Woman in the Nineteenth Century*, 15.

18. "The Minutemen's Pledge," 177.

19. Popkin, "Facing Racial Revolution," 512.

20. Dayan, *Haiti*, 213–15.

21. [Drayton], *The South Vindicated*, 263.

22. Whittier, *Anti-Slavery Poems*, 14.

23. Garrison, "The Dangers of the Nation," 59.

24. See Bell, *Toussaint Louverture*, 18–56.

25. Whittier, *Anti-Slavery Poems*, 19.

26. James, *The Black Jacobins*, ix.

27. Hawthorne, *Peter Parley's Universal History*, 465. For an excellent account of Hawthorne's minimal original contributions to this series, see Brown, "Hawthorne and Parley's Universal History."

28. Emerson, *Antislavery Writings*, 31 (hereafter cited parenthetically as *AW*).

29. Emerson, *Essays and Lectures*, 498.

30. Vesey's planned revolt may not have been a reality but a fabrication by whites intent on gaining political power in the town of Charleston; see Johnson, "Denmark Vesey and His Co-Conspirators."

31. Turner, "Confessions," 136.

32. Turner, "Confessions," 139.

33. Higginson, "Nat Turner's Insurrection," 188.

34. Douglass, *Frederick Douglass Papers*, 2: 131 (hereafter cited parenthetically as *FDP*).

35. *Liberator* 1 (September 17, 1831), 151.

36. See Mayer, *All on Fire*, 120–21.

37. Richards, *"Gentlemen of Property,"* 40.

38. Lovejoy, *Memoir of Rev. Elijah P. Lovejoy*, 171.

39. Lovejoy, "The Mob," 181.

40. "Horrid Tragedy," 1.

41. Useful accounts of Lovejoy's murder can be found in Lincoln, *Alton Trials;* Lovejoy, *Memoir,* 282–92; and Simon, *Freedom's Champion,* 127–32.

42. Demos, "The Antislavery Movement," 507.

43. Lincoln, *Alton Trials,* 7.

44. Lovejoy, *Memoir,* 12.

45. Gougeon, *Virtue's Hero,* 38.

46. "Public Meeting," 202.

47. J. Newton Brown, "The Beginning," 157.

48. Oates, *To Purge This Land with Blood,* 42.

49. Garrison, "Dr. Webster's Address," 111.

50. This summary is based upon Jones, "The Peculiar Institution," 28–50.

51. Rogin, *Subversive Genealogy,* 102.

52. Lowell, *The Biglow Papers,* 51.

53. Fuller, *"These Sad But Glorious Days,"* 230 (hereafter cited parenthetically as *SG*).

54. Quoted in Demos, "The Antislavery Movement," 519.

55. *New York Herald,* September 26, 1848, quoted in Edelstein, *Strange Enthusiasms,* 86.

56. For an analysis of this development, see Demos, "The Antislavery Movement," 501–26.

57. Weld, "Feelings of a Woman," 106.

58. Emerson, *The Journals and Miscellaneous Notebooks,* 11: 352, 412 (hereafter cited parenthetically as *JMN*).

59. Parker, "The Function and Place of Conscience," 147–48.

60. Parker, "The Fugitive Slave Law," 150–51.

61. Petrulionis, *To Set This World Right,* 78.

62. For an excellent comprehensive study of the Burns case, see von Frank, *Trials of Anthony Burns.*

63. Quoted in Edelstein, *Strange Enthusiasms,* 190.

64. Higginson, "1854: Letters on the Anthony Burns Affair," Houghton Library, MS AM 784 (481).

65. Higginson, "Attempted Rescue of Burns," 134.

66. "The Rescue of Burns," 142.

67. Higginson, *Cheerful Yesterdays,* 158.

68. Sophia Hawthorne to Nathaniel Peabody (father), July 4, 1854, Berg Collection, New York Public Library.

69. Thoreau, *Journal*, 8: 175.

70. Conway, *Autobiography*, 1: 162.

71. Conway, *Autobiography*, 1: 162–63.

72. Conway, *Autobiography*, 1: 163.

73. Quoted in Edelstein, *Strange Enthusiasms*, 162.

74. Higginson, *Cheerful Yesterdays*, 155.

75. Quoted in Pease and Pease, "Confrontation and Abolition in the 1850s," 936 n.48.

76. Potter, *The Impending Crisis*, 219.

77. *New-York Tribune*, May 30, 1856.

78. *New York Herald*, June 8, 1856, quoted in Stauffer, "Advent among the Indians," 253.

79. See Carton, *Patriotic Treason*, 178–79.

80. Utter, "Kansas History," 118.

81. Quoted in Oates, *To Purge This Land*, 134.

82. Reynolds, *John Brown*, 164–65.

83. Higginson, *Cheerful Yesterdays*, 207–8.

84. "Annual Meeting of the Massachusetts Anti-slavery Society," 19.

85. "Annual Meeting," 19. When Brown and Garrison first met in 1857 in Theodore Parker's parlors, "[t]hey discussed peace and nonresistance together, Brown quoting the Old Testament against Garrison's citations from the New, and Parker from time to time injecting a bit of Lexington into the controversy" (Phillips and Garrison, *William Lloyd Garrison*, 3: 487–88).

86. "Annual Meeting of the Massachusetts Anti-slavery Society," 19.

87. Demos, "The Antislavery Movement," 522.

88. See Emerson, *JMN*, 8: 368–69.

89. See Meyer, "Thoreau's Rescue of John Brown from History."

90. Thoreau, *Reform Papers*, 133.

91. Details about Brown's activities are taken from Ruchames, *John Brown*; Quarles, *Allies for Freedom*; and Oates, *To Purge This Land with Blood*.

92. Garrison, "The Virginia Insurrection," 166.

93. Garrison, "John Brown and the Principle of Nonresistance," 198.

94. Renehan, *The Secret Six*, 115.

95. Quoted in Renehan, *Secret Six*, 273–74.

96. Thoreau, *Journal*, 8: 165–66.

97. Thoreau, quoted in Renehan, *Secret Six*, 109.

98. Mitchell, "Massachusetts Reacts," 65.

99. Channing, *Crisis of Fear*, 271.

100. "Sentiment at the South," 38.

101. Whitman, "Year of Meteors. (1859–60.)," 51.

102. Utter, "Kansas History," 117.

103. Melville, *Poems of Herman Melville*, 34.

104. Milder, "The Rhetoric of Melville's *Battle-Pieces*," 177.

105. Melville, *Poems of Herman Melville*, 163.

106. Gregory Jay has argued that Melville's *Billy Budd* rehearses the "the unjust killings of African Americans in the period" ("Douglass, Melville, and the Lynching of Billy Budd" 370). While race is certainly an issue in *Billy Budd*, political violence in the North, I will argue, informed Melville's novella most intently in the 1880s.

107. Green, *Death in the Haymarket*, 17.

108. Quoted in Foner, *History of the Labor Movement*, 11.

109. Trachtenberg, *The Incorporation of America*, 88–89. For studies of labor unrest during these years, see Avrich, *The Haymarket Tragedy;* David, *The History of the Haymarket Affair;* Foner, *The Great Labor Uprising;* Foner, *History of the Labor Movement;* and Montgomery, "Strikes in Nineteenth Century America."

110. Quoted in Green, *Death in the Haymarket*, 7.

111. The facts here are taken from Foner, *History of the Labor Movement*, 106.

112. Quoted in Foner, *History of the Labor Movement*, 111.

113. Foner, *History of the Labor Movement*, 116.

114. *Harper's Weekly* 31 (1 October 1887), 702.

115. *New York Times*, November 25, 1887, 4.

116. Avrich, *Haymarket Tragedy*, 262–66.

117. *Harper's Weekly* 31 (26 November 1887), 849–52.

118. For an account of the pardon and reaction to it, see Avrich, *Haymarket Tragedy*, 415–27.

CHAPTER ONE. *Margaret Fuller's Revolutionary Example*

1. Reynolds, *European Revolutions*, 171. For an extended discussion of Fuller's achievement in the dispatches, see Reynolds and Smith, "Introduction," 1–35.

2. Packer, "The Transcendentalists," 544.

3. Fuller, *Woman in the Nineteenth Century*, 7.

4. Fuller, *Margaret Fuller, Critic*, 150.

5. Quoted in Ossoli, *At Home and Abroad*, vii.

6. Quoted in Ossoli, *At Home and Abroad*, x.

7. See Reynolds, *European Revolutions*, 16–19.

8. Quoted in Peterson, "Echoes of the Italian Risorgimento," 228. Lowell, perhaps, was trying to make amends for his hurtful satire of Fuller in his *Fable for Critics.* See von Mehren, *Minerva and the Muse,* 311.

9. Quoted in Peterson, "Echoes of the Italian Risorgimento," 228.

10. Whitman, *Leaves of Grass* (1855), 88. For Fuller's influence on Whitman, see Reynolds, *European Revolutions,* 137–39.

11. Roberts, *Distant Revolutions,* 62.

12. *Boston Post,* June 29, 1849, 1. See also Marraro, *American Opinion on the Unification of Italy,* 68–69.

13. Trevelyan, *Garibaldi's Defense of the Roman Republic,* 149–50.

14. London *Times,* May 11, 1849, 4.

15. Longfellow, *Letters,* 3: 208.

16. Emerson, *Letters,* 4: 39.

17. Emerson, *Essays and Lectures,* 913.

18. Emerson, *Essays and Lectures,* 48.

19. Fuller, *Woman in the Nineteenth Century,* 74.

20. Emerson, *Essays and Lectures,* 945, 946.

21. Zwarg, *Feminist Conversations,* 293–94.

22. Emerson, *Essays and Lectures,* 957.

23. For a useful discussion of this topic and its relevance to the Emerson-Fuller relationship, see Steele, "The Limits of Political Sympathy," 115–35.

24. Hawthorne, *The Letters, 1857–1864,* 18: 544.

25. Quoted in Edward Emerson, "Notes," 579.

26. See Breunig, *The Age of Revolution and Reaction,* 227–29.

27. Fuller, *Letters,* 5: 147.

28. Fuller, *Letters,* 5: 295–96.

29. See Capper, *Margaret Fuller,* 1: 144–45.

30. Quoted in Fuller, *Woman in the Nineteenth Century,* 177.

31. Rostenberg, "Margaret Fuller's Roman Diary," 217–18.

32. As Charles Capper has observed, the greatest danger to Rossi was "he often displayed a proud and sarcastic demeanor toward his legion of adversaries, both Gregorians, who loathed him for his religious liberalism, and Democrats, whose Club of the People he reviled" (*Margaret Fuller* 2: 413)

33. Lowell, *Poems,* 253, 250.

34. Steele, "'Freeing the Prisoned Queen,'" 169.

35. Fuller, *Letters,* 5: 293.

36. Hawthorne, *The Scarlet Letter,* 1: 165.

37. Hawthorne, *The Scarlet Letter*, 1: 51.

38. Hawthorne, *The Blithedale Romance*, 3: 78.

39. Mitchell, *Hawthorne's Fuller Mystery*, 235.

40. Hawthorne, *Elixir of Life*, 13: 67.

41. Howe, *Passion-Flowers*, 61–63.

42. Quoted in Bean, "Margaret Fuller on the Early Poetry of Julia Ward Howe," 78.

43. Howe, "Battle Hymn of the Republic," 145.

44. Wilson, *Patriotic Gore*, 96.

45. Howe, *Margaret Fuller*, 278. For an excellent discussion of Fuller's influence on Howe, see Williams, *Hungry Heart*, 108–14, 165–66, 210–12.

46. Solomon, *Margaret Fuller Ossoli*, xiii.

47. Higginson, *Margaret Fuller Ossoli*, xiv, 2, 6, 314.

48. Higginson, "Massachusetts in mourning!," 20.

49. *New-York Tribune*, October 10, 1856, quoted in Edelstein, *Strange Enthusiasm*, 188.

50. William Henry Channing to Higginson, July 4, 1855, Higginson-Burns Collection, Boston Public Library.

51. Rossbach, *Ambivalent Conspirators*, 274.

52. Douglass, "John Brown: An Address," 66.

53. McPherson, *Battle Cry of Freedom*, 208, 213.

54. Quoted in Ruchames, *John Brown*, 86–87. As von Frank has shown, Brown was influenced by "refugees from the English and Continental revolutions of 1848" ("John Brown, James Redpath, and the Idea of Revolution" 143). Brown and Hugh Forbes eventually quarreled over tactics and money; Forbes threatened to expose the Harpers Ferry plan, forcing Brown to postpone it for a year.

55. Stowe, *Uncle Tom's Cabin*, 510.

CHAPTER TWO. *Emerson, Guns, and Bloodlust*

1. See Packer, "The Transcendentalists," 329–604; Gougeon, *Virtue's Hero* and "Emerson's Abolition Conversion"; von Frank, *The Trials of Anthony Burns* and "Mrs. Brackett's Verdict"; Johnson, "Emerson, Thoreau's Arrest, and the Trials of American Manhood"; Strysick, "Emerson, Slavery, and the Evolution of the Principle of Self-Reliance"; Bush, "Emerson, John Brown, and 'Doing the Word'"; Robinson, "Emerson's 'American Civilization'" and "Introduction:

Emerson as a Political Thinker"; Garvey, *The Emerson Dilemma* and "Emerson, Garrison, and the Anti-Slavery Society"; and Ziser, "Emersonian Terrorism."

2. Gougeon, "'Fortune of the Republic,'" 309.

3. Emerson, *Essays and Lectures*, 48.

4. Emerson, "Hymn," 125.

5. Emerson, "Dedication of the Soldiers' Monument in Concord," 352.

6. Garrison, "A Martyr for Liberty," 191.

7. Channing, "A Letter to Abolitionists," 206.

8. Gougeon, *Virtue's Hero*, 48. Gougeon relies on Edward Emerson, who, in his notes to his father's essay "War," contends that though opposed to war, Emerson never really shared the sentiments of Garrison's nonresistants. One explanation for Edward's misunderstanding of his father's pacifism is that Edward was not born until 1844 and came of age during the Civil War, when his father's ferocity was at its peak.

9. Emerson, *Essays and Lectures*, 380.

10. Emerson, *Collected Poems*, 62.

11. Emerson, "War," 151. Additional references will appear parenthetically in the text.

12. Emerson, *Later Lectures*, 2: 240.

13. Emerson, *Later Lectures*, 2: 240–41.

14. Emerson, *Essays and Lectures*, 744–45.

15. Emerson, *Later Lectures*, 1: 185–86.

16. Reynolds, *European Revolutions*, 36–43.

17. Emerson, *Later Lectures*, 1: 147.

18. Emerson, *Letters*, 4: 73, 74.

19. Emerson, *Essays and Lectures*, 909.

20. Emerson, *Essays and Lectures*, 1021

21. Carlyle, *Oliver Cromwell's Letters and Speeches*, 1: 72.

22. Emerson, *Letters*, 8: 183–84.

23. Emerson, *Lectures and Essays*, 922.

24. Emerson, *Correspondence of Emerson and Carlyle*, 443.

25. Gougeon, "Emerson and the British," 179–213.

26. Cole, "Emerson, England, and Fate," 90.

27. Emerson, *Lectures and Essays*, 964.

28. Cole, "Emerson, England, and Fate," 93.

29. Rowe, *At Emerson's Tomb*, 21.

30. Reynolds, *John Brown, Abolitionist*, 226.

31. Emerson, *Letters*, 4: 444.

32. Quoted in Oates, *To Purge This Land with Blood*, 129.

33. See Petrulionis, *To Set This World Right*, 116.

34. Quoted in Sanborn, *Life and Letters of John Brown*, 244.

35. See Oates, *To Purge This Land with Blood*, 139–46.

36. Thoreau, *Journal*, 2: 1333.

37. Longfellow, *Life*, 2: 325.

38. Storey and Emerson, *Ebenezer Rockwood Hoar*, 146–47.

39. Stillman, "The Philosophers' Camp," 601 (hereafter cited by page number in the text). For an engaging account of a 2002 trip to the remote Philosophers' Camp, see Burkholder, "(Re)Visiting 'The Adirondacs.'"

40. Emerson, *Collected Poems*, 152.

41. Thoreau, *Journal*, 2: 1344.

42. Emerson, *Collected Poems*, 151.

43. McAleer, *Ralph Waldo Emerson*, 553.

44. Emerson, *Essays and Lectures*, 414.

45. Emerson, *Letters*, 5: 178.

46. Emerson, *Essays and Lectures*, 1083–84.

47. Lopez, "*The Conduct of Life*," 257.

48. Emerson, *Emerson-Clough Letters*, 32.

49. Cabot, *Memoir*, 2: 600 (hereafter cited parenthetically in the text).

50. Rusk, *The Life of Emerson*, 428.

51. Conway, *Autobiography*, 1: 297.

52. Emerson, *Letters*, 5: 253.

53. Conway, *Autobiography*, 1: 297.

54. Emerson, *Later Lectures*, 2: 253–54.

55. Richardson, *Emerson*, 550.

56. Emerson, "American Civilization," 173.

57. Rusk, *The Life of Emerson*, 410.

58. Quoted in Rusk, *The Life of Emerson*, 420.

59. Emerson, "Man of Letters," 257.

60. Quoted in Bray, "'Not a *pure* idealist,'" 85–86.

61. Bray, "'Not a *pure* idealist,'" 88–89.

62. Emerson, *Collected* Poems, 168.

63. Melville, *Poems*, 85.

64. Emerson, *Correspondence of Emerson and Carlyle*, 542.

65. Emerson, *Correspondence of Emerson and Carlyle*, 548.

CHAPTER THREE. *Douglass, Insurrection, and* The Heroic Slave

1. In his journal for 1844, Emerson described Douglass as a heroic figure, whose existence outweighed the arguments of abolitionists (see *JMN* 9: 125).

2. Douglass, *Autobiographies*, 760. Hereafter abbreviated and cited in text as *A*.

3. Foner argues that Douglass's "sympathy for Brown's project grew as his confidence in the efficacy of moral suasion waned" (*The Life and Writings* 2: 87). Cited in text as *LW*.

4. This is not to say Douglass disregarded the Old Testament. As Sundquist has pointed out, when Douglass revised his *Narrative* (1845) into *My Bondage and My Freedom* (1855), he identified "himself both with Moses (planning an escape 'out of Egypt') and with Christ ('if any one is to blame for disturbing the quiet of the slaves and slave-masters . . . *I am the man*')" (*To Wake the Nations* 84).

5. Takaki has made the important point that unlike John Brown, Douglass as a slave "had been forced into close and intimate relations with slaveowners, and he had come to know many of them as persons as well as masters. . . . Bondage as Douglass experienced it enabled him to regard white Southerners as fellow human beings trapped like himself in a tragic and absurd system" (*Violence in the Black Imagination* 26).

6. These enduring feelings, according to Blight, led Douglass to regard the Civil War with anticipation and satisfaction (*Frederick Douglass' Civil War* 80–81).

7. Sale has written extensively about Douglass's use of the rhetoric of the American revolution. See her "Critiques from Within," "To Make the Past Useful," and *The Slumbering Volcano*, 173–97. See also, Sundquist, *To Wake the Nations*, 83–87; and Yarborough, "Race, Violence, and Manhood."

8. Other accounts of the development of Douglass's attitudes can be found in Stepto, "Sharing the Thunder," 135–53; Sundquist, *To Wake the Nations*, 83–87; and Wallace, "Violence, Manhood, and War in Douglass," 73–88. My discussion is indebted to these studies.

9. Emerson, *Collected Poems*, 161.

10. Douglass, *The Heroic Slave*, 135. Hereafter cited parenthetically in the text.

11. McFeely, *Frederick Douglass*, 175.

12. Takaki, *Violence in the Black Imagination*, 18.

13. Karcher, "White Fratricide, Black Liberation," 355, 357.

14. For a discussion of the influence of Turner on Douglass, see Sundquist, *Wake the Nations*, 83–93.

15. Garnet, "Call to Rebellion," 36.

16. *Minutes of National Convention of Colored Citizens, Buffalo, New York, August, 1843*, quoted in Brewer, "Henry Highland Garnet," 45. Douglass and Charles Lenox Remond "cast the only two votes against cooperation with the recently organized Liberty Party" (McFeely, *Frederick Douglass*, 106).

17. White, "The Hundred Conventions," 163.

18. Quoted in Goldstein, "Violence as an Instrument for Social Change," 64.

19. Rogers captures an important feature of Douglass's revolutionary models, for as Robert Levine has shown, Douglass's thinking about black revolution was inspired not only by "the principles of 1776" but also by "the Haitian revolutionaries of 1791–1804" ("Frederick Douglass, War, Haiti" 1865).

20. Levine, "Frederick Douglass, War, Haiti," 1865–66.

21. For analyses of how Douglass equates manhood with force and violence, see Franchot, "The Punishment of Esther"; and Leverenz, *Manhood and the American Renaissance*, 108–34. For a critique of Douglass's discursive treatment of women, especially black women, see McDowell, "In the First Place."

22. Aikin, "Dialogue between a Master and a Slave," 240–42.

23. Garrison, "The Dangers of the Nation," 59.

24. Fuller, *Margaret Fuller, Critic*, 132.

25. Leverenz has suggested that the split between Douglass and Garrison "came not only over the issue of voting and the Constitution but also over Douglass's increasingly vehement argument for other kinds of political action, including the use of force" (*Manhood and the American Renaissance* 124); see also Stepto, who observes that with *The Heroic Slave*, Douglass made "clear he had indeed broken from the Garrisonian policies condemning agitation and armed force" ("Storytelling in Early Afro-American Fiction," 359).

26. Quoted in Rossbach, *Ambivalent Conspirators*, 96.

27. Rossbach, *Ambivalent Conspirators*, 97.

28. McKivigan, "The Frederick Douglass–Gerrit Smith Friendship," 216. For an account of Smith as "a white man seeking to become black," see Stauffer, *The Black Hearts of Men*, 62.

29. Stepto has pointed out that the praise of Smith in *The Heroic Slave* is not only a thank-you but also "a clear signal from Douglass that he has broken with the Garrisonian abolitionists and aligned himself with new friends" ("Storytelling" 367 n.12). Levine has made a persuasive case for regarding the Listwell-Washington relation as allegorically related to the Douglass–Harriet Beecher Stowe relation. See "*Uncle Tom's Cabin* in *Frederick Douglass' Paper*."

30. For an account of Brown's visit with Douglass, see Oates, *To Purge This Land with Blood*, 221–22. For the effect of Brown on Douglass's religion, see Wallace, "Violence, Manhood, and War," 76, 79.

31. In a letter to Elizabeth Cady Stanton on his second marriage, Douglass declared, "How good it is to have a wife who can read and write, and who can as Margaret Fuller says cover one in all his range" (*LW* 4: 410). (Anna Douglass, his first wife, was illiterate.)

32. See Reynolds, *European Revolutions*, 16–17.

33. Douglass, "To Captain Thomas Auld, formerly my Master."

34. For details about the relation of Douglass to Thomas Auld, see Preston, *Young Frederick Douglass*, 140–41, 172–75.

35. McFeely, *Frederick Douglass*, 41.

36. Douglass, "To Captain Thomas Auld, formerly my Master."

37. Levine has coined the term "temperate revolutionism" to describe Douglass's "muted attitude toward revolutionary violence"(*Martin Delany, Frederick Douglass* 101).

38. Davis, "The Emergence of Immediatism in British and American Antislavery Thought," 228.

39. Ivy Wilson credits Douglass in *The Heroic Slave* with "a transnational and comparative method in his thinking about liberation as a historical phenomenon" ("On Native Ground: Transnationalism, Frederick Douglass, and 'The Heroic Slave,'" 459).

40. Yarborough, "Race, Violence, and Manhood," 176.

41. For a discussion of Douglass's "double-edged" attitude toward the Irish, see Paul Giles, "Narrative Reversals and Power Exchanges," 798–800; for a discussion of Douglass's antipathy toward the Irish in the United States, see Richard Hardack, "The Slavery of Romanism."

42. Stauffer, "Frederick Douglass's Self-fashioning," 209–10.

43. Gleason, "Volcanoes and Meteors," 111.

44. *Frederick Douglass' Paper* (January 16, 1857), quoted in Gleason, "Volcanoes and Meteors," 130.

45. Sundquist, *To Wake the Nations*, 115.

46. Blight, *Frederick Douglass' Civil War*, 64.

47. For an excellent account of the effect of the mob on Douglass's speech, see Wallace, "Violence, Manhood, and War in Douglass," 82–84.

48. Yarborough, "Race, Violence, and Manhood," 172.

49. For discussion of the relation between Emerson and Douglass, see

Leverenz, *Manhood and the American Renaissance,* 132; and Martin, *Mind of Frederick Douglass,* 263–66.

50. Quoted in McFeeley, *Frederick Douglass,* 318.

51. Walker, *Moral Choices,* 254, 257.

52. Moses, "Where Honor Is Due," 187, 179.

53. Levine, *Martin Delany, Frederick Douglass,* 227.

54. Martin observes that for Douglass, "the liberating spirit of humanism ideally subsumed and eventually overrode the stifling spirit of race" (*The Mind of Frederick Douglass* 96); Sundquist credits Douglass with "a dignity that embraced race while transcending it; an identity forged in an act of revolutionary revision; and a narrative that was nothing less than the story of liberty" (*To Wake the Nations* 134); and Gene Andrew Jarrett makes the point that Douglass's faith in Enlightenment ideals "ended up sustaining him from his early youth to his death" ("Douglass, Ideological Slavery, and Postbellum Racial Politics" 170).

55. Douglass, "Speech at the Dedication of Manassas (Virginia) Industrial School," September 3, 1894, Frederick Douglass Papers, Library of Congress, quoted in Martin, *Mind of Frederick Douglass,* 1.

CHAPTER FOUR. *Contemplation versus Violence in Thoreau's World*

1. Quoted by Edward Emerson, "Notes," 134.

2. Cousin, quoted in Cameron, *Young Emerson's Transcendental Vision,* 578.

3. Richardson, *Emerson,* 115.

4. Thoreau, *A Week,* 137. Hereafter cited parenthetically in the text as *WK.* For informative discussions of the influence of the Gita on Thoreau, see Christy, *The Orient in American Transcendentalism,* 185–234; and Versluis, *Transcendentalism and Asian Religions,* 79–104. Christy makes the important point that the Gita "is a merging of the Yoga and Sankhya philosophies; and it advocates ways of life that are inherently incompatible" (25).

5. Friedrich, *The Gita within Walden,* 26.

6. *The Bhagavad-Gita,* 37. Hereafter cited parenthetically in the text.

7. Thoreau, *Journal,* 2: 240.

8. Thoreau, *Walden,* 161. Hereafter cited parenthetically in the text as *W.*

9. Thoreau, *Journal,* 1: 124.

10. Dimock, "Planetary Time and Global Translation," 503, 505, 504.

11. Thoreau, *Reform Papers,* 13. Hereafter cited parenthetically in the text as *RP.*

12. Thoreau, *Journal*, 8: 165–66.

13. Thoreau, *Journal*, 8: 185.

14. Thoreau, *Journal*, 8: 501, 200. As Petrulionis has shown, many of Thoreau's more furious journal entries (including those I have quoted here) did not make it into his "Slavery in Massachusetts" speech. She argues that he thus worked to cultivate the potential audience for *Walden*, which was soon to appear. See "Editorial Savoir Faire."

15. Sophia Hawthorne, speaking for her husband and herself, told her sister Elizabeth, "When you get so far out of my idea of right as to talk of its being proper to violate laws sometimes, because we 'can obey higher laws than we break' — this, dear Elizabeth, U used to hear in days past and I consider it a very dangerous and demoralizing doctrine and have always called it 'transcendental slang.' . . . I am just on the point of declaring that I hate transcendentalism because it is full of such immoderate dicta" (quoted in Tharp, *The Peabody Sisters of Salem*, 288–89).

16. Thoreau's admiration for Cromwell most likely derived from Thomas Carlyle's praise of him in his *On Heroes, Hero-Worship and the Heroic in History* (1841) and *Oliver Cromwell's Letters and Speeches* (1845), which Thoreau reviewed in *Graham's Magazine* for March and April 1847. See Richardson, *Henry David Thoreau*, 163–65.

17. Quoted in Harding, *The Days of Henry Thoreau*, 434.

18. Harding, *The Days of Henry Thoreau*, 423.

19. Mitchell, "Introduction," 28.

20. For the most thorough studies of Thoreau's readings in and use of Hindu texts, see Jeswine, "Henry David Thoreau." See also Hodder, "Concord Orientalism, Thoreauvian Autobiography, and the Artist of Kouroo."

21. Thoreau, *Journal*, 3: 213–14.

22. Emerson, *Collected Poems*, 159.

23. See Sattelmeyer, *Thoreau's Reading*, 68.

24. See Christy, *The Orient in American Transcendentalism*, 220–21. For detailed analysis of the influence of yoga discipline and the Gita on Thoreau's Walden experience, see MacShane, "*Walden* and Yoga"; and Stein, "Thoreau's *Walden* and the *Bhagavad Gita*."

25. Thoreau, *Correspondence*, 251.

26. Alcott, *Journals*, 190–91.

27. Alcott, *Journals*, 192–94.

28. Quoted in Peple, "Hawthorne on Thoreau, 1853–1857," 2–3.

29. Hawthorne, *The Scarlet Letter*, 1: 25.

30. Emerson, *Letters and Essays*, 48.

31. Paul, *Shores of America*, 353.

32. Johnson, *Thoreau's Complex Weave*, 96.

33. For a detailed discussion of Thoreau's views of slavery, see Meyer, "Thoreau and Black Emigration."

34. For a thorough discussion of the context of "Slavery in Massachusetts," see Albrecht, "Conflict and Resolution."

35. Lemire, *Black Walden*, 1.

36. See Jeswine, "Henry David Thoreau," 142–43.

37. Thoreau, *Correspondence*, 262–63.

38. Thoreau, *Correspondence*, 265.

39. Thoreau, *Journal*, 3: 95.

40. Thoreau, *Journal*, 8: 247.

41. Thoreau, *Correspondence*, 330.

42. Buell, *The Environmental Imagination*, 38.

43. Richardson, *Henry David Thoreau*, 372.

44. Thoreau, *Correspondence*, 583.

45. Thoreau, *Correspondence*, 611.

46. Conway, *Life of Nathaniel Hawthorne*, 206.

47. See Jones, "'The Hall of Fantasy' and the Early Hawthorne-Thoreau Relationship"; Predmore, "Thoreau's Influence in Hawthorne's 'The Artist of the Beautiful,'"; and Peple, "The Personal and Literary Relationship of Hawthorne and Thoreau," 94–127.

48. Hawthorne, *The American Notebooks*, 369.

49. On July 3, 1854, Sophia Hawthorne wrote to her sister Mary Mann, "We receive hundreds of newspapers — whig, democrat, free soil & all kinds, from Washington, New York, Boston & Salem, giving us every one of the speeches in Congress, and all the comments, criticisms, abuse, vituperation, and every thing else going on in those great United States" (quoted in Hawthorne, *The Letters, 1853–1856*, 17: 238 n.1).

50. For a discussion of *The Marble Faun* and its relation to Thoreau, see Reynolds, *Devils and Rebels*, 202–16.

51. Thoreau could have been referring to Bronson Alcott, past owner of Hawthorne's house. In *Walden*, Thoreau describes Alcott as "a true friend of man; almost the only friend of human progress. An Old mortality, say rather an Immortality, with unwearied patience and faith making plain the image engraven in men's bodies, the God of whom they are but defaced and leaning monuments. . . . I do not see how he can ever die" (*W* 269).

52. Hawthorne, *Elixir of Life Manuscripts*, 13: 499. Hereafter cited parenthetically in the text.

53. Hawthorne, *The Letters, 1857–1864*, 18: 605.

CHAPTER FIVE. *Violent Virtue and Alcott's* Moods

1. Alcott, "Recollections of My Childhood," 261; and "Reminiscences of Ralph Waldo Emerson," 284.

2. For details of Alcott's relations with Thoreau, see Stern, *Louisa May Alcott*, 20–22; Elbert, *A Hunger for Home*, 88–89; and Shealy, "Louisa May Alcott's Juvenilia."

3. Saxton, *Louisa May*, 226.

4. Alcott, *Moods* (1865), 1. Hereafter cited parenthetically in the text.

5. Elbert has speculated that Alcott "named him after Warwick Castle in England" and observed that he "is a confusing if attractive New World product constructed out of Old World materials" (*A Hunger for Home* 129).

6. Alcott, *Moods* (1882), v. This is the revised version of the 1865 *Moods*.

7. Major feminist studies that discuss Alcott's critiques of patriarchy include Auerbach, *Communities of Women*, 55–75; Judith Fetterley, "Little Women," 369–83; Showalter, *Alternative Alcott*; Fetterley, "Impersonating 'Little Women'"; and Keyser, *Whispers in the Dark*.

8. Deese, "Louisa May Alcott's 'Moods,'" 450.

9. Alcott, *Moods* (1882), 356.

10. Alcott, *Moods* (1882), 359.

11. Alcott, "Thoreau's Flute," 280.

12. Alcott, *The Journals of Bronson Alcott*, 316.

13. Alcott, *Selected Letters of Louisa May Alcott*, 49.

14. Alcott, *Journals of Bronson Alcott*, 320–21.

15. John Brown's daughter Anne told Bronson Alcott that Thoreau "reminded her of her father" (Petrulionis, *To Set This World Right*, 147).

16. Alcott, *Journals of Bronson Alcott*, 322.

17. Alcott, *Journals of Louisa May Alcott*, 95.

18. Alcott, *Journals of Louisa May Alcott*, 95.

19. For a thorough account of the arrest and rescue, see Petrulionis, *To Set This World Right*, 148–52.

20. Petrulionis, *To Set This World Right*, 98.

21. Petrulionis, *To Set This World Right*, 99–100. In the spring and summer of 1861, Anne and Sarah Brown returned to Concord and boarded with the

Alcotts, which created some frustrations for Louisa, whose sympathy for them had waned a bit. "John Brown's daughters came to board," she wrote in her journal, "and upset my plans of rest and writing when the report and the sewing were done. I had my fit of woe up garret on the fat rag-bag, and then put my papers away, and fell to work at housekeeping" (*Journals of Louisa May Alcott* 105).

22. Alcott, *Journals of Louisa May Alcott*, 104.

23. James, "Moods," 277.

24. Alcott, *Selected Letters of Louisa May Alcott*, 109.

25. Deese, "Louisa May Alcott's 'Moods,'" 452.

26. Keyser, *Whispers in the Dark*, 25.

27. John Stauffer, "Advent among the Indians," 238, 239.

28. Thoreau, *Journal*, 2: 177.

29. Alcott, *Journals of Bronson Alcott*, 325.

30. Emerson, *Essays and Lectures*, 1084.

31. Alcott, *Selected Letters of Louisa May Alcott*, 253.

32. Alcott, *Selected Letters of Louisa May Alcott*, 51–52.

33. Moulton, "Louisa May Alcott," 49.

34. Julian Hawthorne, "'By One Who Knew Her' (1932)," 209.

35. Alcott, *Little Women*, 63, 68.

36. Quoted in Matteson, *Eden's Outcasts*, 63.

37. Cheney, *Louisa May Alcott*, 73.

38. Alcott, *The Feminist Alcott*, 1.

39. Alcott, *The Feminist Alcott*, 238.

40. Abate in her study of the figure of the tomboy makes the important point that "[w]hile critics have frequently cast Jo as longing to enjoy the freedoms associated with a generic form of middle-class white masculinity, she wishes to partake in a more specific, heroic and politicized version of Northern white male bellicosity" (*Tomboys* 28).

41. Alcott, *Selected Letters of Louisa May Alcott*, 22.

42. Alcott, *Hospital Sketches*, 100. Hereafter cited parenthetically in the text.

43. Alcott, *Journals of Louisa May Alcott*, 109.

44. Matteson, *Eden's Outcasts*, 304, 306.

45. Alcott, *Louisa May Alcott on Race, Sex, and Slavery*, 27.

46. Stern, "Introduction," xxviii.

47. Paola Gemme, *Domesticating Foreign Struggles*, 124.

48. Greeley, "Margaret Fuller," 2.

49. Fuller, *Woman in the Nineteenth Century*, 25.

50. Elbert, "Introduction," xxiv.

51. Fuller, *Woman in the Nineteenth Century*, 15.

52. Alcott, *Selected Letters of Louisa May Alcott*, 253.

53. Alcott, *Journals of Louisa May Alcott*, 95.

54. Alcott, *Selected Letters of Louisa May Alcott*, 65.

55. Alcott, *Journals of Louisa May Alcott*, 105.

56. Cheney, *Louisa May Alcott*, 73.

57. Young, *Disarming the Nation*, 71. Young links Alcott's cross-gender iden-
tifications to "Alcott's own psychic conflicts as woman and as writer and to the
larger self-divisions of nineteenth-century female subjectivity to which her writings testify" (76–77).

58. Alcott, "With a Rose," 12.

59. Alcott, "Thoreau's Flute," 280–81.

60. Matteson, *Eden's Outcasts*, 279.

61. Alcott, *Louisa May Alcott on Race, Sex, and Slavery*, 57.

62. Alcott, *Louisa May Alcott on Race, Sex, and Slavery*, 67.

63. Alcott, *Louisa May Alcott on Race, Sex, and Slavery*, 77.

64. Alcott, *Louisa May Alcott on Race, Sex, and Slavery*, 77.

65. Alcott, *Louisa May Alcott on Race, Sex, and Slavery*, 86.

66. Davis, "'Brother against Brother,'" 146.

67. Matteson, *Eden's Outcasts*, 290–91.

68. Alcott, *Selected Letters of Louisa May Alcott*, 92–93.

69. Hawthorne, "'The Woman Who Wrote *Little Women*,'" 197.

70. Fite, "From Savage Passion to the Sweetness of Self-Control," 447.

71. Alcott, *Moods* (1882), 148.

72. Alcott, *Moods* (1882), 84.

73. Alcott, *Moods* (1882), 141–42.

74. Alcott, *Moods* (1882), 148.

75. Alcott, *Moods* (1882), 150–51.

76. Alcott, *Moods* (1882), 220.

77. Fuller, *Letters*, 5: 258.

CHAPTER SIX. *Pacifism, Savagery, and Hawthorne's Last Romances*

1. Quoted in Worthington, *Miss Alcott of Concord*, 109–10.

2. Alcott, *The Journals of Bronson Alcott*, 335–36.

3. Adams, "[Louisa May Alcott in the Early 1860s]," 8–9.

4. Alcott, *The Journals of Bronson Alcott*, 411–12.

5. Hawthorne, *The Letters, 1857–1864*, 18: 543.

6. Hawthorne, *The Elixir of Life Manuscripts*, 13: 23.

7. Hawthorne, *Miscellaneous Prose and Verse*, 23: 350.

8. Hawthorne, *American Notebooks*, 8: 112.

9. Hawthorne, *The Letters, 1857–1864*, 18: 590.

10. Hawthorne, *The Letters, 1857–1864*, 18: 420–421.

11. Hawthorne, *The Letters, 1857–1864*, 18: 543.

12. Hawthorne, *True Stories*, 6: 87–88.

13. Hawthorne, *True Stories*, 6: 50.

14. Hawthorne, *The Scarlet Letter*, 1: 95.

15. Hawthorne, *The Scarlet Letter*, 1: 256.

16. Hawthorne, *Miscellaneous Prose and Verse*, 23: 561, 562.

17. Webster, *Speech*, 32.

18. Hawthorne, *Tales and Sketches*, 1349. Hereafter cited parenthetically in the text.

19. Hawthorne, *Letters, 1857–1864*, 18: 387.

20. Hawthorne, *Letters, 1857–1864*, 18: 590.

21. Hawthorne, *Letters, 1853–1856*, 17: 294.

22. Conway, *Emerson, At Home and Abroad*, 303.

23. Curtis, "The Works of Nathaniel Hawthorne," 540.

24. Reynolds, *John Brown, Abolitionist*, 230.

25. Sanborn, "The John Brown Raid," 414.

26. Reynolds, *John Brown, Abolitionist*, 230, 231.

27. Phillips, "Wendell Phillips on the Puritan Principle," 111.

28. Hawthorne, *Miscellaneous Prose and Verse*, 23: 427.

29. Hawthorne, *Tales and Sketches*, 114.

30. Hawthorne, *True Stories*, 6: 259.

31. See Reynolds, *European Revolutions*, 79–96.

32. Hawthorne, *Peter Parley's Universal History*, 400.

33. Guizot, *History of the English Revolution*, 1: 450.

34. Marvell, "An Horatian Ode," 692–93.

35. Hawthorne, *The Scarlet Letter*, 1: 250.

36. Hawthorne, *True Stories*, 6: 258.

37. Hawthorne, *The English Notebooks, 1853–1856*, 21: 458.

38. Quoted in Hawthorne, *The English Notebooks, 1853–1856*, 21: 678.

39. Hawthorne, *The English Notebooks, 1856–1860*, 22: 218.

40. Newberry, *Hawthorne's Divided Loyalties*, 215.

41. Elsewhere I argue that *The Marble Faun* is also a sustained exploration of this issue (*Devils and Rebels* 202–16).

42. Hawthorne, *Tales and Sketches*, 132.

43. Hawthorne, *American Notebooks*, 8: 297.

44. Hawthorne, *The Scarlet Letter*, 1: 9.

45. According to the Quaker historian William Sewel, "When she was to be whipped at Dedham, and fastened to a cart, deputy Bellingham having seen Hawthorn's warrant, said, 'The warrant is firm,' and then bade the executioner go on; who, thus encouraged, laid on so severely, that with the knot of the whip he split the nipple of her breast, which so tortured her, that it had almost cost her her life; and she, who was a little weakly woman, thinking this would have been her lot, said once that if she should happen to die thus, she was willing that her body should be laid before Bellingham's door, with a charge from her mouth that he was guilty of her blood" (*The History of the Quakers* 1: 566–67).

46. Gollin, "Estranged Allegiances," 163.

47. Hawthorne, *American Claimant Manuscripts*, 12: 203. Hereafter cited parenthetically in the text.

48. Hawthorne, *Tales and Sketches*, 706.

49. Whittier, "Brown of Osawatomie," 304.

50. Hawthorne, *Miscellaneous Prose and Verse*, 23: 427.

51. Hawthorne, *Tales and Sketches*, 1492.

52. Hawthorne, *Miscellaneous Prose and Verse*, 23: 453.

53. Quoted in Lasseter, "Hawthorne's Legacy to Rebecca Harding Davis," 173. My paragraph is indebted to Lasseter's essay.

54. Quoted in Lasseter, "Hawthorne's Legacy," 174.

55. Davidson, *Hawthorne's Last Phase*, 66.

56. Mellow, *Nathaniel Hawthorne in His Times*, 547.

57. Hawthorne, *Letters, 1813–1843*, 15: 590.

58. Hawthorne, *Elixir of Life Manuscripts*, 13: 14. Hereafter cited parenthetically in the text.

59. Wineapple, *Hawthorne*, 347.

60. Hawthorne, *Miscellaneous Prose and Verse*, 23: 416. Hereafter cited parenthetically in the text.

61. Hawthorne, *The Letters, 1857–1864*, 18: 455.

62. "Misconceptions of Peace," 133.

63. Hawthorne, *The Letters, 1857–1864*, 18: 590–91.

64. Hawthorne, *Our Old Home*, 5: 342.

65. Higginson, "Hawthorne's Last Bequest," 103. Hereafter cited parenthetically in the text.

66. See Reynolds, *Devils and Rebels*, 1–13.

CHAPTER SEVEN. *The Revolutionary Times of Melville's* Billy Budd

1. See Reynolds, *European Revolutions,* 97–124.

2. Melville, *White-Jacket,* 315.

3. Melville, *Poems,* 163. Hereafter cited parenthetically in the text.

4. Carolyn Karcher has pointed out the problem with Melville's postwar emphasis on renewed brotherhood: "Reconciliation between northern and southern whites was exactly what Douglass most dreaded, for he knew it would mean once again sacrificing African Americans" ("White Fratricide, Black Liberation" 357).

5. Quoted in Parker, *Herman Melville,* 2: 617–18.

6. *Harper's Weekly* 30 (13 March 1886), 172.

7. Trachtenberg, *Incorporation of America,* 203.

8. See Robert K. Wallace, "*Billy Budd* and the Haymarket Hangings"; Rogin, *Subversive Genealogy,* 284; and Franklin, "From Empire to Empire: *Billy Budd, Sailor.*"

9. Melville, *Billy Budd, Sailor (An Inside Narrative),* 62. Hereafter cited parenthetically in the text.

10. Stern, *Billy Budd,* 10 n.12.

11. See Reynolds, "Kings and Commoners."

12. Melville, *Pierre,* 212.

13. Melville, *Moby-Dick,* 466.

14. Melville, *Mardi,* 499. Hereafter cited parenthetically in the text.

15. Quoted in Moody, *The Astor Place Riot,* 116.

16. Berthold, "Class Acts," 440.

17. As Berthold points out, "the mob constructed a barricade at Fourth Avenue and Ninth Street, within eyeshot of Melville's house. For at least one agonizing night Melville and his family must have slept uneasily, dreading a workers' assault on their home" ("Class Acts" 438).

18. Garner, *The Civil War World of Herman Melville,* 97. Garner points out that when the war began, Melville put his pacifism temporarily aside: "Although he had always loathed the gore and the carnage of war, the contrary elements in his nature now condoned them" (89).

19. Melville, *Poems,* 43.

20. Melville, *Poems,* 74.

21. Stern, "Introduction," xxvii.

22. Melville, *Clarel,* 478–79.

23. Bezanson, "Explanatory Notes," in *Clarel,* 587.

24. Brook Thomas has also noted that plans for celebrating the centenary of the first French revolution turned American attention to the subject; see his *Cross-examinations of Law and Literature*, 239.

25. Melville, *Billy Budd*, edited by Stern, 97–98. This quotation does not appear in the Hayford and Sealts edition of *Billy Budd*, but as Stern has argued, there is no absolute proof Melville discarded the manuscript leaves on which it appears and thus they should be included rather than excluded in editions of the work.

26. Melville, *Billy Budd: The Genetic Text*, 313.

27. Melville, *Billy Budd: The Genetic Text*, 300.

28. See Garner, "Fraud as Fact in Herman Melville's *Billy Budd*."

29. Reynolds, *European Revolutions*, 122.

30. Melville, *Moby-Dick*, 424.

31. Melville, *The Piazza Tales*, 49.

32. Richards, "Melville's (Inter)National Burlesque," 83.

33. Melville, *Clarel*, 157.

34. Melville, *Billy Budd*, ed. Stern, 98.

35. Garner, "Melville in the Custom House, 1881–1882,"14.

36. Garner, "Melville in the Custom House," 9.

37. Leyda, *The Melville Log*, 2: 731.

38. Sealts, "Innocence and Infamy," 416.

39. Cohen and Yannella, *Herman Melville's Malcolm Letter*, 56–60. Cohen and Yannella show that members of the Melville-Gansevoort family, including Melville himself, used authoritarian methods of childrearing to produce dutiful children and to maintain family strength and solidarity.

40. Andrew Delbanco has suggested that *Billy Budd* can be read as a eulogy to Malcolm, written twenty years after the boy's death; Melville "poured his heart into *Billy Budd*, the story of a beautiful boy whose last act is to bless the severe yet tender man who has ordered that he be put to death" (*Melville* 278–79).

41. Metcalf, *Herman Melville*, 38; James Duban has identified the source of the quotation as Thomas Carlyle's translation of Goethe's *Wilhelm Meister's Travels* ("'Visible Objects of Reverence'" 7).

42. Leyda, *Log*, 2: 830, 832.

43. Quoted in Leyda, *Log*, 2: 296.

44. Quoted in Schnapper, *American Labor*, 113.

45. Quoted in Schnapper, *American Labor*, 111.

46. See Foner, *History of the Labor Movement*, 2: 107–11.

47. Mizruchi, "Cataloging," 297.

EPILOGUE

1. Fuller, *"These Sad But Glorious Days,"* 321.

2. Douglass, *Life and Writings*, 3: 318.

3. Thoreau, *Journal*, 8: 165–66.

4. Alcott, *Journals of Louisa May Alcott*, 109.

5. Hawthorne, *The Letters, 1857–1864*, 18: 420–21.

6. Alcott, *Moods* (1865), 199–200.

7. Hawthorne, *Elixir of Life Manuscripts*, 13: 43.

8. Hawthorne, *The Letters, 1857–1864*, 18: 387–88.

9. Dower, *Cultures of War*, 302.

BIBLIOGRAPHY

Abate, Michelle Ann. *Tomboys: A Literary and Cultural History*. Philadelphia: Temple University Press, 2008.

Adams, Anne Brown. "[Louisa May Alcott in the Early 1860s.]" In *Alcott in Her Own Time*, ed. Daniel Shealy, 7–11. Iowa City: University of Iowa Press, 2005.

Aikin, John. "Dialogue between a Master and a Slave." In *Columbian Orator: Containing a Variety of Original and Selected Pieces Together with Rules Calculated to Improve Youth and Others in the Ornamental and Useful Art of Eloquence*, ed. Caleb Bingham, 240–42. Boston: J.H.A. Frost, Lincoln and Edmands, et al., 1832.

Albrecht, Robert C. "Conflict and Resolution: 'Slavery in Massachusetts.'" *ESQ* 19 (1973): 179–88.

Alcott, Bronson. *The Journals of Bronson Alcott*. Ed. Odell Shepard. Boston: Little, Brown, 1938.

Alcott, Louisa May. *The Feminist Alcott: Stories of a Woman's Power*. Ed. Madeleine B. Stern. Boston: Northeastern University Press, 1996.

———. *Hospital Sketches*. Ed. Alice Fahs. 1863. Reprint, Boston: Bedford/St. Martin's, 2004.

———. *The Journals of Louisa May Alcott*. Ed. Joel Myerson and Daniel Shealy. Athens and London: University of Georgia Press, 1997.

———. *Little Women: or, Meg, Jo, Beth and Amy*. Ed. Anne K. Phillips and Gregory Eisenlein. 1868–69. Reprint, New York: Norton, 2004.

———. *Louisa May Alcott on Race, Sex, and Slavery*. Ed. Sarah Elbert. Boston: Northeastern University Press, 1997.

———. *Moods*. Ed. Sarah Elbert. 1865. Reprint, New Brunswick, N.J.: Rutgers University Press, 1991.

————. *Moods, A Novel.* Boston: Roberts Brothers, 1882.

————. "Recollections of My Childhood." *Youth's Companion,* May 24, 1888, 261.

————. "Reminiscences of Ralph Waldo Emerson." In *Some Noted Princes, Authors, and Statesmen of Our Time,* ed. James Parton, 284–88. New York: Thomas Y. Crowell, 1885.

————. *The Selected Letters of Louisa May Alcott.* Ed. Joel Myerson and Daniel Shealy. Athens: University of Georgia Press, 1995.

————. "Thoreau's Flute." *Atlantic Monthly* 12 (September 1863): 280–81.

————. "With a Rose." *The Liberator* 30 (January 20, 1860): 12.

"Annual Meeting of the Massachusetts Anti-Slavery Society." *Liberator* 29 (February 4, 1859): 18–19.

Auerbach, Nina. *Communities of Women: An Idea in Fiction.* Cambridge: Harvard University Press, 1978.

Avrich, Paul. *The Haymarket Tragedy.* Princeton, N.J.: Princeton University Press, 1984.

Bean, Judith Mattson. "Margaret Fuller on the Early Poetry of Julia Ward Howe: An Uncollected Letter." *ANQ: A Quarterly Journal of Short Articles, Notes, and Reviews* 7, no. 2 (April 1994): 76–80.

Bell, Madison Smartt. *Toussaint Louverture: A Biography.* New York: Pantheon, 2007.

Berthold, Dennis. "Class Acts: The Astor Place Riots and Melville's 'The Two Temples.'" *American Literature* 71 (September 1999): 429–61.

Bezanson, Walter E. "Explanatory Notes." In *Clarel,* by Herman Melville. Ed. Walter E. Bezanson. New York: Hendricks House, 1960.

The Bhagvat-Gita. Trans. Charles Wilkins. 1785. Reprint, Gainesville, Fla.: Scholars' Facsimiles & Reprints, 1959.

Blight, David W. *Frederick Douglass' Civil War: Keeping Faith in Jubilee.* Baton Rouge: Louisiana State University Press, 1989.

Bosco, Ronald A., and Joel Myerson, eds. *Emerson: Bicentennial Essays.* Boston: Massachusetts Historical Society, 2006.

Bray, Jessie. "'Not a *pure* idealist': Ralph Waldo Emerson, Edward Waldo Emerson, and the Civil War." *Resources for American Literary Study* 32 (2007): 85–97.

Breunig, Charles. *The Age of Revolution and Reaction: 1789–1850.* New York: Norton, 1970.

Brewer, W. M. "Henry Highland Garnet." *The Journal of Negro History* 13 (January 1928): 36–52.

Brown, J. Newton. "The Beginning of John Brown's Career." *The Nation* 98 (February 12, 1914): 157.

Brown, Merle Elliott. "Hawthorne and Parley's Universal History." *Papers of the Bibliographical Society of America* 48 (1954): 77–90.

Buell, Lawrence. *The Environmental Imagination: Thoreau, Nature Writing, and the Formation of American Culture.* Cambridge: Harvard University Press, 1995.

Burkholder, Robert E. "(Re)Visiting 'The Adirondacs': Emerson's Confrontation with Wild Nature." In *Emerson: Bicentennial Essays*, ed. Bosco and Myerson, 247–69.

Bush, Harold K. "Emerson, John Brown, and 'Doing the Word': The Enactment of Political Religion at Harpers Ferry, 1859." In *The Emerson Dilemma*, ed. Garvey, 197–217.

Cabot, James Elliot. *A Memoir of Ralph Waldo Emerson.* 2 vols. Boston: Houghton Mifflin, 1887.

Cameron, Kenneth Walter. *Young Emerson's Transcendental Vision: An Exposition of His World View with an Analysis of the Structure, Background and Meaning of Nature (1836).* Hartford, Conn.: Transcendental Books, 1971.

Capper, Charles. *Margaret Fuller: An American Romantic Life.* 2 vols. New York: Oxford University Press, 1992, 2007.

Capper, Charles, and Conrad Edick Wright, eds. *Transient and Permanent: The Transcendentalist Movement and Its Contexts.* Boston: Massachusetts Historical Society, 1999.

Carlyle, Thomas, ed. *Oliver Cromwell's Letters and Speeches.* 5 vols. 3rd ed. London: Robson and Sons, 1849.

Carton, Evan. *Patriotic Treason: John Brown and the Soul of America.* New York: Free Press, 2006.

Channing, Steven A. *Crisis of Fear: Secession in South Carolina.* New York: Norton, 1974.

Channing, William E. "A Letter to Abolitionists." *Liberator* 7 (December 22, 1837): 206.

Cheney, Edna, ed. *Louisa May Alcott: Life, Letters and Journals.* New York: Gramercy Books, 1995.

Christy, Arthur. *The Orient in American Transcendentalism: A Study of Emerson, Thoreau, and Alcott.* 1932. Reprint, New York: Octagon Books, 1963.

Cohen, Hennig, and Donald Yannella. *Herman Melville's Malcolm Letter: "Man's Final Lore."* New York: Fordham University Press and the New York Public Library, 1992.

Cole, Phyllis. "Emerson, England, and Fate." In *Emerson: Prophecy, Metamorphosis, and Influence,* ed. David Levin, 83–105. New York: Columbia University Press, 1975.

Conway, Moncure Daniel. *Autobiography: Memories and Experiences.* 2 vols. New York: Cassell, 1904.

———. *Emerson, At Home and Abroad.* 1883. Reprint, New York: Haskell House, 1968.

———. *Life of Nathaniel Hawthorne.* 1890. Reprint, New York: Haskell House, 1968.

Curtis, George W. "The Works of Nathaniel Hawthorne." *North American Review* 99 (October 1864): 539–57.

David, Henry. *The History of the Haymarket Affair: A Study in the American Social-Revolutionary and Labor Movements.* New York: Russell & Russell, 1936.

Davidson, Edward Hutchins. *Hawthorne's Last Phase.* New Haven: Yale University Press, 1949.

Davis, David Brion. "The Emergence of Immediatism in British and American Antislavery Thought." *The Mississippi Valley Historical Review* 49, no. 2 (September 1962): 209–30.

Davis, Matthew R. "'Brother against Brother': Reconstructing the American Family in the Civil War Era." *ESQ: A Journal of the American Renaissance* 55, no. 2 (2009): 135–63.

Dayan, Joan Dayan. *Haiti, History, and the Gods.* Berkeley: University of California Press, 1995.

"Declaration of Sentiments." In *Report of the Woman's Rights Convention, Held at Seneca Falls, N.Y., July 19th and 20th, 1848,* 7–8. Rochester: John Dick, at the North Star Office, 1848.

Deese, Helen R. "Louisa May Alcott's 'Moods': A New Archival Discovery." *New England Quarterly* 76 (Sept. 2003): 439–55.

Delbanco, Andrew. *Melville: His World and Work.* New York: Knopf, 2005.

Demos, John. "The Antislavery Movement and the Problem of Violent 'Means.'" *New England Quarterly* 37 (December 1964): 501–26.

Dimock, Wai Chee. "Planetary Time and Global Translation: 'Context' in Literary Studies." *Common Knowledge* 9, no. 3 (2003): 488–507.

Douglass, Frederick. *Autobiographies: Narrative of the Life of Frederick Douglass, an American Slave; My Bondage and My Freedom; Life and Times of Frederick Douglass.* New York: Library of America, 1994. Abbreviated as *A.*

———. *The Frederick Douglass Papers,* ser. 1, *Speeches, Debates, and Interviews.* 5 vols. Ed. John W. Blassingame et al. New Haven: Yale University Press, 1979–92. Abbreviated as *FDP.*

———. *The Heroic Slave.* In *The Oxford Frederick Douglass Reader,* ed. William L. Andrews, 131–63. New York: Oxford University Press, 1996.

———. "John Brown: An Address at the Fourteenth Anniversary of Storer College." In Quarles, *Allies for Freedom and Blacks on John Brown,* 54–66.

———. *The Life and Writings of Frederick Douglass.* 5 vols. Ed. Philip S. Foner. New York: International Publishers, 1950–75. Abbreviated as *LW.*

———. "To Captain Thomas Auld, Formerly My Master." *North Star,* September 7, 1849.

Dower, John W. *Cultures of War: Pearl Harbor / Hiroshima / 9-11 / Iraq.* New York: Norton / New Press, 2010.

[Drayton, William]. *The South Vindicated from the Treason and Fanaticism of the Northern Abolitionists.* 1836. Reprint, New York: Negro Universities Press, 1969.

Duban, James. "'Visible Objects of Reverence': Quotations from Goethe in Melville's Annotated New Testament." *Leviathan: A Journal of Melville Studies* 9 (June 2007): 1–23.

Edelstein, Tilden G. *Strange Enthusiasm: A Life of Thomas Wentworth Higginson.* New Haven: Yale University Press, 1968.

Elbert, Sarah. *A Hunger for Home: Louisa May Alcott and "Little Women."* Philadelphia: Temple University Press, 1984.

———. Introduction to *Moods,* by Louisa May Alcott, ed. Sarah Elbert, xi–xlii. 1865. Reprint, New Brunswick, N.J.: Rutgers University Press, 1991.

Emerson, Edward. "Notes." In *Miscellanies,* by Ralph Waldo Emerson, ed. Edward Emerson, 547–648. 1904. Reprint, New York: AMS Press, 1968.

Emerson, Ralph Waldo, "American Civilization (1862)." In *The Political Emerson: Essential Writings on Politics and Social Reform,* ed. David M. Robinson, 158–76. Boston: Beacon, 2004.

———. *Collected Poems and Translations.* New York: Library of America, 1974.

———. *The Correspondence of Emerson and Carlyle.* Ed. Joseph Slater. New York: Columbia University Press, 1964.

———. "Dedication of the Soldiers' Monument in Concord." In *Miscellanies.* Vol. 11 of *The Complete Works of Ralph Waldo Emerson,* ed. Edward Emerson, 347–79. 1904. Reprint, New York: AMS Press, 1968.

———. *Emerson-Clough Letters.* Ed. Howard F. Lowry and Ralph Leslie Rusk. N.p.: Archon Books, 1968.

———. *Emerson's Antislavery Writings.* Ed. Len Gougeon and Joel Myerson. New Haven: Yale University Press, 1995. Abbreviated as *AW.*

———. *Essays and Lectures.* Ed. Joel Porte. New York: Library of America, 1983.

———. "Hymn: Sung at the Completion of the Concord Monument, April 19, 1838." In Emerson, *Collected Poems*, 125.

———. *The Journals and Miscellaneous Notebooks of Ralph Waldo Emerson*. Ed. William H. Gilman et al. 16 vols. Cambridge: Harvard University Press, Belknap Press, 1960–82. Abbreviated as *JMN*.

———. *The Later Lectures of Ralph Waldo Emerson, 1843–1871*. Ed. Ronald A. Bosco and Joel Myerson. 2 vols. Athens: University of Georgia Press, 2001.

———. *The Letters of Ralph Waldo Emerson*. Ed. Ralph L. Rusk and Eleanor M. Tilton. 10 vols. New York: Columbia University Press, 1939–95.

———. "Man of Letters." In *Lectures and Biographical Sketches*. Vol. 10 of *The Complete Works of Ralph Waldo Emerson,* ed. Edward Emerson, 239–58. 1904. Reprint, New York: AMS Press, 1968.

———. "War." In *Miscellanies*. Vol. 11 of *The Complete Works of Ralph Waldo Emerson*, ed. Edward Emerson, 151–76. 1904. Reprint, New York: AMS Press, 1968.

Erkkila, Betsy. "Revolution in the Renaissance." *ESQ* 49, nos. 1–3 (2003): 17–32.

Fetterley, Judith. "Impersonating 'Little Women': The Radicalism of Alcott's *Behind a Mask*." *Women's Studies* 10 (1983): 1–14.

———. "Little Women: Alcott's Civil War." *Feminist Studies* 5 (Summer 1979): 369–83.

Fite, Keren. "From Savage Passion to the Sweetness of Self-Control: Female Anger in *Little Women* and 'Pauline's Passions and Punishment.'" *Women's Writing* 14 (December 2007): 435–48.

Foner, Philip S. *The Great Labor Uprising of 1877*. New York: Monad Press, 1977.

———. *From the Founding of the American Federation of Labor to the Emergence of American Imperialism*. Vol. 2 of *History of the Labor Movement in the United States*. New York: International Publishers, 1955.

Franchot, Jenny. "The Punishment of Esther: Frederick Douglass and the Construction of the Feminine." In *Frederick Douglass: New Literary and Historical Essays*, ed. Eric J. Sundquist, 141–65. Cambridge: Cambridge University Press, 1990.

Franklin, H. Bruce. "From Empire to Empire: *Billy Budd, Sailor*." In *Herman Melville: Reassessments*, ed. A. Robert Lee, 199–216. Totowa, N.J.: Barnes & Noble, 1984.

Friedrich, Paul. *The Gita within Walden*. Albany: State University of New York Press, 2008.

Fuller, Margaret. "'The Impulses of Human Nature': Margaret Fuller's Journal from June through October 1844." Ed. Martha L. Berg and Alice de V. Perry. *Massachusetts Historical Society Proceedings* 102 (1990): 38–126.

———. *The Letters of Margaret Fuller.* Ed. Robert N. Hudspeth. 6 vols. Ithaca, N.Y.: Cornell University Press, 1988.

———. *Margaret Fuller, Critic: Writings from the "New-York Tribune," 1844–1846.* Ed. Judith Mattson Bean and Joel Myerson. New York: Columbia University Press, 2000.

———. *"These Sad But Glorious Days": Dispatches from Europe, 1846–1850.* Ed. Larry J. Reynolds and Susan Belasco Smith. New Haven, Conn.: Yale University Press, 1991. Abbreviated as *SG.*

———. *Woman in the Nineteenth Century.* Ed. Larry J. Reynolds. 1845. Reprint, New York: Norton, 1998.

Fuller Ossoli, Margaret. *At Home and Abroad, or, Things and Thoughts in America and Europe.* Ed. Arthur B. Fuller. 1856. Reprint, Port Washington, N.Y.: Kennikat Press, 1971.

Garner, Stanton. *The Civil War World of Herman Melville.* Lawrence: University of Kansas Press, 1993.

———. "Fraud as Fact in Herman Melville's *Billy Budd.*" *San Jose Studies* 4 (1978): 85–105.

———. "Melville in the Custom House, 1881–1882: A Rustic Beauty Among the Highborn Dames of Court." *Melville Society Extracts* 35 (1978): 12–15.

Garnet, Henry Highland. "Call to Rebellion." In *Words That Changed America,* ed. Alex Barnett, 33–36. N.p.: Lyons Press, 2003.

Garrison, William Lloyd. "The Dangers of the Nation" (1832). In *Selections from the Writings and Speeches of William Lloyd Garrison,* 44–61. 1852. Reprint, New York: Negro Universities Press, 1968.

———. "Dr. Webster's Address at Bunker Hill." *Liberator* 13 (July 14, 1843): 111.

———. "John Brown and the Principle of Nonresistance." *Liberator* 29 (December 16, 1859): 198.

———. "A Martyr for Liberty: Slain by the Hands of His Own Countrymen!" *Liberator* 7 (November 24, 1837): 191.

———. "The Virginia Insurrection." *Liberator* 29 (October 21, 1859): 166.

Garvey, T. Gregory. "Emerson, Garrison, and the Anti-Slavery Society." In *Emerson: Bicentennial Essays,* ed. Bosco and Myerson, 153–82.

———, ed. *The Emerson Dilemma: Essays on Emerson and Social Reform.* Athens: University of Georgia Press, 2001.

Gemme, Paola. *Domesticating Foreign Struggles: The Italian Risorgimento and Antebellum American Identity.* Athens: University of Georgia Press, 2005.

Giles, Paul. "Narrative Reversals and Power Exchanges: Frederick Douglass and British Culture." *American Literature* 73 (December 2000): 779–810.

Gleason, William. "Volcanoes and Meteors: Douglass, Melville, and the Poetics of Insurrection." In *Frederick Douglass and Herman Melville: Essays in Relation,* ed. Robert S. Levine and Samuel Otter, 110–33. Chapel Hill: University of North Carolina Press, 2008.

Goldstein, Leslie Friedman. "Violence as an Instrument for Social Change: The Views of Frederick Douglass (1817–1895)." *Journal of Negro History* 61 (January 1976): 61–72.

Gollin, Rita K. "Estranged Allegiances in Hawthorne's Unfinished Romances." In *Hawthorne and the Real,* ed. Millicent Bell, 159–80. Columbus: Ohio State University Press, 2005.

Gougeon, Len. "Emerson and the British: Challenging the Limits of Liberty." In *Liberty Ltd.: Civil Rights, Civil Liberties, and Literature.* Vol. 22 of *Real: Yearbook of Research in English and American Literature,* ed. Brook Thomas, 179–213. Tübingen: Gunter Narr Verlag, 2006.

———. "Emerson's Abolition Conversion." In *The Emerson Dilemma,* ed. Garvey, 170–96.

———. "'Fortune of the Republic': Emerson, Lincoln, and Transcendental Warfare." *ESQ: A Journal of the American Renaissance* 45, nos. 3–4 (1999): 259–324.

———. *Virtue's Hero: Emerson, Antislavery, and Reform.* Athens and London: University of Georgia Press, 1990.

Greeley, Horace. "Margaret Fuller." *New-York Daily Tribune,* May 12, 1860, 2.

Green, James. *Death in the Haymarket: A Story of Chicago, the First Labor Movement and the Bombing That Divided Gilded Age America.* New York: Anchor Books, 2007.

Gross, Robert A. *The Minutemen and Their World.* New York: Hill & Wang, 1976.

Guizot, François. *History of the English Revolution of 1640, Commonly Called the Great Rebellion: From the Accession of Charles I to His Death.* 2 vols. Trans. William Hazlitt. New York: Appleton, 1846.

Hallahan, William H. *The Day the American Revolution Began: 19 April 1775.* New York: William Morrow, 2000.

Hancock, John. "Monthly Intelligence." *Pennsylvania Magazine; or, American Monthly Museum* 1 (July 1775): 333.

Hardack, Richard. "The Slavery of Romanism: The Casting Out of the Irish in the Work of Frederick Douglass." In *Liberating Sojourn: Frederick Douglass and Transatlantic Reform*, ed. Alan J. Rice and Martin Crawford, 115–40. Athens: University of Georgia Press, 1999.

Harding, Walter. *The Days of Henry Thoreau.* New York: Knopf, 1970.

Hawthorne, Julian. "'By One Who Knew Her' (1932)." In *Alcott in Her Own Time*, ed. Daniel Shealy, 188–210. Iowa City: University of Iowa Press, 2005.

———. "'The Woman Who Wrote *Little Women*' (1922)." In *Alcott in Her Own Time*, ed. Daniel Shealy, 189–201. Iowa City: University of Iowa Press, 2005.

Hawthorne, Nathaniel. *The American Claimant Manuscripts.* Vol. 12 of *The Centenary Edition of the Works of Nathaniel Hawthorne.* Ed. Edward H. Davidson, Claude M. Simpson, and L. Neal Smith. Columbus: Ohio State University Press, 1977.

———. *The American Notebooks.* Vol. 8 of *The Centenary Edition of the Works of Nathaniel Hawthorne.* Ed. Claude M. Simpson. Columbus: Ohio State University Press, 1972.

———. *The Blithedale Romance; and, Fanshawe.* Vol. 3 of *The Centenary Edition of the Works of Nathaniel Hawthorne.* Ed. Fredson Bowers et al. Columbus: Ohio State University Press, 1971.

———. *The Elixir of Life Manuscripts.* Vol. 13 of *The Centenary Edition of the Works of Nathaniel Hawthorne.* Ed. Edward H. Davidson, Claude M. Simpson, and L. Neal Smith. Columbus: Ohio State University Press, 1977.

———. *The English Notebooks, 1853–1856.* Vol. 21 of *The Centenary Edition of the Works of Nathaniel Hawthorne.* Ed. Thomas Woodson and Bill Ellis. Columbus: Ohio State University Press, 1997.

———. *The English Notebooks, 1856–1860.* Vol. 22 of *The Centenary Edition of the Works of Nathaniel Hawthorne.* Ed. Thomas Woodson and Bill Ellis. Columbus: Ohio State University Press, 1997.

———. *The Letters, 1813–1843.* Vol. 15 of *The Centenary Edition of the Works of Nathaniel Hawthorne.* Ed. Thomas Woodson, L. Neal Smith, and Norman Holmes Pearson. Ohio State University Press, 1985.

———. *The Letters, 1853–1856.* Vol. 17 of *The Centenary Edition of the Works of Nathaniel Hawthorne.* Ed. Thomas Woodson et al. Columbus: Ohio State University Press, 1987.

———. *The Letters, 1857–1864.* Vol. 18 of *The Centenary Edition of the Works of Nathaniel Hawthorne.* Ed. Thomas Woodson et al. Columbus: Ohio State University Press, 1987.

———. *Miscellaneous Prose and Verse.* Vol. 23 of *The Centenary Edition of the Works of Nathaniel Hawthorne.* Ed. Thomas Woodson, Claude M. Simpson, and L. Neal Smith. Columbus: Ohio State University Press, 1995.

————. *Mosses from an Old Manse.* Vol. 10 of *The Centenary Edition of the Works of Nathaniel Hawthorne.* Ed. William Charvat, Roy Harvey Pearce, and Claude M. Simpson. Columbus: Ohio State University Press, 1974.

————. *Our Old Home.* Vol. 5 of *The Centenary Edition of the Works of Nathaniel Hawthorne.* Ed. Fredson Bowers and L. Neal Smith. Columbus: Ohio State University Press, 1970.

————. *Peter Parley's Universal History on the Basis of Geography.* London: John W. Parker, 1837.

————. *The Scarlet Letter.* Vol. 1 of *The Centenary Edition of the Works of Nathaniel Hawthorne.* Ed. William Charvat, Roy Harvey Pearce, and Claude M. Simpson. Columbus: Ohio State University Press, 1962.

————. *Tales and Sketches; A Wonderbook for Girls and Boys; Tanglewood Tales for Girls and Boys.* New York: Library of America, 1982.

————. *True Stories.* Vol. 6 of *The Centenary Edition of the Works of Nathaniel Hawthorne.* Ed. Fredson Bowers, L. Neal Smith, and John Manning. Columbus: Ohio State University Press, 1974.

Higginson, Thomas Wentworth. "1854: Letters on the Anthony Burns Affair." Houghton Library, MS AM 784, 481.

————. "Attempted Rescue of Burns." *Liberator* 25 (August 24, 1855): 134.

————. *Cheerful Yesterdays.* 1898. Reprint, New York: Arno Press, 1968.

————. "Hawthorne's Last Bequest." *Scribner's Monthly* 5 (November 1872): 100–105.

————. *Margaret Fuller Ossoli.* 1898. Reprint, New York: Confucian Press, 1980.

————. "Massachusetts in Mourning! A SERMON." *National Anti-Slavery Standard,* June 24, 1854, 20.

————. "Nat Turner's Insurrection." *Atlantic Monthly* 8 (August 1861): 173–87.

Hodder, Alan D. "Concord Orientalism, Thoreauvian Autobiography, and the Artist of Kouroo." In *Transient and Permanent: The Transcendentalist Movement and Its Contexts,* ed. Charles Capper and Conrad Edick Wright, 190–226. Boston: Massachusetts Historical Society, 1999.

"Horrid Tragedy." *Philanthropist* 2 (November 21, 1837): 1.

Howe, Julia Ward. "Battle Hymn of the Republic." *Atlantic Monthly* 9 (February 1862): 145.

————. *Margaret Fuller.* Boston: Roberts Brothers, 1883.

————. *Passion-Flowers.* Boston: Ticknor, Reed, Fields, 1854.

James, C.L.R. *The Black Jacobins: Toussaint L'Ouverture and the San Domingo Revolution.* 2nd ed. rev. New York: Random House, 1963.

James, Henry. "Moods." *The North American Review* 101 (July 1865): 276–81.

Jarrett, Gene Andrew. "Douglass, Ideological Slavery, and Postbellum Racial Politics" In *The Cambridge Companion to Frederick Douglass*, ed. Maurice S. Lee, 160–72. New York: Cambridge University Press, 2009.

Jay, Gregory. "Douglass, Melville, and the Lynching of Billy Budd." In *Frederick Douglass and Herman Melville: Essays in Relation*, ed. Robert S. Levine and Samuel Otter, 369–95. Chapel Hill: University of North Carolina Press, 2008.

Jeswine, Miriam Alice. "Henry David Thoreau: Apprentice to the Hindu Sages." PhD diss., University of Oregon, 1971.

Johnson, Linck C. "Emerson, Thoreau's Arrest, and the Trials of American Manhood." In *The Emerson Dilemma*, ed. Garvey, 35–64.

———. *Thoreau's Complex Weave: The Writing of "A Week on the Concord and Merrimack Rivers."* Charlottesville: University Press of Virginia, 1986.

Johnson, Michael P. "Denmark Vesey and His Co-Conspirators." *William and Mary Quarterly* 58 (October 2001): 915–76.

Jones, Buford. "'The Hall of Fantasy' and the Early Hawthorne-Thoreau Relationship." *PMLA* 83 (1968): 1429–38.

Jones, Howard. "The Peculiar Institution and National Honor: The Case of the Creole Slave Revolt." *Civil War History* (1975): 28–50.

"The Jubilee—Glorious Demonstration." *Liberator* 14 (August 9, 1844): 127.

Karcher, Carolyn L. "White Fratricide, Black Liberation: Melville, Douglass, and Civil War Memory." In *Frederick Douglass and Herman Melville: Essays in Relation*, ed. Robert S. Levine and Samuel Otter, 349–68. Chapel Hill: University of North Carolina Press, 2008.

Keyser, Elizabeth Lennox. *Whispers in the Dark: The Fiction of Louisa May Alcott.* Knoxville: University of Tennessee Press, 1993.

Lasseter, Janice Milner. "Hawthorne's Legacy to Rebecca Harding Davis." In *Hawthorne and Women: Engendering and Expanding the Hawthorne Tradition*, ed. John L. Idol Jr. and Melinda M. Ponder, 168–78. Amherst: University of Massachusetts Press, 1999.

Lemire, Elise. *Black Walden: Slavery and Its Aftermath in Concord, Massachusetts.* Philadelphia: University of Pennsylvania Press, 2009.

Leverenz, David. *Manhood and the American Renaissance.* Ithaca: Cornell University Press, 1989.

Levine, Robert S. "Frederick Douglass, War, Haiti." *PMLA* 124 (October 2009): 1864–68.

———. *Martin Delany, Frederick Douglass, and the Politics of Representative Identity.* Chapel Hill: University of North Carolina Press, 1997.

———. "*Uncle Tom's Cabin* in *Frederick Douglass' Paper:* An Analysis of Reception." *American Literature* 64 (March 1992): 71–93.

Leyda, Jay. *The Melville Log: A Documentary Life of Herman Melville, 1819–1891.* 2 vols. 1951. Reprint, with additional material, New York: Gordian Press, 1969.

Lincoln, William S. *Alton Trials: Of Winthrop S. Gilman.* New York: J. F. Trow, 1838.

Longfellow, Henry Wadsworth. *The Letters of Henry Wadsworth Longfellow.* Vol. 3. *1844–1856.* Ed. Andrew Hilen. Cambridge, Mass.: Harvard University Press, Belknap Press, 1972.

———. *Life of Henry Wadsworth Longfellow.* Volume 2. Ed. Samuel Longfellow. Boston: Ticknor, 1886.

Lopez, Michael. "*The Conduct of Life:* Emerson's Anatomy of Power." In *The Cambridge Companion to Ralph Waldo Emerson,* ed. Joel Porte and Saundra Morris, 243–66. New York: Cambridge University Press, 1999.

Lovejoy, Elijah P. "The Mob at St. Charles, Illinois." *Liberator* 7 (November 10, 1837): 181.

Lovejoy, Joseph C., Owen Lovejoy, and John Quincy Adams. *Memoir of Rev. Elijah P. Lovejoy: Who Was Murdered in Defence of the Liberty of the Press, at Alton, Illinois, Nov. 7, 1837.* New York: John S. Taylor, 1838.

Lowell, James Russell. *The Biglow Papers [First Series].* Critical ed. Ed. Thomas Wortham. DeKalb: Northern Illinois University Press, 1977.

———. *The Poems of James Russell Lowell.* New York: Thomas Crowell, 1892.

MacShane, Frank. "*Walden* and Yoga." *New England Quarterly* 37 (1964): 322–42.

Marraro, Howard R. *American Opinion on the Unification of Italy, 1846–1861.* New York: Columbia University Press, 1932.

Martin, Waldo E., Jr. *The Mind of Frederick Douglass.* Chapel Hill: University of North Carolina Press, 1984.

Marvell, Andrew. "An Horatian Ode Upon Cromwell's Return from Ireland." In *The Longman Anthology of British Literature: Compact Edition,* gen. ed. David Damrosch, 691–94. New York: Longman, 2000.

Matteson, John. *Eden's Outcasts: The Story of Louisa May Alcott and Her Father.* New York: Norton, 2005.

Mayer, Henry. *All on Fire: William Lloyd Garrison and the Abolition of Slavery.* New York. St. Martin's, 1998.

McAleer, John. *Ralph Waldo Emerson: Days of Encounter.* Boston: Little, Brown, 1984.

McDowell, Deborah E. "In the First Place: Making Frederick Douglass and the Afro-American Narrative Tradition." In *African American Autobiography: A Collection of Critical Essays*, ed. William L. Andrews, 36–58. Englewood Cliffs, N.J.: Prentice Hall, 1993.

McFeely, William S. *Frederick Douglass.* New York: Norton, 1991.

McKivigan, John R. "The Frederick Douglass–Gerrit Smith Friendship and Political Abolitionism in the 1850s." In *Frederick Douglass: New Literary and Historical Essays*, ed. Eric J. Sundquist, 205–32.

McPherson, James. *Battle Cry of Freedom: The Civil War Era.* New York: Oxford University Press, 1988.

McWilliams, John. "Lexington, Concord, and the 'Hinge of the Future.'" *American Literary History* 5 (Spring 1993): 1–29.

Mellow, James R. *Nathaniel Hawthorne in His Times.* Boston: Houghton Mifflin, 1980.

Melville, Herman. *Billy Budd: The Genetic Text.* Ed. Harrison Hayford and Merton M. Sealts Jr. Chicago: University of Chicago Press, 1962.

———. *Billy Budd, Sailor (An Inside Narrative).* Ed. Harrison Hayford and Merton M. Sealts Jr. Chicago: University of Chicago Press, 1962.

———. *Clarel.* Ed. Walter E. Bezanson. New York: Hendricks House, 1960.

———. *Mardi: And a Voyage Thither.* Ed. Harrison Hayford, Hershel Parker, and G. Thomas Tanselle. Evanston and Chicago: Northwestern University Press and the Newberry Library, 1970.

———. *Moby-Dick.* Ed. Harrison Hayford, Hershel Parker, and G. Thomas Tanselle. Evanston and Chicago: Northwestern University Press and the Newberry Library, 1988.

———. *The Piazza Tales, and Other Prose Pieces, 1839–1860.* Ed. Harrison Hayford, Alma A. MacDougall, and G. Thomas Tanselle. Evanston and Chicago: Northwestern University Press and the Newberry Library, 1987.

———. *Pierre: or, the Ambiguities.* Ed. Harrison Hayford, Hershel Parker, and G. Thomas Tanselle. Evanston and Chicago: Northwestern University Press and the Newberry Library, 1971.

———. *Poems of Herman Melville.* Ed. Douglas Robillard. New Haven, Conn.: College and University Press, 1976.

———. *White-Jacket: or, The World in a Man-of-War.* Ed. Harrison Hayford,

Hershel Parker, and G. Thomas Tanselle. Evanston and Chicago: Northwestern University Press and the Newberry Library, 1970.

Metcalf, Eleanor. *Herman Melville: Cycle and Epicycle.* Cambridge, Mass.: Harvard University Press, 1953.

Meyer, Michael. "Thoreau and Black Emigration." *American Literature* 53 (1981): 380–96.

———. "Thoreau's Rescue of John Brown from History." In *Studies in the American Renaissance 1980*, ed. Joel Myerson, 301–16. Charlottesville: University of Virginia Press, 1980.

Milder, Robert. "The Rhetoric of Melville's *Battle-Pieces.*" *Nineteenth-Century Literature* 44 (September 1989): 173–200.

"The Minutemen's Pledge." *Liberator* 30 (November 9, 1860): 177.

"Misconceptions of Peace." *Advocate of Peace*, September/October 1864, 133.

Mitchell, Betty L. "Massachusetts Reacts to John Brown's Raid." *Civil War History* 19 (March 1973): 65–79.

Mitchell, Stephen. Introduction to *Bhagavad Gita: A New Translation.* New York: Three Rivers Press, 2000.

Mitchell, Thomas R. *Hawthorne's Fuller Mystery.* Amherst: University of Massachusetts Press, 1998.

Mizruchi, Susan. "Cataloging the Creatures of the Deep: 'Billy Budd, Sailor' and the Rise of Sociology." *Boundary* 2 17 (1990): 272–304.

Montgomery, David. "Strikes in Nineteenth Century America." *Social Science History* (February 1980): 81–104.

Moody, Richard. *The Astor Place Riot.* Bloomington: Indiana University Press, 1958.

Moses, Wilson J. "Where Honor Is Due: Frederick Douglass as Representative Black Man." *Prospects* 17 (1992): 177–89.

Moulton, Louisa Chandler. "Louisa May Alcott." In *Our Famous Women*, ed. Elizabeth Stuart Phelps, 29–52. Hartford Conn.: A. D. Worthington, 1885.

Murdock, Harold. *The Nineteenth of April, 1775.* Boston: Houghton Mifflin, 1923.

Newberry, Frederick. *Hawthorne's Divided Loyalties: England and America in His Works.* Rutherford, N.J.: Associated University Presses, 1987.

Oates, Stephen B. *To Purge This Land with Blood: A Biography of John Brown.* Amherst: University of Massachusetts Press, 1984.

Packer, Barbara. "The Transcendentalists." In *Prose Writing, 1820–1865*. Vol. 2 of *The Cambridge History of American Literature*, ed. Sacvan Bercovitch, 329–604. Cambridge: Cambridge University Press, 1995.

Parker, Hershel. *Herman Melville: A Biography.* Vol. 2. *1851–1891.* Baltimore: Johns Hopkins University Press, 2002.

Parker, Theodore. "The Fugitive Slave Law." In *The Rights of Man in America,* ed. F. B. Sanborn, 143–52. 1911. Reprint, New York: Negro Universities Press, 1969.

———. "The Function and Place of Conscience in Relation to the Laws of Men." In *Discourses of Slavery: The Collected Works of Theodore Parker. Part 5,* ed. Frances Power Cobbe, 134–63. 1863. Reprint, n.p.: Kessinger, 2004.

Paul, Sherman. *The Shores of America: Thoreau's Inward Exploration.* Champaign: University of Illinois Press, 1958.

Pease, Jane H., and William H. Pease. "Confrontation and Abolition in the 1850s." *Journal of American History* 58 (March 1972): 923–37.

Peple, Edward Cronin, Jr. "Hawthorne on Thoreau, 1853–1857." *Thoreau Society Bulletin* 119 (Spring 1972): 2–3.

———. "The Personal and Literary Relationship of Hawthorne and Thoreau." PhD diss., University of Virginia, 1970.

Peterson, Roy M. "Echoes of the Italian Risorgimento in Contemporaneous American Writers." *PMLA* 47 (March 1932): 220–40.

Petrulionis, Sandra Harbert. "Editorial Savoir Faire: Thoreau Transforms His Journal into 'Slavery in Massachusetts.'" *Resources for American Literary Study* 25 (1999): 206–31.

———. *To Set This World Right: The Antislavery Movement in Thoreau's Concord.* Ithaca and London: Cornell University Press, 2006.

Phillips, Wendell. "Wendell Phillips on the Puritan Principle." In *Echoes of Harper's Ferry,* ed. James Redpath, 105–18. 1860. Reprint, Westport, Conn.: Negro Universities Press, 1970.

Phillips, Wendell, and Francis Jackson Garrison. *William Lloyd Garrison, 1805–1879: The Story of His Life Told by His Children.* 4 vols. Boston: Houghton Mifflin, 1885–89.

Popkin, Jeremy D. "Facing Racial Revolution: Captivity Narratives and Identity in the Saint-Domingue Insurrection." *Eighteenth-Century Studies* 36, no. 4 (2003): 511–33.

Potter, David J. *The Impending Crisis, 1848–1861.* New York: Harper & Row, 1976.

Predmore, Richard. "Thoreau's Influence in Hawthorne's 'The Artist of the Beautiful.'" *ATQ* 40 (1978): 329–34.

Preston, Dickson J. *Young Frederick Douglass: The Maryland Years.* Baltimore: Johns Hopkins University Press, 1980.

"Public Meeting in Faneuil Hall." *Liberator* 7 (December 15, 1837): 202.

"The Rescue of Burns." *Liberator* 25 (September 7, 1855): 142.

Quarles, Benjamin. *Allies for Freedom and Blacks on John Brown.* Cambridge, Mass.: Da Capo, 2001.

Renehan, Edward J., Jr. *The Secret Six: The True Tale of the Men Who Conspired with John Brown.* New York: Crown, 1995.

Reynolds, David. *John Brown, Abolitionist: The Man Who Killed Slavery, Sparked the Civil War, and Seeded Civil Rights.* New York: Knopf, 2005.

Reynolds, Larry J. *Devils and Rebels: The Making of Hawthorne's Damned Politics.* Ann Arbor: University of Michigan Press, 2008.

———. *European Revolutions and the American Literary Renaissance.* New Haven: Yale University Press, 1988.

———. "Kings and Commoners in *Moby-Dick.*" *Studies in the Novel* 12 (Summer 1980): 101–13.

Reynolds, Larry J., and Susan Belasco Smith. Introduction to *"These Sad But Glorious Days": Dispatches from Europe, 1846–1850,* by Margaret Fuller, ed. Larry J. Reynolds and Susan Belasco Smith, 1–35. New Haven: Yale University Press, 1991.

Richards, Jason. "Melville's (Inter)National Burlesque: Whiteface, Blackface, and 'Benito Cereno.'" *ATQ* 22 (June 2007): 73–94.

Richards, Leonard I. *"Gentlemen of Property and Standing": Anti-Abolition Mobs in Jacksonian America.* New York: Oxford University Press, 1970.

Richardson, Robert D., Jr. *Emerson: The Mind on Fire.* Berkeley: University of California Press, 1995.

———. *Henry David Thoreau: A Life of the Mind.* Berkeley: University of California Press, 1986.

Roberts, Timothy Mason. *Distant Revolutions: 1848 and the Challenge to American Exceptionalism.* Charlottesville: University of Virginia Press, 2009.

Robinson, David M. "Emerson's 'American Civilization': Emancipation and the National Destiny." In *The Emerson Dilemma,* ed. Garvey, 221–33.

———. "Introduction: Emerson as a Political Thinker." In *The Political Emerson: Essential Writings on Politics and Social Reform,* ed. David M. Robinson, 1–26. Boston: Beacon, 2004.

Rogin, Michael Paul. *Subversive Genealogy: The Politics and Art of Herman Melville.* Berkeley: University of California Press, 1985.

Rossbach, Jeffery. *Ambivalent Conspirators: John Brown, the Secret Six, and a Theory of Slave Violence.* Philadelphia: University of Pennsylvania Press, 1982.

Rostenberg, Leona. "Margaret Fuller's Roman Diary." *Journal of Modern History* 12 (June 1940): 209–20.

Rowe, John Carlos. *At Emerson's Tomb: The Politics of Classic American Literature.* New York: Columbia University Press, 1997.

Ruchames, Louis, ed. *John Brown: The Making of a Revolutionary.* New York: Grosset & Dunlap, 1969.

Rusk, Ralph L. *The Life of Ralph Waldo Emerson.* New York: Columbia University Press, 1949.

Sale, Maggie Montesinos. "Critiques from Within: Antebellum Projects of Resistance." *American Literature* 64 (December 1992): 695–718.

———. *The Slumbering Volcano: American Slave Ship Revolts and the Production of Rebellious Masculinity.* Durham: Duke University Press, 1997.

———. "To Make the Past Useful: Frederick Douglass' Politics of Solidarity." *Arizona Quarterly* 52, no. 3 (Autumn 1995): 25–60.

Sanborn, Franklin. "The John Brown Raid. II. Comment by a Radical Abolitionist." *The Century* 26 (July 1883): 411–16.

———. *The Life and Letters of John Brown: Liberator of Kansas, and Martyr of Virginia.* 1885. Reprint, New York: Negro Universities Press, 1969.

Sattelmeyer, Robert. *Thoreau's Reading: A Study in Intellectual History.* Princeton, N.J.: Princeton University Press, 1988.

Saxton, Martha. *Louisa May: A Modern Biography of Louisa May Alcott.* Boston: Houghton Mifflin, 1977.

Schnapper, M. B. *American Labor: A Pictorial Social History.* Washington, D.C.: Public Affairs Press, 1972.

Sealts, Merton M. "Innocence and Infamy: *Billy Budd, Sailor.*" In *A Companion to Melville Studies,* ed. John Bryant, 407–30. New York: Greenwood, 1986.

"Sentiment at the South." *New York Observer and Chronicle,* November 22, 1860, 38.

Sewel, William. *The History of the Rise, Increase, and Progress of the Christian People Called Quakers. Intermixed with Several Remarkable Occurrences. Written Originally in Low Dutch, and Also Translated by Himself into English.* 4th ed. 2 vols. London, 1799–1800. *Eighteenth Century Collections Online,* Gale Digital Collections, http://gdc.gale.com.

Shealy, Daniel. "Louisa May Alcott's Juvenilia." In *The Child Writer from Austen to Woolf,* ed. Christine Alexander and Juliet McMaster, 222–36. Cambridge: Cambridge University Press, 2005.

Showalter, Elaine. Introduction to *Alternative Alcott,* ed. Elaine Showalter, ix–xliii. New Brunswick and London: Rutgers University Press, 1988.

Simon, Paul. *Freedom's Champion—Elijah Lovejoy.* Carbondale: Southern Illinois University Press, 1994.

Solomon, Barbara Miller. Introduction to *Margaret Fuller Ossoli,* by Thomas Wentworth Higginson, xi–xxvi.

Stauffer, John. "Advent among the Indians: The Revolutionary Ethos of Gerrit Smith, James McCune Smith, Frederick Douglass, and John Brown." In *Antislavery Violence: Sectional, Racial, and Cultural Conflict in Antebellum America,* ed. John R. McKivigan and Stanley Harrold, 236–73. Knoxville: University of Tennessee Press, 1999.

———. *The Black Hearts of Men: Radical Abolitionists and the Transformation of Race.* Cambridge, Mass.: Harvard University Press, 2002.

———. "Frederick Douglass's Self-fashioning and the Making of a Representative American Man." In *The Cambridge Companion to the African American Slave Narrative,* ed. Audrey Fisch, 201–17. New York: Cambridge University Press, 2007.

Steele, Jeffrey. "'Freeing the Prisoned Queen': The Development of Margaret Fuller's Poetry." In *Studies in the American Renaissance 1992,* ed. Joel Myerson, 137–75. Charlottesville: University Press of Virginia, 1992.

———. "The Limits of Political Sympathy: Emerson, Margaret Fuller, and Woman's Rights." In *The Emerson Dilemma,* ed. Garvey, 115–35.

Stein, William Bysshe. "Thoreau's *Walden* and the *Bagavad Gita.*" *Topic* 3 (1963): 38–55.

Stepto, Robert B. "Sharing the Thunder: The Literary Exchanges of Harriet Beecher Stowe, Henry Bibb, and Frederick Douglass." In *New Essays on "Uncle Tom's Cabin,"* ed. Eric J. Sundquist, 135–53. New York: Cambridge University Press, 1986.

———. "Storytelling in Early Afro-American Fiction: Frederick Douglass' 'The Heroic Slave.'" *Georgia Review* 36 (Summer 1982): 355–68.

Stern, Madeleine. Introduction to *Behind a Mask: The Unknown Thrillers of Louisa May Alcott,* ed. Madeleine Stern, vii–xxxiii. New York: Perennial, 2004.

———. *Louisa May Alcott: A Biography.* New York: Random House, 1996.

Stern, Milton R. Introduction to *Billy Budd,* by Herman Melville, ed. Milton R. Stern, vii–xliv. Indianapolis: Bobbs-Merrill, 1975.

Stillman, William James. "The Philosophers' Camp: Emerson, Agassiz, Lowell, and Others in the Adirondacks." *Century Magazine,* August 1893, 598–606.

Storey, Moorfield, and Edward W. Emerson. *Ebenezer Rockwood Hoar: A Memoir.* Boston and New York: Houghton Mifflin, 1911.

Stowe, Harriet Beecher. *Uncle Tom's Cabin, or, Life among the Lowly.* 1852. Reprint, New York: Collier Macmillan, 1962.

Strysick, Michael. "Emerson, Slavery, and the Evolution of the Principle of Self-Reliance." In *The Emerson Dilemma,* ed. Garvey, 139–69.

Sundquist, Eric J. *Empire and Slavery in American Literature, 1820–1865.* Jackson: University Press of Mississippi, 2006.

————. *To Wake the Nations: Race in the Making of American Literature.* Cambridge, Mass.: Harvard University Press, Belknap Press, 1993.

Takaki, Ronald T. *Violence in the Black Imagination: Essays and Documents.* New York: Putnam's, 1972.

Tharp, Louise Hall. *The Peabody Sisters of Salem.* Boston: Little, Brown, 1950.

Thomas, Brook. *Cross-examinations of Law and Literature: Cooper, Hawthorne, Stowe, and Melville.* Cambridge: Cambridge University Press, 1987.

Thoreau, Henry David. *The Correspondence of Henry David Thoreau.* Ed. Walter Harding and Carl Bode. New York: New York University Press, 1958.

————. *Journal.* Vol. 1. *1837–1844.* Ed. Elizabeth Hall Witherell et al. Princeton, N.J.: Princeton University Press, 1981.

————. *Journal.* Vol. 2. *1842–1848.* Ed. Robert Sattelmeyer. Princeton, N.J.: Princeton University Press, 1984.

————. *Journal.* Vol. 3. *1848–1851.* Ed. Robert Sattelmeyer, Mark R. Patterson, and William Rossi. Princeton, N.J.: Princeton University Press, 1990.

————. *Journal.* Vol. 8. *1854.* Ed. Sandra Harbert Petrulionis. Princeton, N.J.: Princeton University Press, 2002.

————. *The Journal of Henry D. Thoreau.* 2 vols. Ed. Bradford Torrey and Francis H. Allen. New York: Dover, 1962.

————. *Reform Papers.* Ed. Wendell Glick. Princeton, N.J.: Princeton University Press, 1973. Abbreviated *RP.*

————. *Walden.* Ed. J. Lyndon Shanley. Princeton, N.J.: Princeton University Press, 1971. Abbreviated *W.*

————. *A Week on the Concord and Merrimack Rivers.* Ed. Carl F. Hovde, William L. Howarth, and Elizabeth Hall Witherell. Princeton, N.J.: Princeton University Press, 1980. Abbreviated *WK.*

Trachtenberg, Alan. *The Incorporation of America: Culture and Society in the Gilded Age.* New York: Hill & Wang, 1982.

Trevelyan, George Macaulay. *Garibaldi's Defense of the Roman Republic, 1848–49.* London: Longmans, Green, 1941.

Turner, Nat. "Full Text of Nat Turner's 'Confessions.'" In Herbert Aptheker, *Nat Turner's Slave Rebellion,* 127–51. New York: Humanities Press, 1966.

Utter, David, "Kansas History (January 24, 1885)." In *Papers Relating to John Brown*, 117–18. Massachusetts Historical Society, MS N-1952.

Versluis, Arthur. *Transcendentalism and Asian Religions*. Oxford University Press, 1993.

von Frank, Albert J. "John Brown, James Redpath, and the Idea of Revolution." *Civil War History* 52, no. 2 (June 2006): 142–60.

———. "Mrs. Brackett's Verdict: Magic and Means in Transcendental Antislavery Work." In *Transient and Permanent: The Transcendentalist Movement and Its Contexts*, ed. Charles Capper and Conrad Edick Wright, 385–407. Boston: Massachusetts Historical Society, 1999.

———. *The Trials of Anthony Burns: Freedom and Slavery in Emerson's Boston*. Cambridge: Harvard University Press, 1998.

von Mehren, Joan. *Minerva and the Muse: A Life of Margaret Fuller*. Amherst: University of Massachusetts Press, 1994.

Walker, Peter. *Moral Choices: Memory, Desire, and Imagination in Nineteenth-Century American Abolition*. Baton Rouge: Louisiana State University Press, 1978.

Wallace, Maurice O. "Violence, Manhood, and War in Douglass." In *The Cambridge Companion to Frederick Douglass*, ed. Maurice S. Lee, 73–88. Cambridge: Cambridge University Press, 2009.

Wallace, Robert K. "*Billy Budd* and the Haymarket Hangings." *American Literature* 47 (1975): 108–13.

Webster, Daniel. *Speech of the Hon. Daniel Webster Upon the Subject of Slavery*. Boston: Redding, 1850.

Weld, Angelina Grimké. "Feelings of a Woman." *Liberator* 24 (July 7, 1854): 106.

White, W. A. "The Hundred Conventions." *Liberator* 13 (October 13, 1843): 163.

Whitman, Walt. *Leaves of Grass*. Brooklyn: Walt Whitman, 1855.

———. "Year of Meteors. (1859–60.)" In Whitman, *Leaves of Grass*, 51. New York: William E. Chapin, 1867.

Whittier, John Greenleaf. *Anti-Slavery Poems: Songs of Labor and Reform*. Boston: Houghton, Mifflin, 1888.

———. "Brown of Osawatomie." In *Echoes of Harper's Ferry*, ed. James Redpath, 303–4. 1860. Reprint, Westport, Conn.: Negro Universities Press, 1970.

Williams, Gary. *Hungry Heart: The Literary Emergence of Julia Ward Howe*. Amherst: University of Massachusetts Press, 1999.

Wilson, Edmund. *Patriotic Gore: Studies in the Literature of the American Civil War*. New York: Farrar, Straus & Giroux, 1962.

Wilson, Ivy G. "On Native Ground: Transnationalism, Frederick Douglass, and 'The Heroic Slave.'" *PMLA* 121, no. 2 (2006): 453–68.

Wineapple, Brenda. *Hawthorne: A Life.* New York: Knopf, 2003.

Worthington, Marjorie. *Miss Alcott of Concord.* Garden City: Doubleday, 1958.

Yarborough, Richard. "Race, Violence, and Manhood: The Masculine Ideal in Frederick Douglass's 'The Heroic Slave.'" In *Frederick Douglass: New Literary and Historical Essays,* ed. Eric J. Sundquist, 166–88. Cambridge: Cambridge University Press, 1990.

Young, Elizabeth. *Disarming the Nation: Women's Writing and the American Civil War.* Chicago and London: University of Chicago Press, 1999.

Ziser, Michael. "Emersonian Terrorism: John Brown, Islam, and Postsecular Violence." *American Literature* 82 (June 2010): 333–60.

Zwarg, Christina. *Feminist Conversations: Fuller, Emerson and the Play of Reading.* Ithaca, N.Y.: Cornell University Press.

INDEX